JULIA M. USHER'S
ultimate cookies

JULIA M. USHER'S
ultimate cookies

PHOTOGRAPHS BY STEVE ADAMS

GIBBS SMITH
TO ENRICH AND INSPIRE HUMANKIND

to my mom

For letting me ride her apron strings and teaching me that baking
from scratch is one of the truest expressions of the heart.

*Mom decorating cookies with me and my sister Betsy, circa 1971. (I'm the one
still in my jammies, wondering if my star cookie is up to snuff!)*

First Edition
15 14 13 12   6 5 4 3

Text © 2011 Julia M. Usher
Photographs © 2011 Steve Adams

Published by
Gibbs Smith
P.O. Box 667
Layton, Utah 84041

1.800.835.4993 orders
www.gibbs-smith.com

Designed by Alison Oliver
Printed and bound in China

Gibbs Smith books are printed on either recycled,
100% post-consumer waste, FSC-certified papers
or on paper produced from sustainable PEFC-
certified forest/controlled wood source. Learn
more at www.pefc.org.

Library of Congress Cataloging-in-Publication Data

Usher, Julia M.
  Julia M. Usher's ultimate cookies / Julia M. Usher ;
photographs by Steve Adams. — 1st ed.
    p. cm.
  Includes index.
  ISBN 978-1-4236-1934-5
1. Cookies. I. Title. II. Title: Ultimate cookies.
  TX772.U84 2011
  641.8'654—dc23
                              2011019611

contents

acknowledgments

I'M ONLY BEING PARTLY FACETIOUS when I say that I wouldn't have finished this book had it not been for C&H and KitchenAid. Most days, my basement test kitchen was a flurry of powdered sugar with me at the center of the storm, kicking up plumes of the stuff as I raced to meet pressing book deadlines. An impressive 600 pounds of powdered sugar were expended to produce the 300 batches of Royal Icing that went into this book! Naturally, I needed something in which to blend all this icing, which is where my KitchenAid mixer, affectionately called Old Faithful, came in. In 1996, Old Faithful dutifully accompanied me from cooking school in Boston to my bakery in St. Louis. Seven years of professional service, thousands of wedding cakes, and one cookbook later, she started the recipes for this book. Nothing, not even frayed electrical cord or missing spokes, stopped her. It wasn't until my final deadline that she had to be replaced—and only because her "off" switch never turned off. Ironic to be retired for working too hard, wouldn't you say?

There are, of course, real live people—not just inanimate objects with names—to thank! My first book *Cookie Swap* was four years in the making, and while this project went from contract to bookstore about four times faster, I leaned on as many people, if not more, along the way. You see, no matter how simple you think creative projects are going to be, they have a way of morphing into more than ever dreamed. So, first, thanks to all of my loyal *Cookie Swap* fans for launching that book into its ninth printing and for providing just the sustenance needed on my 120-stop book tour. Without your support, I probably wouldn't have written a second book—and certainly not so close on the heels of the first. Thank you, too, for asking me the hard decorating questions and always answering those I posted to Facebook. I am especially grateful to Jane Bonacci, Carolyn Lawrence, Debbie Lynskey, Kathie Reuter, Joanne Shellan, and Robin Traversy for the cookie decorating conundrums they posed for sidebars in the book and the companion FAQ pdf on my website, and to Marian Poirier of the popular blog Sweetopia for promoting my first book and standing at the ready to push this one.

While there were many suppliers who, wittingly and unwittingly, contributed wonderful props and products for *Ultimate Cookies,* I feel compelled to single out a few. First, Nancy Lee Quist, Sally Rue, and the rest of the staff at fancyflours.com. I'm sure they know how many last-minute orders they filled for me. (I lost count months ago!) All I remember is that they filled each and every one with incredible style and speed. Second, the folks at Chicago Metallic. What a privilege it was to experiment (for free) with their very fine bakeware. And last but not least, Carol Fyhrie and Chris Priest of Warson Woods Antiques Gallery, and the Culbertson family of Quintessentials Antiques. I routinely raided their stores in quest of the perfect accessory, and they never once flinched.

My gratitude also goes to my immensely supportive agent (and sometimes therapist) Sorche Fairbank, my capable editors Lisa Anderson and Jennifer Adams, and the many other talented folks at Gibbs Smith, Publisher. Of course, not to be forgotten is Steve Adams, my always clear-headed photographer, who kept up with an unprecedented 30-plus shots a day, over nine 10-hour days. (Phew! I still get tired thinking about those numbers.)

Now that the powdered sugar has settled, there's one person, though, who rises above the plumes. Bryan, my soul mate and strength, thank you for listening patiently, for making (I won't say how many) dinners after I had baked myself silly all day, for critiquing the occasional snake or lizard cookie, and, most important, for not retiring me for working too hard. I love you.

introduction

MY EDUCATION IN FOOD BEGAN as early as I can remember. There were the berries plucked plump and juicy from our backyard brambles, the eggs still warm from our flock of Rhode Island Reds, and the many herbs and edible flowers that Mom grew in her beloved country-style (read "overgrown") garden. The ingredients were just the beginning though. The greatest learning came after these goodies landed in the kitchen, where Mom turned them into everything from Anadama bread and rose geranium jelly to blackberry cobbler and Christmas croissants. My mom worked hard to provide her young family with the food she thought was best: food with a direct connection to the earth as well as to her heart and hands.

I rode her apron strings at every opportunity, and, as it turned out, I was a quick study. It didn't take too many bites of Mom's chocolate-nut wafers or cinnamon-kissed stollen to understand why Chips Ahoy and Sara Lee's had no place in our house. (Occasionally, Dad would sneak home a bag of store-bought cookies or a boxed cake, only to find that Mom had promptly banished the item to the back of a cabinet, well out of the kids' reach.) But Mom's lessons weren't only about weighty matters such as quality of ingredients and local sourcing. She showed me and my sibs, Betsy and Chris, the value of shared fun in the kitchen, too. While semi-homemade, 30-minute meals have sadly become de rigueur these days, they were a foreign concept to us. We were taught from the get-go that time in the kitchen, no matter how long, was time well spent.

One of our most anticipated kitchen adventures was in the weeks preceding Christmas when we donned Mom's frilly June Cleaver-esque aprons and gathered all of our creative reserve for our annual cookie decorating spree. Mom would mix up her famous anise-scented sugar cookie and gingerbread doughs and we three kids would "help" by adding gingerbread people, invariably maimed or disfigured, and other cutouts to the cookie sheets. While we got more icing in and on us than on our cookies, it didn't matter. Even crooked cutouts and errant icing blobs garnered Mom's highest praise, and so I always ended up beaming. What an amazing sense of accomplishment this time together gave me. It was hard to let my cookies go (we often trundled them into tins and off to cookie swaps), but seeing others' eyes light up when I unveiled my treats made the giving easy.

And what more personal gift than a cookie made from scratch and beautifully decorated by hand? The present of a lovely cookie is truly transcendent. We all know this instinctively. We bask in its fragrance as it takes shape in the oven. We ooh and ahh over its artful decoration. We smile as its buttery crumbs caress our tongues. It's a rare gift that not only tickles the fancy and teases the palate, but satisfies all the way to the heart. So there you have it: cookie decorating isn't a frivolity to me. It's fun, for sure, but it's also a passion that gives my life a strong sense of meaning.

Despite this passion, I never intended for my first book, *Cookie Swap,* to be a decorating book. Party guide or cookbook? Sure. But, decorating how-to? Not so much. That said, you can probably imagine my surprise when the emails from readers started mounting—most with pleas for cooking decorating help. Evidently, my passion for decorating had peeked through and readers liked what they saw, but . . . I hadn't completely satisfied their cravings. It dawned on me then, around mid-*Cookie Swap* tour, that *Ultimate Cookies* was in me, calling out to be written the way a naked sugar cookie calls out to be cloaked with icing and sprinkles. *Cookie Swap* had only scratched the surface. I needed and wanted to give my readers more.

Ultimate Cookies was a labor of love, as most cookie decorating is. It challenged my skill and creativity for 365 days straight! As proud as I was to share my first misshapen gingerbread man with my mom, I am even prouder of *Ultimate Cookies*. I offer it to you now with the sincerest hope that it brings you and your loved ones the joy I found long ago in Mom's kitchen, learning this most meaningful craft.

HELLO, *ULTIMATE COOKIES*! (OR WHAT YOU'LL FIND IN THIS BOOK)

EXCEPT FOR THE VERY SIMPLEST of cookie decorating techniques, most cookie decorating takes time, patience, and practice. If you feel your blood pressure rising at the thought of making a batch of cookies or icing from scratch, then this book is probably not for you. But if you've got even the slightest cookie-decorating urge, you're in the right place. In addition to its many never-before-seen cookie projects, such as peacocks, lizards, and jewelry (oh my!), *Ultimate Cookies* offers a plethora of concrete technique tips and tools to help you master these projects and then move onto your own inventions. I'm a firm believer that if you make the investment upfront to understand basic decorating principles, then you can extrapolate and make just about anything.

With that premise in mind, I start this book with a section called "Cookie Craft," which I highly recommend you read first. This section explores everything from the essential tools of a decorating kit to specialty decorating items and processes designed to give cookies extra pizzazz, such as custom templates and cutters, modeling media, and 3-D cookie construction. If you're just getting started and want to ease into decorating without buying a bunch of gadgets, no worries. The vast majority of cookie decorating in this book is done with three very inexpensive items: a parchment pastry cone, a metal trussing needle or toothpick, and a craft paintbrush. Plus, a pricing key is associated with other tools so you can decide which ones to invest in next. In this section, you'll also find one of the most comprehensive discussions of decorating technique anywhere. I've expanded upon the techniques first introduced in *Cookie Swap* with additional details about wafer-papering and stenciling and discussions of four new techniques, including wet-on-wet layering, rubber-stamping, dipping, and embossing.

As you get into the projects, you'll find more tools to guide you, too. At the top of each project is a key that provides an at-a-glance view of project complexity, the recipes used, and any advance preparation and planning tips unique to that project. "Stand-in," also in the key, suggests simpler alternatives to certain projects and/or ideas for displaying or packaging the project for gift giving. "Short and Sweet," a special photo feature that accompanies the multi-component projects, shows in one shot and three brief steps how each project is built. And the many crafting shots sprinkled throughout the chapters are further testament that a picture speaks a thousand words. My hope is that they remove any lingering decorating mystery.

Of course, food should taste as good as it looks, as my mom taught me so well so many years ago. I give you several decorating shortcuts in this book, but I never compromise by suggesting store-bought cookies or icing as some other decorators do. All of my basic building blocks are made from scratch, and you'll find them, each with its own cookie key, at the back of the book, along with icing consistency adjustments, my favorite resources, and custom templates used in some of the projects.

So, why decorated cookies and not cupcakes, cake pops, or some other treat? In addition to being every bit as colorful and fun as these trendy sweets, cookies are the ultimate in practicality. The icing most often used in this book (Royal Icing) dries to a crunchy candy-like coating that requires no refrigeration and allows cookies to be infinitely stacked. (Handy, if you're making many dozens in advance or transporting the goodies to a cookie swap.) What's more, the cookie doughs in this book can be made well in advance, frozen, and baked when needed to offer peak freshness. Once baked, they also typically stay tasty for at least a week. If you're going to put time into an inspirational treat, it's nice to make one that won't get stale or dry in the matter of a few days, don't you think? Lastly, cookies are immensely adaptable, in part because of their longer shelf life. As you'll see throughout this book, most of my projects serve at least two purposes. Naturally, the first is to be eaten. But many also work wonders as invitations, favors, or centerpieces, thereby eliminating the need to plan—and pay for—other party accoutrements. That's quite a deal if you ask me!

Let me end this section by saying that while some of my projects may look elaborate, rest assured, none of them requires any more skill than is needed for a very basic gingerbread house. Though I went to culinary school in my early thirties, I never had any formal decorating training. If you've got the decorating bug but not any experience, just pick up this book and go for it. Granted, I may have a few years of practice on you, but there's plenty of support in these pages to get you started. And I'm only ever an email away. (Just try me at sweetlife@juliausher.com!)

Make every moment a special event,

Julia M. Usher

www.juliausher.com
sweetlife@juliausher.com
Facebook: Julia M Usher
Twitter: JuliaMUsher

COOKIE CRAFT
Tips and Tools of the Trade

No trivial amuse-bouche, this intro chapter is fully loaded. It starts with "Basics" (p. 13), which includes an inventory of the decorating tools that no decorator, beginner or otherwise, should be without, as well as tips for using my favorite decorating tool and icing. It then moves to "Bedazzlers" (p. 23), which introduces what I call the "nice-to-have" tools and ingredients that accompany some of the more advanced or uncommon decorating methods introduced in "15 Bottom-to-Top Decorating Techniques" (p. 27). "Beyond Bedazzled" (p. 48) brings up the rear, but does so boldly with information about 3-D cookie construction, custom cookie templates, and other decorating possibilities designed to take your cookie art to the highest level. I strongly urge you to taste these pages before you read any further and to nibble your way through in order from "Basics" to "Beyond Bedazzled." If you do, your first crack at the projects is sure to be its sweetest.

basics

TOOLS I CAN'T LIVE WITHOUT

You have it. I have it. We all have that special kitchen gadget or piece of equipment whose absence—even if only misplaced—provokes complete meltdown. Maybe it's a trusty wooden spoon, a muffin tin rich with the patina of years of greasing with real butter, or a workhorse of a mixer. When it comes to cookie baking and decorating, my list of indispensable tools is short, but very particular. I call on the following few items over and over throughout the book and believe they're essential elements in everyone's tool kit. For a sense of how deep you may have to dig, take a look at my pricing key below. And, remember, if you're a beginner, you can get a lot of mileage out of three inexpensive *decorating* tools: a parchment pastry cone, a metal trussing needle, and the handle-end of a craft paintbrush!

PRICE:	$ less than $20	$$ $21 to $50	$$$ $51 and above

1. Parchment pastry cone, aka cornet ($). I do 95 percent of my cookie detailing with this simple DIY tool, hence its top billing here as my favorite item. I prefer cones to reusable pastry bags with metal tips for most icing applications, partly because there's nothing I dislike more than reaching into a goopy pastry bag to remove the coupler (the plastic piece that holds the tip to the bag) for cleaning. With parchment pastry cones, once you're done, just snip off the tip, squeeze out the leftover icing, and toss out the cone. Extremely tiny holes (smaller than any pastry tip) can also be cut in cone tips, allowing for very precise decorating. Disposable plastic piping bags or baggies with holes cut in their corners can substitute for cones, though I find them floppier and harder to handle. What's worse, they're not biodegradable. Some decorators use squeeze bottles, but they also offer inferior control.

2. Parchment paper ($). If I love parchment pastry cones, I've got to love parchment paper, right? You betcha. I usually stock two types of parchment paper: rolled parchment paper for making cones and sheet parchment for lining storage containers and cookie sheets for easy cookie removal.

3. Silicone baking mats ($$). These mats can be pricey, which is why I suggest parchment paper as an alternative for lining cookie sheets, when appropriate. But, truth be told, silicone baking mats are the superior liner. They promote more even heating and browning; plus, they're a requirement when baking very thin, delicate wafers, such as my Traditional Tuiles (p. 255). Parchment paper almost always buckles under these lightweight cookies, leading to misshapen cookies. What's more, tuiles are harder to remove from paper without breaking.

4. Heavy-gauge aluminized steel (12 to 13 x 16- to 18-inch) jelly roll pans, for cookie sheets ($). Avoid flimsy cookie sheets whenever you can. The heft of these pans promotes more even heating and browning, and their short walls keep the pans from warping over time—God forbid you should ever throw a hot one into cold water! Better yet, their ample size fits more cookies than smaller (10 x 15-inch) jelly roll pans. I'm partial to Chicago Metallic's very affordable commercial line of these pans, but there are many brands from which to choose.

5. Digital scale ($-$$$). You won't need a scale to make my cookie recipes if you follow my method for measuring dry ingredients (p. 233). However, my project yields are based on dough weight, simply because weighing is far more accurate than eyeballing one-half or some other fraction of a cookie recipe. While prices for scales vary widely from brand to brand, you'll find many inexpensive options available—and, fortunately, inexpensive is all you need for my projects.

6. Offset spatulas, small and large ($). Offset spatulas are characterized by having a blade that is offset from the handle at roughly a 45-degree angle. These spatulas are super for a couple of reasons: (1) they allow you to spread batters or icings, as I often do with the stenciling technique, without racking your knuckles on the tabletop and (2) the crook where the handle and blade come together gives cookies extra support. For stenciling, I usually use a small spatula (blade about $3/4$ x $3^1/2$ inches, pictured middle, p. 12) for greater control. I reserve wider (2-inch or more) spatulas for transferring large pieces of cut dough from work surface to cookie sheet to minimize misshaping, or to lift recently iced cookies so my fingers don't mess them up.

7. Electric stand mixer ($$$). I already told you in "Acknowledgments" (p. 6) just how much I loved Old Faithful, my 15-year old KitchenAid mixer, but I'm not sure I fully explained why. Many of the projects in this book rely on rolled sugar or gingerbread cookies decorated with Royal Icing, and I like to mix my icing until very thick and white to start. Simply put, an electric stand mixer makes light of this task. A handheld mixer will also work, but beating to the desired point will take a lot longer.

8. Nontapered rolling pins ($-$$). When it comes to rolling out cookie dough, I require nothing fancy. I actually work most of the time with a standard ($2^1/8$ x 10-inch) nontapered wooden rolling pin, just like the one my mom had except the handles are broken off! Only when rolling out very large cookies (greater than about 10 inches) will I swap in a longer (3 x 18-inch) wooden rolling pin; but, generally, this pin is too bulky for my confined countertop space.

Some words on other types of pins, because there are many: For whatever reason, I have a difficult time rolling dough to a uniform thickness with tapered French-style rolling pins. Similarly, heavy marble rolling pins are harder for me to control—apply a bit too much pressure and I end up with a large dent in the dough. Nontapered French-style and silicone pins without handles are another story: they yield nice, even results. But they are a bit longer than my standard pin (between 16 and 20 inches), again making them somewhat hard to navigate in my workspace. Further, silicone pins are no less prone to sticking than wooden pins, despite manufacturers' claims to the contrary. So when all is said and done, it's difficult for me to justify their price, which can be three to four times that of wooden pins.

9. Soft-gel (aka liquid-gel or liqua-gel) food coloring ($). Okay, so this item isn't really a tool, but it's an essential ingredient when decorating with Royal Icing, as I love to do. Because icing consistency can determine success or failure with any given decorating technique, you're playing the decorator's equivalent of Russian Roulette if you use anything but a very concentrated food coloring, such as soft-gel. Liquid food coloring is extremely unconcentrated and simply messes with the icing consistency too much. Gel and paste food colorings are also very concentrated and fine to use, but unlike soft-gel, which comes in a mess-free squeeze bottle, gel and paste food colorings typically come in lidded jars and must be doled out in a hit-or-miss fashion with a toothpick. Because I always work with soft-gel food coloring, you'll see that when I specify quantity of coloring, I always measure in drops. As for brand, watch out: some brands have a strong odor and taste. You'll know what I'm talking about as soon as you take a whiff. My favorite brand is Chefmaster.

10. Graduated cookie cutter sets ($). Several of my projects call for similar cookie shapes (i.e., rounds, ovals, squares, daisies, or diamonds) in a number of different sizes. Rather than hunting and pecking for these cutters from various sources, you'll be better off purchasing an inexpensive cutter set. Ateco is, hands down, my favorite— and the most widely available—set supplier. Projects that call for cutter sets also indicate the individual cutters used in that set (in the dough cutting step), so you can quickly check your existing inventory before you purchase.

11. Metal trussing needles (aka turkey lacers) or tooth-picks ($). When icing cookies, I always have a metal trussing needle around. I use it to pop air bubbles in icing, to scrape unwanted icing out of small areas on cookies, and for marbling, one of my favorite decorating techniques. Toothpicks also work perfectly well for these same tasks, but I prefer the wash-and-reuse aspect of trussing needles.

12. Small craft paintbrushes ($). I always have one or more of these tools on hand for decorating, too, but as strange as it may sound, I more often use the handle-end than the brush-end. The former comes in handy for quickly top-coating cookies (i.e., covering cookie tops smoothly with icing). By "small," I mean a brush with a $^1/_4$-inch-diameter handle, or sometimes smaller for top-coating tiny (1-inch or less) cookies.

13. A few reusable pastry bags and tips ($). Though I'm a diehard parchment pastry cone fan, you really do need pastry bags and metal tips to give icing certain textures. But hang on! There's no reason to immediately run out and snatch up every pastry tip ever made. As you'll see in this book, I do a lot with just a few tips, specifically small ($^1/_4$-inch) round, leaf, and star styles. Fortunately, tip manufacturers number their tips to make it easier to find the size and style you need; unfortunately, this numbering isn't always consistent from manufacturer to manufacturer, especially in the larger tip sizes. Since Ateco seems to dominate the tip market, I've chosen to reference their tips in this book, as well as provide general tip descriptions.

My Druthers for Cutters

All else being equal (that is, when shape or size of a cookie cutter isn't a constraint), I prefer to work with open tin cutters as opposed to copper cutters or cutters with closed backs and/or handles. Tin cutters are less expensive and tend to cut more crisply than blunter copper cutters. Open cutters can also be flipped over, allowing for cutting of mirror images. Further, if the dough gets stuck in an open cutter, it's easy enough to gently poke it out with your finger or a soft-bristled brush.

HANDLING ROLLED COOKIE DOUGH

Though *Ultimate Cookies* is primarily a cookie decorating book, I'd be remiss if I didn't first share some tips on the rolling, cutting, and baking of sugar cookie and gingerbread doughs. These rolled doughs are the "canvas" for many of the projects in this book, and if this canvas isn't properly prepared, painting it with icing can become more difficult than it should be. Trust me, it takes a lot more decorating skill and patience to conceal the flaws of a misshapen or bumpy cookie than it does to dress up one that is well shaped and smooth on top.

Flawless Cookies: *Flat, well shaped, and evenly baked.*

So what's the key to getting flawless rolled cookies like those pictured above? Some bakers will exhort you to buy specialty nonstick rolling pins, guides for the ends of your rolling pin that keep every roll the same thickness, or even expensive marble surfaces to prevent the dough from getting warm too fast. And me? I'll tell you that you need absolutely none of these things. For me, the key isn't in fancy tools, but in the techniques spelled out in "7 Steps to Flawless Rolled Cookies," (p. 16).

7 Steps to Flawless Rolled Cookies

1. Properly mixed and well chilled dough. The most important point to remember about mixing rolled cookie dough is to avoid overcreaming the butter (or shortening) and sugar. Overcreaming incorporates more air into the dough than necessary and results in domed cookie tops, which invariably lead to messy icing runoff! I generally recommend creaming no longer than about 1 minute. As for chilling, it's much easier to get an even roll if the dough is well chilled. If the dough is too warm and soft, even small variations in pressure applied to the rolling pin can lead to hills and valleys in the top of the dough. Always chill my doughs until firm following the instructions in each of my recipes. And as you're rolling, never hesitate to rechill the dough if it gets difficult to handle.

2. A work surface lightly dusted with flour. No special work surface is required if the dough is well chilled; the surface just needs to be smooth and easy to clean—and lightly dusted with flour. Here, the operative word is "lightly." If you find yourself having to dust your surface heavily, it's probably because your dough is too soft. It's always better to rechill the dough than to introduce excess flour, as the latter will have a drying and toughening effect on the cookies. My rule of thumb: if you can see spots of flour on the underside of the dough after a roll or two, you've probably dusted too heavily.

3. Application of direct pressure to the roller. It's also easier to get an even roll if you can feel the dough beneath the roller. For this reason, it's best to roll directly from the roller rather than the handles (see right) or to use a rolling pin without handles, such as a nontapered French-style pin. Now you know why I covet my old broken rolling pin without any handles!

4. Rotating the dough while rolling. To ensure an even roll, some bakers also recommend rolling outward from the center of the dough and changing the direction of the pin as you roll. This is good practice, for sure, though I prefer to rotate the dough (rather than the pin) and to roll across the entire surface of the dough on each pass. The advantage of rotating the dough is that it provides a simultaneous check on whether the dough is sticking to the work surface. If you can't easily rotate the dough, then you need to dust (lightly!) with flour.

5. Rolling the dough to a relatively thin ($\frac{1}{8}$- to $\frac{3}{16}$-inch) thickness. I recommend rolling gingerbread and sugar cookies no thicker than $\frac{3}{16}$ inch for a couple of reasons. One, I prefer the delicacy of a thinner, crisper cookie. But, two, thick cookies, even if evenly rolled to start, tend to dome more upon baking, which can subsequently lead to troubles with icing runoff. Shortbread is an exception to this rule, at least for me. I think its buttery texture is better accentuated in cookies closer to $\frac{1}{4}$ inch thick.

6. Transferring the cut dough with an offset spatula. If you've followed Steps 1 to 5 and have a nice, even piece of rolled dough before you, the last thing you want to do is disfigure it in the cutting process. Always transfer cut cookies to cookie sheets with an offset spatula wide enough to support the cookies' largest dimension. Cookies that are especially slender or delicately shaped, or ones too big to be easily supported by a spatula, are best cut directly on a prepared cookie sheet, as pictured here.

Alternatively, you can roll and cut on a piece of parchment paper or a silicone baking mat and then transfer the paper (or mat) with cookies atop to the cookie sheet. Once the cookies are cut, carefully remove the dough from around the cookie shapes.

7. Baking to ensure even browning. Wondering why my cookie sheets are always upside down throughout the book? No, it's not a careless oversight! It's a purposeful technique that I use to ensure even browning. For reasons noted on page 13, I prefer to use a heavy-gauge jelly roll pan as my cookie sheet. However, the pan's sides are efficient heat conductors, meaning that cookies set near them will brown more quickly than those in the pan's interior. By flipping over the pan and baking on the back side, I effectively eliminate the sides and encourage more uniform air circulation around the cookies. One word of caution with this approach: remember to secure parchment paper liners to the pan with a dab of butter or shortening in each corner. Otherwise, you run the risk of the paper—and any cookies on it—sliding off!

I also recommend baking only like-size cookies on a single cookie sheet so that all cookies bake at close to the same rate. Lastly, place only one cookie sheet in the oven at a time and position that sheet in the center of the oven. If all of these tips fail and your cookies still bake unevenly, then don't hesitate to rotate your pans in the oven (the back of the oven is typically hotter) and/or to remove finished cookies as others are baking.

ROYAL ICING

Now that you know how to perfect your cookie canvas, let's talk about getting the icing on top. After all, the icing is the pièce de résistance, wouldn't you agree?

Confectioners' icing and Royal Icing (p. 242) are the two icings generally used on rolled cookies, since, unlike buttercream, both icings eventually set up, allowing for easier cookie storage and transport. While I was schooled by my mom in the use of confectioners' icing, I now vastly prefer the royal variety. I've used it on nearly every iced cookie in this book, with rare exception, and this section tells you why!

Both icings contain powdered sugar and a touch of cream of tartar, which helps keep the icing white, among other things. Where they depart from one another is in the liquid that brings the dry ingredients together. Confectioners' icing typically calls for water, milk, cream, and/or lemon or other juice, whereas Royal Icing calls for egg whites or rehydrated meringue powder (essentially dried egg whites mixed with water). This may not seem like a big difference, but it is. The use of egg whites changes the handling and performance of Royal Icing rather dramatically.

To be specific, the protein in the egg whites causes Royal Icing to dry faster than confectioners' icing, which translates into less waiting time between the application of different icing colors and less likelihood of icing colors bleeding into one another. Royal Icing also tends to hold sharper, more defined lines, which is critical for very detailed or delicate piped patterns.

Some decorators like to completely cover their cookies with thin sheets of rolled fondant (as distinct from poured fondant), Chocolate Dough (p. 260), marzipan, or rolled buttercream—all pliable doughs of one form or another. However, I generally don't like to do this for texture reasons. Like any icing, Royal Icing needs to be well flavored with an extract or oil to taste its best, but it dries to a crunchy candy-like coating that enhances the snap of a cookie. Conversely, rolled fondant and other doughs start out chewy, dry crisp, and then revert to chewy once they hit your mouth, detracting from a cookie's crunchiness, in my opinion. I can only assume that those who routinely cover cookies with these doughs haven't mastered top-coating with Royal Icing and find it easier to smoothly cover their cookies this way. But I assure you: if you mix Royal Icing to the right consistency (p. 244), you'll get equally smooth results.

Last but not least, Royal Icing is simply more versatile than these doughs. Not only can you get a smooth finish with it, but you can marble, stencil, and pipe with it! Now this is not to say that I completely shun rolled fondant et al., because I definitely don't. They're wonderful modeling media, which I tend to use in smaller doses as appliqués and embellishments that can easily be removed from cookie tops by those who are less fond of their texture or taste.

THE PARCHMENT PASTRY CONE

I've already extolled the virtues of the parchment pastry cone in "Tools I Can't Live Without" (p. 13), so let me show you how to make and handle my favorite decorating tool. There are probably as many ways to make a cone as there are ways to decorate a sugar cookie, but the method described here is what I was taught in culinary school and I'm sticking with it! Making cones properly can take some practice, but I urge you to keep at it until the process becomes second nature. Remember, disposable plastic piping bags (or baggies with holes snipped in the corners) are ready alternatives. However, paper cones provide superior control because they can be made to any size and they're less floppy.

It's important to touch briefly on reusable pastry bags, too. While I don't use them nearly as often as pastry cones, they are required for certain textured icing applications, as described in "7 Essential Piping Techniques" (p. 46). Filling and handling a pastry bag is fairly similar to filling and handling a parchment pastry cone, but there are a few important differences to understand, so read on!

Making a Parchment Pastry Cone

You can buy precut parchment paper triangles for making cones, but I prefer to use ordinary parchment paper on rolls for making mine. It's easier to find and less expensive (per cone); plus, it has some built-in curvaceousness, which makes it easier to shape into cones.

1. Start by cutting a perfect square off the end of the roll. The more perfect the square to start, the easier it will be to apply my litmus test in Step 7 that tells you if you've made the cone properly. Cut the square along the diagonal to end up with two isosceles triangles—that is, two triangles, each with two equal sides and one longer side. You will get one cone from each triangle. *Note:* If you use parchment paper from a standard (15-inch-wide) roll, the cone should end up $7^1/2$ to 8 inches long and about $3^1/2$ inches wide at the mouth. If you prefer working with a smaller or larger cone, then start by cutting smaller or bigger triangles in this step.

2. Hold the triangle from the corners on either end of the long side, with the long side facing away from you. Also, hold the paper so that its natural curve is facing up. It will be easier to shape the cone in the next step if you're not fighting the bend in the paper.

3. Turn in the right corner to make a half-cone with a point (or tip) at the center of the long side of the triangle. Be careful not to over-rotate the paper; if you do, your cone will end up very small and narrow. If you've properly rotated the paper, the right corner and corner facing you should be closely aligned, as pictured above.

4. Guide the other half of the triangle around the half-cone just created.

5. Rotate the cone so the corners of the triangle face you. Grab onto all three corners to keep the now fully formed cone from unraveling.

6. Check the tip of the cone. If it's open at all, as it often is at this point, gently pull the two outer corners of the cone toward you to shimmy the hole completely closed. I prefer to start with no hole to give me the flexibility to later cut the hole as small or large as needed.

7. Here's the litmus test I spoke of earlier: If you started with a perfect square and made the cone properly, the three corners of the triangle should be equidistant from one another (1 to 2 inches apart) at the open end of the cone.

8. To keep the cone together for good, fold down the corners to the outside of the cone; then tear or cut a notch at the point where all three corners intersect. Voilà, you're done. Now practice this one more time with the remaining triangle!

Filling and Handling a Parchment Pastry Cone

So how to use this fabulous tool once it's made? Regardless of the decorating technique you choose, there are some basic cone handling instructions to always apply:

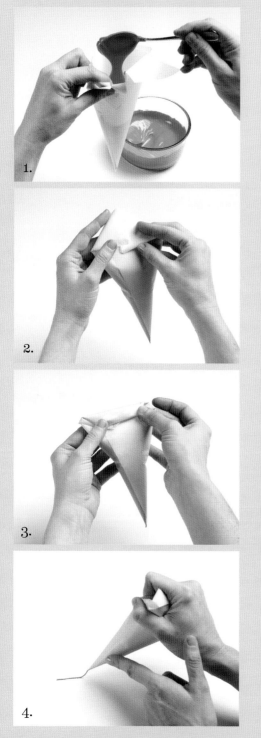

1. Fill the cone about half to two-thirds full with Royal Icing. Never fill all the way up, as some unfilled paper at the top is needed to create a grip in Step 2; plus, if you do, the icing is more likely to backflow out the top as you work. If you start with a bag much less than half full, your piping hand will too quickly get close to the work surface and obscure the cookies you're trying to decorate.

For cones made from standard parchment paper rolls (about $7^{1}/_{2}$ to 8 inches long; $3^{1}/_{2}$ inches wide at the mouth), you'll need about $^{1}/_{4}$ to $^{1}/_{2}$ cup icing to fill the cone to this extent. Hold the cone at the notch as you fill so the weight of the icing doesn't unravel the cone.

2. As a safeguard to prevent icing backflow while piping, fold down the two top corners of the bag toward the center of the bag.

3. Make the grip by rolling down the top of the bag until it meets the icing. Cut a hole of the desired size in the tip. Be sure to cut straight across the tip if you want to create beads and perfectly rounded lines. Cutting at an angle will make more irregular shapes, and is something I don't often do.

4. Before you work on any cookies, press some icing onto your work surface to release any trapped air in the tip of the cone and to test the icing flow. (Don't do this, and you can experience minor icing explosions on your cookies!) Apply steady pressure from the grip to push the icing out the tip. Do not squeeze from the middle of the cone, or you will constrict the icing flow to the tip and increase the chances of icing backflow out the top. You can steady the tip of the cone with your forefinger, but don't apply any pressure at the tip.

As you use icing, continue to fold down the top of the cone. Constant tension is needed on the cone to help push the icing through the tip.

Filling and Handling a Pastry Bag

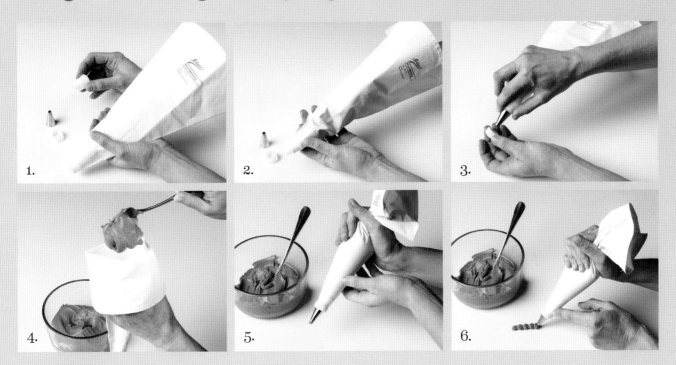

1. Grab a pastry bag, a pastry tip of your choice, and a coupler (the two-part threaded plastic unit that keeps the pastry tip in place). I like to work with a 14- to 16-inch bag for optimum control. Anything smaller usually gets emptied too fast or puts my hand too close to my work area; anything larger is overkill for the relatively small quantities of icing used in cookie detailing.

2. Insert the larger part of the coupler inside the pastry bag. If the bag is new, you may need to cut a larger hole in the end to accommodate the coupler.

3. Fit the pastry tip over the exposed end of the coupler. Screw on the smaller part of the coupler to hold the tip in place. Be sure the coupler grabs the end of the bag.

4. Fold down the top of the bag a little less than halfway. (This step prevents icing from slopping on the upper parts of the bag and later squeezing out the top.) Hold the bag from under the fold with one hand; with the other hand, spoon in icing until it reaches the fold. As with filling parchment pastry cones, the bag should never be fully loaded; you'll need room at the top for a grip.

5. Make the grip by twisting the top of the bag until the twist meets the icing. Continue to twist the top until the bag is taut.

6. Squeeze out some icing to release trapped air and proceed to pipe as you would with a parchment pastry cone, but apply steady pressure at the point where the twist meets the icing. Again, avoid squeezing the middle of the bag. Twist down the top of the bag as it loses tension and steady the tip with your fingertip, as needed.

1.

2.

3.

Make your own Cookie Cutter

Can't find that special cookie cutter shape?

Make it yourself!

Also included are recipes and tips for Crafts

Make your own Cookie Cutter

4.

5.

6.

7.

8.

9.

UNINKED FOAM PAD

STANDARD FELT PAD

bedazzlers

NICE-TO-HAVE TOOLS

Here's the shortlist of items that I use for more advanced or unusual decorating techniques, such as stenciling, appliqué work, wafer-papering, and rubber-stamping, along with some other gadgets that I use on occasion in the book. I've given a shout-out to certain sources and brands in cases where I have a strong preference and also a rough gauge of relative price to help you decide whether to make the investment in these tools.

PRICE:	$ less than $20	$$ $21 to $50	$$$ $51 and above

1. Hand-cranked pasta machine ($$-$$$). If you intend to make more than a few ribbons or bands with modeling media (p. 27), then a pasta rolling machine is an essential tool. You can certainly use a rolling pin to roll these doughs into sheets, but a pasta machine will allow you to roll thinner, more uniform sheets a lot more quickly. Atlas is probably the most recognized brand and the one I use with absolutely no complaint. It has nine thickness settings, which I refer to in the book, ranging from #1 (largest, about $1/8$ inch between rollers) to #9 (smallest).

2. Decorative silicone molds ($). For reasons noted on page 18, I'm not a fan of covering cookies completely with rolled fondant, or any other modeling medium for that matter. However, I do like to turn these doughs into small 3-D embellishments that can be readily plucked off if not to the eater's taste. Silicone molds are a great way to create embellishments that are especially rich in texture and detail. I used molds from firstimpressionsmolds.com (hands down my favorite source) for the cameos and necklaces in Pendant Perfect (p. 67).

3. Textured rolling pins and impression mats ($-$$). I typically use these textured tools for embossing modeling media before cutting it into ribbons or bands. Textured pins are rolled over a sheet of dough that has already been rolled through a pasta machine or with a plain rolling pin, whereas the mats are pressed into the sheet, often by rolling a plain pin over the top of the mat. Pins and mats come in a variety of textures ranging from a grosgrain pattern (for which I have a particular fondness) to basket-weave, cobblestone, and more. Both tools are easiest to locate online; globalsugarart.com, kitchenkrafts.com, and thebakerskitchen.net have wide selections.

4. Heavy-gauge (about $2/100$-inch-thick) acetate ($). Commonly found in hobby and art supply stores, this stiff acetate is used for making templates for cutting out custom cookie shapes or for making custom stencils for tuiles or decorating cookie tops (aka decorative stencils, item #8, p. 24). But to be perfectly honest, I rarely turn acetate into decorative stencils mostly because designerstencils.com does such a great job of hooking me up. Decorative stencils also tend to be quite intricate, which makes cutting them a task better left to die-cutting machines! However, I do call for very simple templates and tuile stencils in a few of the projects that follow, so be sure to read my how-tos on cutting and working with templates and stencils (p. 48).

5. Cookie cutter making kit ($$). If you find yourself in the position of having to cut out many custom cookies with a template, then it's time to turn that template into a cookie cutter. (Cutting with templates is fine in small batches, but it can quickly get tedious as cookie count rises or if your template is complex.) Fortunately, cookie cutter making kits are simple to use and easily found online. Contents of these kits are relatively standard: most come equipped with rolls of 1-inch-wide tin stripping for the cutters, a couple of tools for making angles and curves in the tin, and double-sided tape to keep cutter ends together.

6. Serrated tracing wheel ($). If you thought something looked funny here, you're right. This isn't a standard kitchen tool; it's one used for sewing. But, why split hairs, when it's the perfect device for embossing stitch-like marks on ribbons made of modeling media!

7. Silicone baking molds ($-$$$). These pans can be pricey depending on the size and brand, but they're wonderful for baking brownie batters into perfectly smooth, individually sized hemispheres, ovals, and other shapes.

8. Decorative stencils ($). Aside from marbling, stenciling is probably my favorite decorating technique. So, I suppose it should come as no surprise that I have boxes and boxes of decorative stencils. As recent as a few years ago, stencils could only be found in art and home decorating stores, but now there are stencils specifically made to fit cake and cookie tops, even cookies of particular sizes and shapes. When in need of a new stencil, designerstencils.com is my primary indulgence.

9. Rubber stamps and un-inked felt or foam ink pads ($). I use rubber stamps and un-inked felt or foam ink pads for rubber-stamping on cookies—naturally, what else?! Just ink the pads with soft-gel food coloring and follow my tips for rubber-stamping (p. 40), and you're good to go. Any rubber stamp that fits your cookie top coats will do. And while some decorators say felt ink pads are better than foam pads, I've found that either type works well. Both stamps and un-inked pads can be found in hobby and office supply stores, but the pads are more reliably found online.

10. Dedicated printer with edible inks ($$$), not pictured. This investment is really only worth making if you plan to do a lot of custom wafer paper-printing (p. 26). You should never use edible inks or wafer paper in a printer that has come in contact with inedible inks before, so a dedicated printer is a must for this task. I use an Epson Stylus NX415 printer, though any ink jet printer will work as long as there are edible ink cartridges designed for it.

THE ICING ON THE COOKIE

There's no better way to bedazzle a plain iced cookie than to top it with other edibles! When I first started decorating cookies with my mom way back when, we had little other than jimmies and standard (3 mm) silver sugar beads, aka dragées, for this purpose. But times have changed (thankfully) and now you can find a veritable gold mine of embellishments at specialty cooking stores, online, and even at your local five-and-dime. Pictured to the right are my favorite decorating elements, along with the name of my preferred online supplier, if I happen to have one. You can venture to make some of these items on your own, such as the sugar gems and royal icing embellishments, but I don't think anyone will object to these lovely shortcuts.

1. Sugar gems. A plethora of isomalt jewels can be found at fancyflours.com and elsewhere online. When exposed to humidity, gems can turn cloudy, so it's best to store them in their original packaging, tightly sealed, along with tiny desiccator packs. The shimmer on cloudy gems can be temporarily restored by coating them lightly with vegetable oil.

2. Isomalt. Isomalt is a form of sugar that withstands humidity with less clouding and wilting than normal sugar. It comes in granular form, as shown right, and needs to be hydrated, dissolved, and boiled before use. You can use it to make sugar gems (by pouring it, liquefied, into gem molds), but I most often use it to make clear sugar panels or windows in my cookies, as pictured in Jack o' Lanterns (p. 191) and Along Came a Spider (p. 185). Crushed hard candies can also be used for windows, but in addition to its humidity advantage, isomalt yields shinier, less bubbly glass. And,

because it's clear when dissolved, you can tint it any color you like. Isomalt is widely available, especially online.

3. Crystallized edible flowers. Expensive, but exquisite, these sugar-coated (real) flowers are completely edible if pesticide-free. I love the selection and service at both crystallizedflowerco.com and sweetfields.com. In addition to the roses used on my May Day Baskets (pictured on pages 25 and 168), you can get organic pansies, violets, snapdragons, strawberry blossoms, and more!

4. Readymade royal icing and rolled fondant embellishments. Up until discovering the royal icing and rolled fondant do-dads on fancyflours.com, I'd have made my own. But the detail, quality, and breadth of their product line is beyond compare—and so now I take a shortcut or two every once in a while! Pictured on page 25 is just a small smattering of what fancyflours.com and others offer.

5. Dragées and sugar beads (aka edible pearls). An online search for these items is bound to leave you scratching your head in confusion. That's because "dragées," "sugar beads," and "edible pearls" are often used inconsistently to describe various types of small round decorative elements. To help clarify matters, I've made a distinction between dragées and sugar beads (which I also refer to as edible pearls) in this book. By my definition, dragées are sugar beads onto which trace amounts of metal (primarily, silver) have been deposited to make them glimmer. They usually come in silver and gold finishes, but you can also find them in other metallic colors. Because of this coating, dragées are not FDA-approved. However, they are nontoxic and safe for use on food, and considered edible in countries outside the US. Regardless of your nation's stance on edibility, the bigger ones can be hard, so I often brush them off before eating. By contrast, sugar beads (edible pearls) are made without any metal in their coatings and look a lot like dragées, albeit less shiny. They come in the same wide range of sizes (2 mm to 8 mm) and a rainbow of colors, making them a great—and FDA-approved—substitute.

6. Sugar confetti (aka quins). Classically, sugar confetti comes in the form of small (about 1/4-inch) flat sugar disks, but you can also find it in a variety of seasonal shapes, such as snowflakes, Christmas trees, leaves, bats . . . you name it. Once again, fancyflours.com is my go-to source due to their broad selection.

7. Printed wafer paper. Nothing more than thin (8 x 11-inch) sheets of dehydrated potato starch, water, and oil, wafer paper is a relatively new decorating medium, which is cut and pasted onto dried Royal Icing or modeling media with corn syrup. Wafer paper is virtually tasteless and quickly dissolves on the tongue, much like a communion wafer if you've ever experienced one! Printed paper is harder to find than most other items on this list; the most extensive selection of patterns I've found—and it's lovely to boot—is at fancyflours.com.

8. Plain wafer paper. If you can't find a printed wafer paper pattern to suit your needs, no worries. You can print your own patterns onto plain wafer paper using a dedicated printer (p. 24) with edible inks or draw or trace on the paper with food-safe marking pens (below). Unlike printed wafer paper, plain paper is readily available online. I like to source mine from kopykake.com, since I can get it there in larger increments and at lower cost than from most other suppliers.

9. Edible inks and marking pens. Edible inks are available in cartridges to fit ink jet printers as discussed on page 24; you can also find a range of marking pens filled with food-safe ink. Before you buy ink cartridges, make sure that they're designed to work with your specific printer model. Kopykake.com has some excellent online reference tools to help you match ink to printer. As for markers, my preferred brand is AmeriColor, as their markers seem to consistently outlast the other major brands I've tried.

10. Sanding sugar, jimmies, nonpareils, and edible glitter. I've grouped these tiny sugar decorations together here, as I generally use them the same way on cookies—that is, I apply them with the flocking technique (p. 42). These items vary in shape and shimmer, but all come in an abundance of colors and are easily found online and off. (Sanding sugar also comes fine- or coarse-grained.)

11. Modeling media. I love to make tiny 3-D elements for cookies, and one can only get so far with Royal Icing. Far more lifelike and delicate elements can often be made with modeling media, such as rolled fondant, Chocolate Dough, and marzipan (pictured left to right on page 25). Each of these media has its pros and cons, as described on page 53.

12. Luster, pearl, petal, and other decorating dusts (or powders). As with dragées and sugar beads, the wealth of decorating dusts, and the differences among them, can boggle the mind. Generally speaking, all dusts can be applied dry to cookies or cookie decorations to add an iridescent glow and/or color highlights. They can also be extended with oil-based colorings, extract, or alcohol, and painted onto edibles to create a stronger, more opaque finish. The various dusts range in shimmer and color intensity. Petal dusts come in a wide range of colors but have a matte finish. Pearl and luster dusts are very similar to one another in that they're shinier than petal dusts and sometimes, but not always, more subtly colored. Other dusts, such as metallic highlighter dusts, are super shiny and create the most opaque paint, and still others, such as disco, sparkle, twinkle, and pixie dusts, are slightly more granular and, as their names suggest, sparkle like glitter.

Most types of dusts are nontoxic, but not FDA-approved. However, some brands, namely Wilton (pearl dust) and Crystal Colors (petal dust), are FDA-approved, so be sure to look carefully at product labels. Regardless of official edibility, I generally use dusts in small quantities on cookies, for "show" cookies, or on elements that can be removed, because they do leave a somewhat powdery residue on the tongue.

13. Dime store candies. Don't ever dis' dime stores. It might take a little more ingenuity to find the right decorating element in their candy aisles, but dreaming up uses for their eye-catching confections is part of the fun. Pictured on page 25 are the candies I use most frequently in the book: licorice lace, Haribo licorice wheels, gumballs, and M&Ms, especially the mini ones. If you can't find what you need locally, candywarehouse.com has an extensive online selection.

15 bottom-to-top decorating techniques

Now that you've got both "Basics" and "Bedazzlers" in your decorating arsenal, the question is: what to do with these tools and ingredients? Here, I discuss the 15 decorating techniques that I use most frequently, starting with those that are generally applied to cookies first, such as top-coating and flooding, and ending with those that are icing on top, such as stenciling, wafer-papering, and flocking. If you attempt to master my techniques in roughly the order presented, you'll end up happier with your results. Having said that, I should point out that I rarely, if ever, apply a single decorating technique to a cookie. In my eye, the layering of two or more techniques usually leads to the greatest interest and beauty.

Given my fondness for Royal Icing, it should come as no surprise that the first 13 of the 15 techniques use Royal Icing directly or assume it's already been applied to the cookies, and only two (embossing and appliqué work) use modeling media. For the techniques that use Royal Icing, it's most important to pay attention to the suggested icing consistency and corresponding consistency adjustments on page 244. If you find yourself getting frustrated with a technique and/or not getting the result you want, chances are good that your icing is either too thick or too thin for what you're trying to do. My best recommendation in these circumstances is to review my consistency adjustments, tweak the icing (either thicken with powdered sugar or thin with water), and try again.

1. Top-coating

Top-coating refers to laying a smooth, glass-like coating of Royal Icing on a cookie top, without first laying a border around the edge to contain the icing. And why would someone want to do this, you might ask? Wouldn't skipping the borders just increase the chances of icing running off? Certainly, you can always outline a cookie first to make a "dam" and then flood the interior with icing to create the same smooth effect. In fact, I'll be talking about outlining and flooding next. However, when icing is mixed to the proper consistency, you can skip the outlining step and save a lot of time—and money if you're paying someone else to decorate. Here's how:

(a) Tint thick Royal Icing to a color of your choice and then thin the icing to top-coating consistency (p. 245) by adding water. (The amount of water needed will vary with cookie size; the larger the cookie, the looser the icing needs to

be to get smooth coverage.) To prevent icing overflow, the Royal Icing should be mixed thicker than for flooding, but thinner than for outlining. Check the icing consistency using the 15-second rule: let the icing drop from a spoon back into the bowl; then watch the icing tracks.

(b) If the tracks disappear in 15 seconds, you're guaranteed to be close to the right consistency.

b.

(c) Get used to working with a craft paintbrush (as I do) for this task; it's quicker to apply top-coating icing this way than with a parchment pastry cone. Simply deposit a teaspoon or so of icing in the center of the cookie with the handle-end of the brush and then push the icing toward the cookie edge. Avoid using the bristle-end, as the bristles flex, making it harder to control the placement of the icing. And be sure to push with the tip of the brush handle and not the side, as you'll be less likely to leave tracks.

a.

c.

e.

(d) Continue to push the icing around the cookie until the entire cookie top is covered, adding more icing as needed as you go. Work quickly, and if an area of the cookie looks smooth, don't touch it again. Royal Icing sets up very fast and you'll only muck it up by retreading old territory. It's best to leave a $^1/_8$- to $^1/_4$-inch margin around the edge as an extra safeguard against icing runoff. This margin is also a perfect place to later put a showy decorative border.

d.

(e) While the icing is still wet, pop any large air bubbles with a metal trussing needle or toothpick.

2. Outlining

Outlining refers to the drawing of lines—such as borders, zigzags, and stripes—onto a cookie top. Outlines can be laid either on naked cookies, most often as a border or "dam" to contain flooding icing (p. 31), or on already top-coated cookies as decorative flourishes. In both cases, you'll get crisper, sharper lines with less spreading if you use a relatively thick Royal Icing—thicker than top-coating icing, but thinner than "glue." Before I get into the details of piping an outline, let me first address the circumstances that would lead me to outline and flood an entire cookie rather than top-coat it. As noted on page 28, I generally prefer to top-coat cookies as the process is faster. However, I do outline first and then flood in instances where I want my icing extremely close to the cookie edge, or on very tiny cookies where the icing may be more likely to flow off. I also outline and flood certain shapes within cookies—particularly angular ones—because a craft paintbrush simply doesn't allow for the precise icing placement that these shapes require. Whether you're outlining in preparation for flooding or for decorative purposes, the basic steps are the same:

(a) Fill a parchment pastry cone about half to two-thirds full with Royal Icing thinned to outlining consistency (p. 244); then cut a hole straight across the tip of the cone.

(The larger the hole, the wider the line.) Alternatively, place the icing in a pastry bag fitted with a small round tip. Hold the cone at a 45-degree angle to the cookie and touch down on the cookie top at the point where you want to start the line.

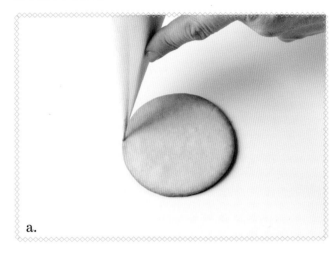

a.

(b) Apply consistent, gentle pressure to the cone while moving its tip in the direction you want the icing to go. Never drag the tip in the icing if you want a well rounded line; rather, hold the tip about $1/4$ inch above the cookie and allow the icing to fall in place.

b.

(c) Touch the tip of the cone to the cookie top at the point where you want to end the line and release pressure on the top of the cone.

c.

The variables that dictate the form of a line (tip or hole size, icing consistency, and piping speed) are also important to understand. For delicate, well-defined lines, keep the icing on the thicker end of my recommended range for this technique (p. 244) and the hole in your cone (or your pastry tip) quite small. Conversely, for wider lines, cut a bigger hole (or use a bigger tip), or for softer, flatter lines, loosen the icing a bit. Just bear in mind that a looser icing should generally dry longer before you set another icing color next to it. (Drying minimizes the risk of colors bleeding, but more on this topic in a bit.) With thick icing, you'll need to pipe a little more slowly, for if you go too fast, the line will break; conversely, if you pipe too slowly with a looser icing, the line can fall back on itself and end up wiggly rather than straight.

Now back to drying. How long should you wait before flooding next to an outline? Or before putting an outline on a freshly top-coated cookie? Both are excellent questions, and ones I get a lot. If the outlining and flooding (or top-coating) colors are the same, there's no need to wait at all. But if they're different, then it's a good idea to allow some drying time, because, as noted earlier, dry icing is less likely to bleed. Drying time depends on many factors, such as icing consistency, quantity of icing, icing color, and ambient conditions, all of which will vary from case to case, and from day to day. But waffling aside, my rule of thumb is: wait long enough for the icing to dry to the touch and lose its sheen, which is typically at least half an hour. If one or the other icing is loose or applied heavily, one of the colors is dark (or black), or it's a humid day, I've been known to wait an hour or more, just to be on the safe side.

3. Flooding (aka Running in Sugar)

Flooding describes the process of "running" a relatively loose Royal Icing into an area defined by a preexisting outline. As noted earlier, it's wise to allow the outline to dry to the touch before flooding in order to reduce the risk of colors bleeding, except, of course, when the outlining and flooding colors are the same.

Because the outline acts as a "dam," you can get away with a looser icing when flooding than you can when top-coating. Even so, I like to mix my flooding icing only as thin as needed to flow into a glass-like coating without any tracks. There's no reason to mix it any looser, as loose icings take longer to dry and, in the process, increase the chance of colors bleeding. As with top-coating, the best icing consistency for flooding varies with cookie size. Generally, larger cookies will require a slightly looser icing in order to get completely smooth coverage before the icing sets up. To flood:

(a) Fill a parchment pastry cone about half to two-thirds full with Royal Icing thinned to flooding consistency (p. 245); then cut a small ($^1/_{16}$-inch or more) hole in the tip of the cone. Alternatively, place the icing in a pastry bag fitted with a small round tip. (I prefer a cone or bag to the craft paintbrush handle used for top-coating, simply because flooding icing is very fluid and I have more control with less mess this way.) Pipe icing into the interior of the outline. For very big areas, you may want to cut a bigger hole in the bag.

a.

(b) Push the icing around with the tip of the cone until you've smoothly flooded the whole area. As with top-coating, do not retread territory that looks smooth. The icing dries quickly and you are likely to mess it up. While the icing is still wet, pop any large air bubbles with a metal trussing needle or toothpick.

b.

4. Wet-on-Wet Layering

Wet-on-wet layering is an extension of top-coating or flooding, insofar as it involves immediate decoration of a just-top-coated or just-flooded cookie with other icings, usually of contrasting colors. Simply put, wet icing gets applied to wet icing—hence the name. The icings can be piped on top in any pattern—dots, lines, zigzags, whatever you please. The only requirement is that you work fast before the top-coating or flooding icing sets up, as the goal of this technique is for the icings to settle into one big, smooth, happy top coat! If instead you were to allow the top coat to dry first and then add details, the resulting cookie would have more dimension, especially when viewed from the side. (See photo, below, for a comparison of wet-on-wet to wet-on-dry layering.)

The icing applied on top can be either relatively loose (a la flooding consistency, p. 245) or relatively thick (a la top-coating or outlining consistency, p. 244). Just remember, if the icing is thinner, it will spread more as it settles into the top coat; its color is also more likely to bleed into the top coat as it dries.

A Wet-on-Wet to Wet-on-Dry Comparison. *(a) Wet-on-wet layering: The cookie was outlined and flooded with green icing; then the white and pink details were immediately piped on top. (b) Wet-on-dry layering: The green icing was allowed to dry before white and pink details were applied. Note this cookie's additional relief.*

5. Dipping

I've added this technique since my first book, *Cookie Swap,* not just because it's needed for the beetles in Beetlemania (p. 145) and some other projects in this book, but because it's the quickest way to smoothly coat cookies with icing.

Having said that, I should point out that I don't use the technique very often for the simple reason that it's messy. Dipping basically involves the immersion of a cookie (and your fingertips) into a relatively loose Royal Icing in order to either fully or partially coat the cookie.

I refer to two dipping methods in this book: Nose-Dive Dipping and Roundabout Dipping, both of which use Royal Icing of roughly the same consistency. Nose-Dive Dipping involves the full immersion of a cookie into the icing in order to smoothly top-coat it and its edges. I choose this approach over top-coating (or outlining and flooding) when covering the cookie edge leads to a more lifelike look. A case in point: imagine how much less convincing my beetles would be if you could see the brownies underneath their Royal Icing! Dipping very large cookies (such as A Good Egg, p. 95) using this technique can require further loosening of the icing (p. 245), but otherwise the most important thing to remember is to dip with a simple down-and-up dunk. Roundabout Dipping, on the other hand, refers to partial dipping of a round, oval, or smoothly contoured cookie to coat only its edge. Rather than dunking, it requires a rotation of the cookie edge through the icing.

Nose-Dive Dipping

(a) Turn your cookie upside down and dip it headfirst into icing of dipping consistency (p. 245), taking care to

fully cover the cookie edge. It's best not to let the cookie touch the bottom of the bowl, or you may not get a smooth coating. If needed, transfer the icing to a smaller bowl, or add more icing, to get the depth you need. Shake off any excess icing over the bowl, with the cookie still upside down.

(b) Turn the cookie right side up and gently shake it again to smooth out any tracks in the icing.

(c) Wipe off the excess icing on the cookie bottom on the edge of the bowl. Wiping minimizes pooling of icing around the cookie as it dries, which leads to a neater edge.

(d) Place the cookie on a rack over parchment paper (to catch any drippings) or a parchment paper-lined cookie sheet. Quickly fill in any fingerprints from holding the cookie with extra icing. While the icing is wet, pop any big air bubbles with a metal trussing needle or toothpick.

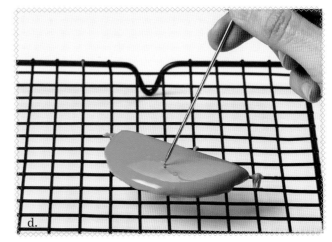

(e) Before the icing fully dries, slide a thin-bladed paring knife under the cookie to sever the drippings from the rack (or paper); then slide the cookie onto a clean area on the rack (or paper). If you don't move the cookie, it may dry onto the surface; plus, sliding straightens the icing along the bottom edge, leaving you with a neater cookie.

Roundabout Dipping

(a) Start on one end of the cookie edge and submerge it in the icing until you've covered the cookie to the point you want.

a.

(b) Slowly rotate the cookie through the icing until you've covered the entire length of the cookie edge. Lift the cookie out of the icing and gently shake it to smooth any icing tracks.

b.

(c) Wipe off the excess icing on the cookie bottom on the edge of the bowl. Again, wiping minimizes the pooling of icing around the cookie as it dries, which leads to a neater edge. Place the cookie on a rack or parchment paper-lined cookie sheet and handle as described in Step (e), p. 33, for "Nose-Dive Dipping."

c.

6. Beadwork

Even though beadwork (the making of perfectly round icing dots) is actually a piping technique similar to those on page 46, I've included it here as a full-fledged decorating technique. Why the extra attention? Well, partly because I love dots and I use them a lot, but also because beadwork is one of the trickier techniques for beginners. I can't tell you how many times I've been asked, "How come my dots always have peaks and yours look so round?" A small question on the surface. But unresolved details like this can gnaw at a perfectionist cookie decorator!

Fortunately, the answer to this question is straightforward, and once you know it, the technique is easy to master. If your dots end up with peaks, it's simply because your icing is too thick. Thin it with water and try again. (For beadwork consistency adjustments, see page 245.) If your dots have no peaks but don't look quite round, check to make sure you've cut the tip on your parchment pastry cone straight across, or use a round metal tip in a pastry bag. (Holes cut at an angle can lead to irregular shapes.) If that doesn't work, be sure you're holding the parchment pastry cone or pastry bag at a 90-degree angle to the cookie. Again, piping at some other angle can lead to oval shapes.

It's also useful to know how to control dot size. For very tiny dots (that is, pinprick size), work with a parchment pastry cone, as you'll always be able to get a smaller dot than with the smallest of standard size pastry tips. Cut a barely perceptible hole in the tip of the cone, apply a small amount of pressure to the top of the cone, and you're done. To make larger dots, there are essentially three things you can do: (1) apply more pressure, (2) cut a bigger hole in your cone, and/or (3) loosen the icing. Though if you loosen the icing much beyond beadwork consistency, watch out. The icing can spread further once it hits the cookie and dots can run together. My best recommendation when piping dots, or anything else for that matter, is to test the icing on a piece of parchment paper before applying it to cookies. Pipe a few dots in a row; if you're satisfied with their initial size, shape, and spread, then you're good to go.

7. Marbling

Marbling is responsible for the wonderfully swirly patterns shown on Lollypalooza (p. 103) and Proud as a Peacock (p. 155), as well as other projects in this book. While marbling gives the appearance of being complex, it's actually one of the quickest and most forgiving decorating methods around. Its foundation is wet-on-wet layering (p. 31), which means that icings are applied next to each other before any have dried (which, in turn, means that extra care must be taken with icing consistency, as I'll explain in a bit). In a nutshell, the technique involves laying a top coat on either a whole cookie or part of one and then piping other icing colors in lines, dots, or other patterns on top. While the icings are wet, a metal trussing needle or toothpick is drawn through the icings to create a marbled effect. In my opinion, the technique looks best when three or more colors are used—one for the top coat and two or more on top. Also, the greater the contrast between the colors, the more striking the final result.

Success with this technique hinges on two key factors: (1) icing consistency (naturally!) and (2) working quickly before the icings set up. Make sure that all icings are at the proper consistency before you start work; that is, top-coating consistency (p. 245) for the top-coating color and marbling consistency (p. 244), which is just slightly thicker than top-coating consistency, for the colors on top. On the one hand, you want the icings to be loose enough to marble smoothly without the trussing needle or toothpick leaving tracks. But, on the other hand, you never want the icings to be too loose. Because the colors are laid next to each other when wet, there is more risk of colors bleeding. So the thicker you can mix the icings without getting tracks, the faster they'll dry without bleeding. Start with my consistency adjustments, but if you can work even thicker (which is sometimes possible on very small cookies), then do so.

As for the second success factor, don't forget that Royal Icing dries very quickly. If you dilly-dally while laying the icings, they may partially set up by the time you draw the trussing needle through them, and the pattern will end up looking rough. See "What Happens When You Marble Slowly," below, for an example of what you don't want! Make sure your marbling icings are in separate parchment pastry cones before you start. If you stop to adjust colors or fill cones mid-marble, you certainly won't get the smooth result that you should.

What Happens When You Marble Slowly. *I waited too long to draw the trussing needle through the icings on the cookie to the right. As a result, the marbled pattern is a lot rougher than the one on the properly marbled cookie to the left.*

One last word on making patterns: I show how to make a basic starburst pattern, below, and other designs throughout the book, but the possibilities are endless—truly. Just remember, there are basically three variables with which you can play to vary patterns: (1) the colors, (2) the way in which you pipe the icings onto the top coat, and (3) the path that you draw the trussing needle through the icings. My best advice on creating patterns is to experiment with these variables—you will not be disappointed with the results!

Marbling a Starburst Pattern

(a) Top-coat a cookie as described on page 28.

a.

(b) Immediately pipe one or more contrasting colors of Royal Icing in concentric circles on top. Don't worry if your

b.

circles aren't perfect. As I said before, marbling is a very forgiving technique; most piping imperfections can be masked in the next step.

(c) Work quickly before the icings set up. Use a metal trussing needle or toothpick to draw a series of straight lines through the icings, starting at the cookie center and ending at the edge. To minimize any blobs or imperfections in the icing piped in Step (b), run the trussing needle through them whenever you can.

c.

(d) Notice how the waviness in my circles has virtually disappeared by the time I'm done!

d.

8. Stenciling

Though I'd categorize this technique as later-stage "icing on the cookie" to master after top-coating, outlining, and flooding, it is by no means a difficult technique. In fact, along with marbling, wafer-papering, and rubber-stamping, it's one of the easiest ways to add eye-catching detail to cookies even if artistic ability isn't your strong suit. If you can stencil paint on a wall, then I guarantee you can stencil icing on a cookie!

Either naked or top-coated cookies can be stenciled, though I generally prefer to use top-coated cookies because they're flatter (and tastier). Before you stencil, make sure to dry top coats completely, ideally overnight. Stenciling requires application of pressure to the cookie tops, which can crack or dent partially dried icing. Success hereafter depends on three factors: (1) choosing the right stencil, (2) mixing the Royal Icing to the right consistency (as always), and (3) having a steady, even hand.

On the first point, it's best to choose a stencil that lies very flat across the cookie and fits the top coat with some room (at least $1/4$ inch) to spare. If your stencil is too large, it can

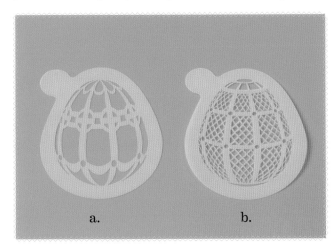

Beginner vs. Advanced Stencil. *(a) Beginner stencil, with relatively large openings and distance between openings. (b) Advanced stencil, with smaller, more closely spaced openings.*

lift off the edge of the top coat and allow the stenciling icing to sneak underneath into areas it shouldn't be. I also urge beginners to start with an easy stencil, meaning one that isn't very intricate and whose openings aren't too closely spaced. When the openings are closer than about $1/8$ inch, it becomes more important to mix the stenciling icing to just the right consistency. If too loose, the icing in one opening will run into the next, resulting in a blurry pattern.

As for stenciling icing, start by tinting thick Royal Icing. (Generally, a color that contrasts the top coat color works best.) Then thin the icing to stenciling consistency (p. 244), a consistency thicker than top-coating consistency and looser than outlining consistency. However, if you find your icing leaving too many tracks, thin it with a bit of water. Conversely, if it flows too freely, especially under intricate stencils, thicken it with powdered sugar.

Lastly, try your hardest not to move the stencil while applying the icing. Even small movements can result in a smudged pattern. Here are some more tips for getting sharp results:

(a) Lay the stencil where you want the design to appear on the cookie. To keep the stencil from moving, hold it firmly in place on the cookie top with a finger or two, or with the tip of a metal trussing needle or toothpick if there's limited holding room on the stencil, as shown here.

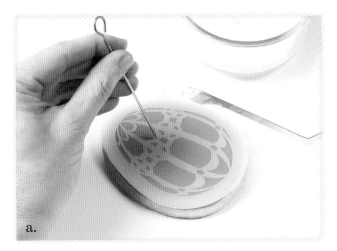

(b) Use a small offset spatula to spread the stenciling icing over the openings in the stencil. To minimize track marks, use as few strokes as possible and avoid lifting the spatula in the middle of the pattern.

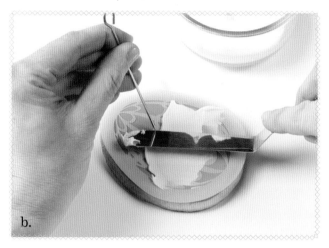

b.

(c) Once the pattern is filled with icing, carefully lift off the stencil to reveal the finished pattern. Wipe off the underside of the stencil before placing on the next cookie. For the sharpest patterns, wash and thoroughly dry the stencil after every two or three icing applications.

c.

9. Wafer-Papering

Another speedy way to add impressive cookie detail, wafer-papering refers to the application of wafer paper (p. 26) to cookie tops using corn syrup as the "glue." Wafer paper is virtually tasteless and quickly dissolves on the tongue, so it doesn't detract from the cookie eating experience the way large pieces of modeling media sometimes do. You can either purchase paper already printed with edible ink or custom-print your own patterns using a dedicated printer with edible ink, as described on page 24.

Although one of the easier techniques in this book, wafer-papering does require attention to detail. First, the paper will not stick to a naked cookie—only to one that has been top-coated or covered with rolled fondant or another modeling medium. The paper is also translucent, so be sure to top-coat cookies with a color that you don't mind seeing through the paper, and which is light enough to allow the pattern to show well. Since some pressure is needed to fix the paper in place, cookie top coats should be dried completely, ideally overnight, before the paper is applied. The paper is also rather delicate, so handle it carefully. And avoid getting it wet or too damp with the corn syrup "glue," as it can tear or even dissolve.

Wafer paper can be applied to an entire cookie surface, or it can be cut or punched out (using craft paper punches) and applied to smaller areas of a cookie. While the technique is basically the same regardless of how much cookie you cover, there is one important exception. To apply paper to an entire cookie, paint the cookie top coat with corn syrup and then lay the paper on top. This is the quickest approach; plus, you're less likely to rip the paper if you don't paint it. However, to apply paper to a small area, always paint the back of the paper and then set the paper on the cookie. Why the difference? Because any corn syrup that gets on the cookie, and which isn't later covered with paper, will end up drying into a shiny and not so attractive spot.

Once the paper is on, dry it for at least an hour before adding borders or other icing details on top. The paper has a tendency to lift, especially along cut edges, if icing is applied too soon. Last but not least, dry the cookies with the paper facing up despite what packaging instructions may tell you. The paper, especially if laid on larger cookies, can buckle if dried face down. It also dries faster if exposed to the air.

Wafer-Papering an Entire Cookie

(a) Trace the outline of the cookie on the back side of the wafer paper using the cookie cutter originally used to cut the cookie.

a.

(b) Remember, wafer paper will not stick to a naked cookie, so the paper must be trimmed to fit the icing (or modeling medium) on the cookie top—and to remove the tracing marks.

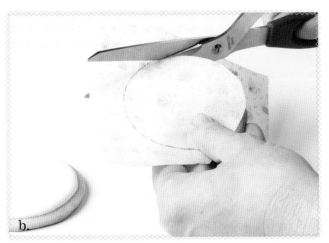

b.

(c) Use a small, soft sponge brush to spread a very thin layer of corn syrup on the icing (or modeling medium). Blot shiny wet spots with paper towel. The surface should only be tacky, as the paper can buckle and dissolve in overly wet spots. Avoid bristle brushes for this task, since the bristles tend to pull off and get stuck in the corn syrup.

c.

(d) Stick the paper on one edge of the cookie and gradually smooth down the rest of the paper, working out any air bubbles as you go. Setting down the paper in one fell swoop can often trap air bubbles, especially if you're working with a large piece of paper. Press down the edges well, as they have a tendency to lift.

d.

(e) Before adding a border, air-dry the paper face up as described on page 38; then trim any paper that overhangs the icing. Extra paper at the edge can sometimes interfere with even piping of borders.

e.

10. Rubber-Stamping

Rubber-stamping on cookies is really no different than rubber-stamping on paper. The only exception is that you must use edible ink and rubber stamps that haven't been touched by anything but edible ink. You can stamp directly on top-coated cookies. Or you can stamp on thin sheets of rolled fondant or other modeling media, either dried or soft, and then stick the stamped dough onto iced or un-iced cookie tops with Royal Icing. If you're stamping on top-coated cookies, it's important to dry top coats completely, ideally overnight, or you can crack the icing when you apply pressure with the stamp on top. Likewise, be careful if you're stamping on dried modeling media, especially rolled fondant, as these doughs are brittle in dry form and can also crack. Lastly, if you stamp on soft modeling media, expect not only to see the stamp, but also to end up with a very cool embossed effect! (The relief of the stamp will transfer into the soft dough, along with the edible ink.)

A quick word on tools: almost any rubber stamp will do, as long as it fits your cookie top or top coat. Rubber stamps

don't conform well to rounded icing edges, so if you're stamping on a top-coated cookie, it's best to allow some icing margin (at least $1/8$ inch) around the edge of the stamp. This way, you're sure to capture the entire stamp on the top coat. As for edible ink, I use soft-gel food coloring applied to an un-inked felt or foam ink pad (p. 24). Both types of pads work just fine, despite what you may have read elsewhere about felt pads being superior. Foam pads are softer and absorb more food coloring than felt pads, which makes it easier to inadvertently over-ink your stamp and then your cookies. But because they hold more coloring, they'll stay moist and well inked for many days if closed and sealed in baggies, whereas felt pads often need to be reinked many times in the course of working with them.

Rubber-Stamping a Top-Coated Cookie

(a) Apply soft-gel food coloring to an un-inked felt or foam ink pad and let the coloring soak into the pad.

a.

(b) Use paper towels to blot any excess coloring that remains pooled on top of the pad. Felt pads will need more blotting than foam pads, because they're less absorbent.

(c) Press the stamp on the pad to evenly coat it with coloring; then gently press it onto the dried cookie top coat.

(d) Carefully lift the stamp to avoid smudging the wet ink; then reink the stamp as needed for the next cookie.

b.

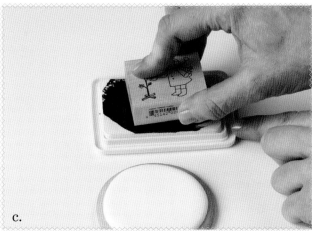

c.

d.

11. Dusting

Dusting refers to the brushing of dry decorating powders (such as luster, pearl, petal, and disco dust, p. 27) onto naked or top-coated cookie tops with a craft paintbrush. These dusts come in a plethora of colors and with varying degrees of shimmer. When applied dry, dusts lend a subtle blush and/or shimmer. If you're dusting on an icing top coat, make sure it is completely dry before you start; otherwise, the dust will cling heavily to damp spots, leaving a spotted or streaked appearance.

You can dust either the entire cookie top or portions of the cookie, but bear in mind that the dust easily launches airborne and can be difficult to contain. If you want to dust a confined area, it's best to use a tiny brush and to shake any excess dust off the brush before setting the brush on the cookie.

12. Painting

You can paint naked or dry top-coated cookies with soft-gel food coloring, but when I say "painting" in this book, I'm referring to painting with a decorating powder, such as luster or petal dust (p. 27). These dusts are not water soluble, so to create paint, you must extend them with an oil-based coloring, flavored extract, or alcohol. I usually choose a clear extract (such as lemon, orange, almond, or anise) that complements the flavor of my cookies or icing and that won't alter the color of the dust.

There are a couple of ways in which painting with dust differs from dusting. One, paint tends to create a more opaque finish, as demonstrated in "Painting with Decorating Powder," on page 42. Second, paint is a lot easier to place exactly where you want it. If mixed relatively thick (about one part dust to one part extract by volume), it can easily be painted on very delicate outlines. For a less opaque finish, simply use a higher ratio of extract to dust, but recognize that the paint will flow more freely and be harder to control. Also be prepared to continually tweak the paint consistency—the extract will evaporate and the paint will become thicker as you work. Because painting only requires a very light touch, it's not critical that your cookie icing be completely dry through and through; however, it should dry until it has crusted and dulled.

Dusts are relatively expensive (about $4 to $5 for a 2 gram/0.07 ounce container), but fortunately a little bit goes a long way and, if you work smartly, you can always recover what you've used and save it for future use, even after mixing it into paint. I rarely work with more than $1/2$ teaspoon dust at a time. (Mixed with $1/2$ teaspoon extract, this quantity is enough to paint accents on at least a few dozen cookies.) I also mix paint in a small lidded container, and when I'm done, all I do is snap on the lid. The paint will dry and revert to dust, so that when it's time to paint again, I just take off the lid and extend the dust as before.

Painting with Decorating Powder

Note: The same general principles for painting an outline, as shown here, apply to painting naked or top-coated cookies, either in whole or in part. *Also note:* This cookie's top coat has already been dusted with gold luster dust. The giveaway? Its telltale soft sheen.

(a) Mix clear extract and decorating powder (p. 27) in equal parts in a reclosable container. I use the nonbristle end of a craft paintbrush to mix the paint, so as not to

a.

mess up the bristles. (If you're painting a large swath of cookie, you may want to increase the quantity of extract to make a looser paint.)

(b) Choose a craft paintbrush sized to your task. A tiny brush ($1/16$- to $1/8$-inch-wide bristle) is best for painting this delicate line. Dip the brush in the paint and carefully apply the paint to the outline. If the paint is too runny and drips off the line, let some of the extract evaporate to thicken the paint and try again. At the proper consistency, the paint should cling neatly to the line. To maintain the desired paint consistency, add more extract as it evaporates. *One last note:* See how opaque the dust looks when it's painted? It's much more showy this way than when dusted on dry.

b.

13. Flocking (aka Sanding)

I'm sure you've seen cookies with patches of sanding sugar, jimmies, or nonpareils (p. 26) on top. Well, flocking is the technique whereby those tidy patches of texture get applied. You can flock a whole cookie, a small area, or even a very thin line, but, in all cases, the key thing to remember is that these tiny sugar items will stick to icing even if it's only slightly tacky. If you don't want them on an area of a cookie, then be very sure that the icing in that area is completely dry. The basic approach to flocking is the same regardless of whether you cover a large swath or a very focused area: simply apply icing where you want the sugar pieces to stick, and while the icing is wet, pour a generous amount of sanding sugar, jimmies, or nonpareils on top. Shake off the excess sugar pieces and voilà! Minor icing consistency and other adjustments are needed, especially when flocking thin lines, as discussed below.

A couple of housekeeping notes: because flocking is one of the more messy techniques, leave it for the end of the decorating process in order to keep stray sugar pieces off cookies that shouldn't have them. If the sugar pieces are packaged in a large (8- to 16-ounce) bag or bottle, they'll be easier to apply (and you'll use less) if funneled through a parchment pastry cone. Otherwise, pouring directly from a smaller (3- to 4-ounce) container onto the cookie is fine. Either way, always flock over a bowl. The bowl catches the sugar overflow, which can sometimes be a lot, and allows you to recover it for future use.

Flocking a Large Swath vs. a Thin Line

Always start by tinting and adjusting the Royal Icing used for flocking "glue." To minimize its visibility, tint it to match existing top coats and/or the sugar pieces you're putting on top. Conversely, if you'd like the glue to show behind the sugar pieces, tint it a contrasting color.

When flocking a large swath, thin the "glue" to top-coating consistency (p. 245) and spread it onto the cookie with a small craft paintbrush. You'll get more even coverage, more quickly, this way. Then simply sprinkle the sugar pieces on top.

(a) When flocking a thin line, pictured right, it's best to use a thicker "glue" of outlining consistency (p. 244) to keep the line from flattening under the weight of the sugar pieces. But because outlining icing is relatively thick, it will dry very fast. Pipe your line(s) quickly.

(b) And waste no time in sprinkling your sugar pieces over the top. If the sugar pieces don't stick to your line(s), you either waited too long to flock or your icing was too thick. If the latter, loosen the icing a tad with water and try again.

a.

b.

(c) The flocked line will always appear fatter than the original piped line, but the thicker your icing is to start, the less it will expand.

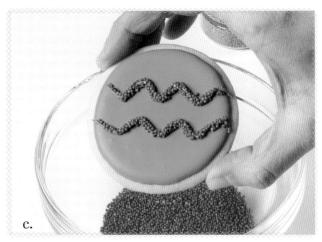

c.

14. Embossing

Embossing refers to creating an impression in rolled fondant or another modeling medium (p. 27) by running a textured rolling pin over the dough, stamping objects into it, or pressing it into molds. Once embossed, the dough is often trimmed with a paring knife or cookie cutter to neaten its edges or to create specific shapes, which, in turn, are applied to cookie tops as 3-D decorative flourishes, aka appliqués (p. 45). The biggest problem encountered when embossing is a tacky modeling medium that sticks to the embossing tool. While the temptation may be to dust the rolling pin (or stamp or mold) with powdered sugar, I prefer to knead more powdered sugar into the dough until it becomes tractable. If you dust the tool instead, small clumps of powdered sugar can imbed themselves in the dough where they become quite difficult to remove.

Embossing with Molds

(a) Choose your mold. I prefer silicone molds to inflexible plastic or resin ones, because they bend easily, allowing the modeling medium to be popped out with minimal to no distortion of the final piece. Press a small amount of modeling medium into the mold, taking care to fully press it into the bottom to capture the full impression. You'll need

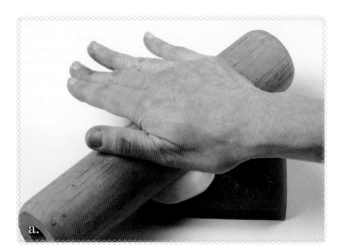

more dough for deeper molds. To ensure the most uniform imprint, firmly run a plain rolling pin over the dough.

(b) Turn the mold upside down and gently press on the bottom until the dough pops out on its own.

(c) Trim around the edge with a cookie cutter or paring knife.

(d) (Optional) To accentuate the pattern, dust the top with a decorating powder (p. 27) or cocoa powder, as I've done here and with the cookie jewelry on page 66.

(e) Lastly, fix the cutout to a cookie using a small amount of Royal Icing. If the embossed piece is thin, avoid using

d.

e.

appliqués aren't integral to the primary cookie, they can easily be plucked off if tastes dictate.

Appliqué work can be as simple as sticking a few dragées on cookies, or as complex as multi-component compound cookies (see "Definition," below). Regardless of complexity, the process for appliqué work is the generally the same: (1) pipe Royal Icing onto the cookie in the place where you want to stick the appliqué, (2) set the appliqué on top, and (3) let the icing dry before you move the cookie. Thick icing of "glue" consistency (p. 243) is a must in most applications. It is less likely to squeeze out from underneath appliqués and sets quickly, thereby preventing slipping and sliding of pieces as the icing dries. However, it's best to use looser icing of top-coating consistency (p. 245) for thin appliqués, such as those in "Embossing with Molds" (p. 44), to ensure that they lie flat against cookies without looking lumpy. For small appliqués, such as dragées, tint the icing "glue" to match the color of the cookie dough or top coat to which they're being applied. In the event that the "glue" does peek out from underneath the appliqué(s), it's less likely to show this way.

For tips on making embossed appliqués and other decorations from modeling media, see "Embossing" (p. 44) and "Made with Modeling Media" (p. 55), respectively.

icing any thicker than top-coating consistency (p. 245), as it can make the cutout look lumpy and/or keep it from lying flat.

15. Appliqué Work

As noted earlier, I'm not a fan of completely covering cookies with modeling media for texture reasons. But small 3-D embellishments can add a lot of visual interest, and Royal Icing can only go so far. Because the making of 3-D decorations is the raison d'être for modeling media, I do use these doughs in appliqué work, a term I use to describe the gluing of small edibles (i.e., 3-D decorations, dragées, cookies, candies, etc.) onto bigger cookies. Since

Definition: Compound Cookie

"Compound cookie" is a term I coined in *Cookie Swap* to refer to cookies stacked on cookies, such as the cookie rings that form the baskets in A Tisket, a Tasket (p. 169) or the moon-owl-and-bat cookies in What a Hoot (p. 195). I like to distinguish compound cookies, where the cookies lay flat on top of one another, from other 3-D cookies, where cookies stand vertically on end, for the simple reason that they're easier to assemble. If you're just venturing into 3-D cookie play, then compound cookies are a safe place to start.

7 ESSENTIAL PIPING TECHNIQUES

Once I've decorated a cookie with one or more of my 15 techniques, I usually give it a final polish with a piped border. There are myriad icing borders that can be piped on cookie edges (or elsewhere on top), but in this section, I focus solely on the ones used in this book. If you're an advanced decorator, you probably know much of this information already, so breeze through it if you wish. However, if you're a beginner, you'll find a good introduction to some quick and easy piping techniques.

Four factors largely determine the look of any piped pattern: (1) the shape and size (or number) of tip used, if any; (2) the piping angle between the bag (or cone) and work surface; (3) the way in which you move the bag (or cone) and/or apply pressure to it; and (4) the Royal Icing consistency. More on the second point: for a perfectly symmetrical application of icing (i.e., a perfectly round dot), it's best to hold your bag at a 90-degree angle to the work surface. Any smaller angle tends to produce a more elongated result. As for the third point, it's most important to remember that smooth and continuous application of pressure (as in a Straight Line, below) will generally result in a pattern of uniform width, whereas application of sustained pressure, followed by a gradual or abrupt release of pressure, will result in patterns of varying width (as in Trailing Beaded Border or Trailing Star Border, below and right). For each of the patterns shown here, I've given direction on how to handle these factors, as well as an indication of the pastry tip(s) most often used for the technique in this book.

Simple Outlines and Beaded Borders

These borders can be made with either a parchment pastry cone or a pastry bag with a round tip.

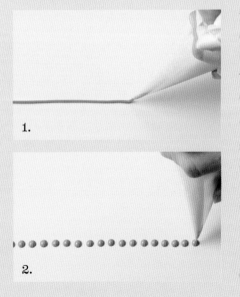

1.

2.

1. Straight Line (also see "Outlining," p. 29): (a) Round tip (Ateco #5 or smaller) or pastry cone; (b) 45-degree angle; (c) Touch down the tip at the start of the line; apply uniform pressure while pulling the cone toward you in a straight line; touch down the tip at the end of the line and release pressure on the top of the cone; (d) For well-defined lines, use Royal Icing of outlining consistency (p. 244).

2. Beaded Border (also see "Beadwork," p. 34): (a) Round tip (Ateco #5 or smaller) or pastry cone; (b) 90-degree angle; (c) Place the tip close to the cookie top, apply uniform pressure until the bead reaches the desired size, release pressure, and then pull up abruptly; repeat to create a series of beads in a row; (d) For well rounded beads with no peaks, use Royal Icing of beadwork consistency (p. 245).

3. Trailing Beaded Border: (a) Round tip (Ateco #5 or smaller) or pastry cone; (b) 45-degree angle; (c) Place the tip close to the cookie top, apply pressure until the bead reaches the desired size, and then abruptly pull the cone toward you as you release pressure to create a tapered point on the bead; repeat to create a series of overlapping tapered beads that run in a straight line; (d) Royal Icing of outlining consistency (p. 244).

4. Zig Zag or Two-Sided Trailing Beaded Border: (a) Round tip (Ateco #5 or smaller) or pastry cone; (b) 45-degree angle; (c) Place the tip close to the cookie top, apply pressure until the bead reaches the desired size, and then abruptly pull the cone toward you as you release pressure to create a tapered point on the bead; rotate the tip of the cone slightly so the next bead starts at an angle to the first and apply and release pressure as just described to create a second overlapping bead; rotate the tip of the cone in the opposite direction (so it's in alignment with the first bead) and repeat until you've created a border of the desired length; (d) Royal Icing of outlining consistency (p. 244).

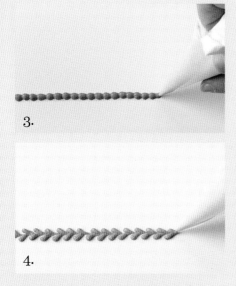

3.

4.

Textured Borders

These borders require use of a pastry bag and a very particular, nonround tip.

1.

1. Leaf or Feather: (a) Leaf tip with a single large notch (Ateco #352); (b) 45-degree angle; (c) Place the tip close to the cookie top, apply pressure until the base of the leaf (or feather) reaches the desired size, and then abruptly pull the bag toward you as you release pressure to create a tapered point; repeat to make a cluster, line, or another pattern, as desired; (d) Thick Royal Icing, close to "glue" consistency (p. 243).

2.

2. Trailing Star Border: (a) Open or closed star tip (Ateco #18 or #27); (b) 45-degree angle; (c) Place the tip close to the cookie top, apply pressure until the textured bead reaches the desired size, and then abruptly pull the bag toward you as you release pressure to create a tapered point; repeat to create a series of overlapping textured beads that run in a straight line; (d) Thick Royal Icing, close to "glue" consistency (p. 243).

3. Grass: (a) Grass tip (Ateco #113); (b) 90-degree angle; (c) Place the tip close to the cookie top, apply pressure until you've created a bead that's about the width of the tip; abruptly pull straight up on the bag while releasing pressure to create tips on the grass; repeat in a tight cluster to create a patch of grass or another pattern, as desired; (d) Thick Royal Icing, close to "glue" consistency (p. 243).

3.

beyond bedazzled

CUSTOM TEMPLATES AND STENCILS

There inevitably comes a time in cookie decorating, especially for diehard decorators, when the craving to design a truly original cookie kicks in, and off-the-shelf cookie cutters start looking tired and bland. I know. Standard cutters just didn't cut it—so to speak—for a few of this book's projects.

So, what did I do in the face of no perfect cutter? Abandon my cookie decorating dreams? No way! When you can't find a cutter of the right size or shape, there are a couple of paths you can take. If you plan to cut a lot of custom cookies, creating a custom cookie cutter (p. 49) is the most expedient approach over the long run. You'll also generally get cleaner, more precise cuts this way. However, if all you need is a few unique cookies, making a custom template to use as a cutting guide will be cheaper and faster in the short run.

Making and Cutting with Custom Templates

(a) To make a template, draw or trace your desired shape onto a piece of thin cardboard or heavy gauge acetate (about $2/100$ inch thick). I generally prefer acetate for templates, since it's easier to clean and reuse. However, if you plan to trim your cookies while hot from the oven (something I do with pieces for tight-fitting 3-D cookie constructions, or to square off rectilinear shapes), then use cardboard. If you place an acetate template on top of a warm cookie, the acetate will buckle and no longer be a useful cutting guide. Cut out the shape to create a template.

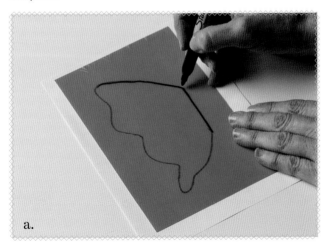

a.

(b) Roll out the dough to a uniform thickness, set the template on top, and cut around it with a thin-bladed paring knife. (Very large shapes—that cannot be easily moved with a wide offset spatula—should be cut directly on a prepared cookie sheet.) Avoid dragging the knife through the dough; you'll generally get cleaner cookie edges if you cut in short up-and-down strokes. If needed, dust the top of the dough and/or the underside of the template lightly with flour to prevent sticking.

b.

(c) Remove the dough around the template. If the cookie edges look at all ragged (a hazard of cutting with templates), neaten them before lifting the template by patting the side of the knife blade against the template and cut cookie edge.

c.

(d) Slowly lift off the template. If you missed any rough edges in Step (c), pat and/or trim these areas.

For outlines of all the custom templates used in this book, see "A Cut Above" (p. 262).

d.

An Aside on Custom Stencils

A stencil is essentially the inverse of a template insofar as the shape is cut out of the interior of the acetate using a utility knife and then icing or cookie batter (i.e., Traditional Tuiles, p. 255) is spread over the opening to make shapes. I always use acetate to make custom stencils, simply because cardboard with tuile batter or icing on it doesn't lend itself well to cleaning and reuse!

CUSTOM COOKIE CUTTERS

As noted earlier, if you're planning a large run of custom cookies, it will ultimately be faster to invest some time upfront in making a cutter. Some cookie cutter suppliers will make cutters to your specification, but getting a single cutter made can cost much more than a cookie cutter making kit (p. 23), which comes with enough tin stripping and all the tools needed to make several cutters. I usually opt to make my own cutters unless the shape I'm seeking is terrifically complex.

Making a Custom Cookie Cutter

(a) Draw or trace the desired shape of the cutter on a piece of paper. Cut a length of tin stripping long enough to form the cutter, adding 1 extra inch for overlap where the ends of the stripping will meet. If you're unsure about the length needed, wind a piece of string around your drawing, taking care to follow all the contours. Cut the string where it meets up with the other end; then straighten out the cut piece and measure it. You'll need this amount of tin plus the 1 inch allowance for overlap. Clean the tin

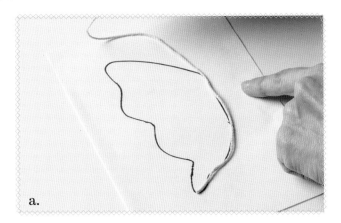

a.

with dishwashing soap if indicated in the kit's instructions. Cleaning can help the tape adhere better in Step (c).

(b) Wind the tin around your drawing using the various tools in the kit to make curves and angles where needed. For easier handling, I often work directly on my work surface, rather than on the board provided with the kit.

(c) Secure the ends of the cutter together with the double-sided tape provided with the kit. Make sure the cutter sits flat on your work surface and trim any extra tape that may extend beyond the tin. Some kits also recommend curing the tape (to set the bond faster) by placing the cutter in a low (200°F) oven for about 1 hour.

b.

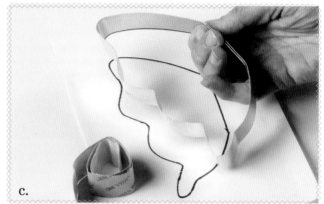

c.

3-D COOKIE CONSTRUCTION

Another way to elevate your cookie designs—both literally and figuratively—is to venture from 2-D to 3-D cookie construction. It's safe to say that the best known example of 3-D cookie construction is the gingerbread house. We've all seen one, many of us have made one or more, and myriad books explain how to make them in great detail. So I don't go there in this book. Instead, I introduce more novel forms of 3-D construction, ranging from jewelry boxes and votive holders to baskets and lizards! (Yes, lizards! Fast forward to page 139.)

More good news: "novel" doesn't equal "complex." Every one of my 3-D projects is simpler to make than the typical gingerbread house, and most rely on the same seven core construction principles:

1. Choose the right cookie dough. As easily said as done. You'll see that I suggest the best dough(s) for each project in "Types" at the project start. However, as a general rule of thumb, Cutout Cookie Gingerbread (p. 236) and Signature Sugar Cookie Dough (p. 234) are more suitable for small-scale projects, whereas Construction Gingerbread (p. 238) is the better building block for projects with exceptionally large (about 10-inch or more) and/or weight-bearing pieces, or ones intended for long-term display. Because it's made with protein-rich bread flour rather than all-purpose flour, Construction Gingerbread is less prone to breaking and bending under humid conditions. It also spreads less than the other two doughs, so it's great for tight-fitting constructions where final, baked cookie dimensions need to be more precise. On the flip side, Construction Gingerbread isn't as delicate on the palate, so I often tailor my projects to the smaller side.

2. Test your templates for fit. If your 3-D project requires custom templates for cutting the dough (as some of mine do), it's best to make sure you cut the templates accurately before you start using them. The last thing you want is to cut and bake a lot of pieces only to find out later that you made a template cutting error. Arrange the templates in 3-D to make sure they fit together as planned. If they don't, trim or recut the templates.

3. For tight-fitting angular constructions, trim the cookie pieces while hot. Even if you've accurately cut your templates and the dough to match the templates, all cookie doughs (even Construction Gingerbread) spread as they bake. Don't be surprised if project pieces need some trimming once they're out of the oven, particularly if they're part of a tight-fitting angular construction such as Open Your Heart Box (p. 165), Jewel Box Gem (p. 81), or other boxes or cubes. Before trimming, let the cookies cool a minute or less, until they can be safely trimmed without putting cracks in the top. And once you start trimming, work fast! If the cookies cool too much, they'll harden to the point that they'll be difficult to trim without breaking.

To trim, simply recut the cookies using the cutter(s) that originally cut them, as pictured below. Or, if they were cut using a template, set the template atop the hot cookie and

cut around it with a sharp knife. Remember, a cardboard template is best for this task. (Acetate templates will curl or melt if they get hot.) For the cleanest cuts, always use a straight up-and-down cutting motion rather than dragging the knife through the dough.

4. For tight-fitting angular constructions, bevel adjoining cookie edges. If left unbeveled, cookie edges generally won't fit snugly together at corners. To bevel an edge, hold a sharp paring knife at a 45-degree angle to the back of the cookie and carefully run the knife along the edge, shaving off cookie as you go.

Once fully beveled, the edge of the cookie will be angled, as pictured on the right cookie below.

5. Reinforce the backs of un-iced cookies. If you don't plan to eat your project immediately, it's a good idea to reinforce the backs of any un-iced cookies before you assemble the project. Reinforcing is especially important to do on large pieces that will bear the weight of other cookies, such as box bottoms, or stand straight up. To reinforce a cookie, simply spread a thin layer of Royal Icing of topcoating consistency (p. 245) on the back and let the icing dry. The added icing will protect the cookie from the evils of humidity and keep it from sagging or cracking over time.

6. Use super thick Royal Icing as the "glue." Decorators' biggest frustration with 3-D cookie construction is usually the slipping and sliding of pieces during assembly. Fortunately, this trouble is easily averted by using Royal Icing of the thickest "glue" consistency (p. 243), meaning icing so thick that it clings (indefinitely) to a spoon or spatula without falling off. Thick icing is less slippery than thin icing to begin with; plus, it sets more quickly.

Before applying any "glue" to a project, tint it to match either the color of the dough (if gluing a corner or visible seam) or the top coat color (if gluing another cookie or decoration onto the top coat). This way, if any "glue" peeks out, it's less likely to show. Speaking of "glue" peeking out,

there's nothing worse than a sloppy "glue" job. To ensure precise placement of "glue," it's best to apply it with a parchment pastry cone, as pictured left.

7. Assemble on a movable, rigid surface and prop, as needed. Once a project is assembled, it can take 30 minutes or more for the icing to dry to the point that the project can be safely picked up. In order to move projects without directly handling them, always assemble on pieces of heavy-duty cardboard sized to fit the final project. (For the ultimate mobility, I assemble most projects, even 2-D ones, this way.) Some projects, especially those with tall vertical pieces, may require propping to keep the pieces in position while the icing dries. I use wooden blocks, though almost any small object will work, even crumpled paper towels.

3-D DECORATING WITH MODELING MEDIA

If you're not quite ready to tackle 3-D construction projects, you can still add dimension to your cookies in a couple of ways. Countless icing patterns and textures can be piped on cookie tops using my "7 Essential Piping Techniques" (p. 46). Likewise, 3-D embellishments can be added using the techniques in "Appliqué Work" on page 45.

Plenty of lovely readymade 3-D do-dads can be found online, but when I've got the time, I prefer to customize my cookies with homemade decorations using modeling media—pliable edible doughs, such as rolled fondant, Chocolate Dough (p. 260), and marzipan. Both rolled fondant and marzipan come ready-to-use and can easily be found online or in cake decorating and kitchen supply stores. Chocolate

Know Your Modeling Media

Wondering which medium to use for your project? There are some tradeoffs to consider, so be sure to take into account the flavor, handling, and tinting characteristics of each dough before you choose.

✪ = okay; ✪✪ = good; ✪✪✪ = better/best

Medium	Flavor	Handling	Tinting
rolled fondant	✪ Most people either love or hate the taste of rolled fondant, a dough consisting primarily of sugar and corn syrup. Rolled fondant is too sugary for my palate, which is why I typically only use it to make very small appliqués that can be plucked off cookies if tastes desire. I usually buy fondant to save time, since it's difficult, even from scratch, to improve on its sugary flavor.	✪✪✪ Rolled fondant handles extremely well under most conditions. It can become very sticky if a lot of food coloring is mixed in, just as all doughs can, but this trouble is easily remedied by kneading in powdered sugar.	✪✪✪ Because rolled fondant is pure white in the formulation described here, food colorings show very true to their original color when kneaded into it, making it the easiest of the doughs to tint.
chocolate dough	✪✪✪ A mixture of corn syrup and chocolate (either white or dark), this dough is my favorite from a taste and texture standpoint—especially when it's made from scratch with a premium chocolate that has no artificial additives or fat substitutes for cocoa butter.	✪✪ Chocolate Dough has a very smooth texture and tends to yield the nicest looking (almost satin-y) ribbons. However, it starts out quite gooey and must sit, wrapped, up to a few days before you can easily shape it. Even if properly set, it can get soft and sticky from the heat of your hands or under warm conditions, because of its high chocolate content. Always work in a cool environment and knead in powdered sugar, as required, to make the dough more manageable.	✪ If you make dark Chocolate Dough, forget about tinting it. Dark brown is its natural color and there's no fighting it! White Chocolate Dough is easier to tint, but food colorings always appear yellower than expected due to the yellowish cast from the cocoa butter in the chocolate.
marzipan	✪✪✪ If you like almonds as I do, then you'll love this dough made of ground almonds and sugar. Very high quality marzipan is readily available in most grocery stores, so I always buy it.	✪ Marzipan is the most difficult dough to handle. It's generally the stickiest, and because of its ground almond content, it's also the least smooth. I avoid twisting and bending it into bows, as it tends to crack, but rolling it into balls or broad ribbons works well.	✪ Marzipan is naturally light brown in color, again due to its almond content. If you're seeking a muted earth tone, then tinting marzipan is no problem. However, brighter colors are nearly impossible to achieve without adding a lot of food coloring.

Dough, in both dark and white varieties, is harder to find and, in my opinion, best made from scratch to ensure the highest flavor. These doughs are, of course, shaped while soft and pliable, but in many applications, they are also allowed to air-dry to set their shape.

Each medium has its pros and cons (see "Know Your Modeling Media," p. 53), but all can be shaped in myriad ways to add pizzazz to cookies. For best results with your decorations, take the time to read these three basic handling principles first; they apply to almost every decoration in "Made with Modeling Media" (p. 55).

1. Tinting. Gradually knead soft-gel food coloring into the dough until the coloring is evenly distributed and you reach the desired shade. (Wearing gloves is advisable; this task is trés messy!)

If you add a lot of coloring to achieve a dark shade, the dough may become too sticky to easily handle. In this case, simply dust your work surface regularly with powdered sugar or knead powdered sugar directly into the dough until it is manageable. (Sometimes, very dark doughs need to sit, wrapped and contained, for a few days in order to firm up.) If you get overzealous with the coloring and end up with a shade that's too dark, knead in more untinted dough. Once the coloring is uniformly incorporated, it's safe to handle without gloves!

2. Rolling into sheets. All of the ribbons and cutout decorations described in "Made with Modeling Media" start with a thin sheet of rolled fondant or another modeling medium. So how does one roll such a sheet? Because modeling media are relatively firm compared to cookie doughs, it's difficult to roll them as uniformly thin as I suggest with a pin. You can certainly try, but I recommend making the relatively small investment in a hand-cranked pasta machine (p. 23) and using it instead.

(a) Before feeding the dough through the machine, knead it until smooth and homogenous; then flatten it to help ease it into the machine in the next step. If you're making long ribbons or bands, it also helps to shape your dough into a long rectangle that approximates the final proportions you want to achieve.

(b) Set your pasta machine so the rollers are as far apart as possible (the #1 setting on an Atlas machine). Guide the dough between the rollers to flatten it further. If you attempt to guide a thick piece of dough through a narrower opening, the dough can tear.

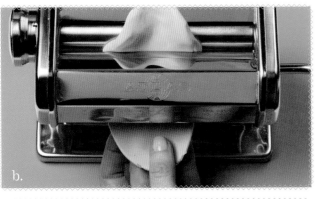

(c) Adjust the machine so that the rollers are closer together and guide the flattened dough through the machine again. (Advance the rollers one setting at a time to avoid ripping the dough.) Repeat this step until the dough is flattened to the desired thickness. For most of the do-dads in "Made with Modeling Media," I roll the dough about $1/16$ inch thick (or to the #3 setting on an Atlas machine).

3. Storing. When not in use, modeling media should be wrapped in plastic and stored in airtight containers at room temperature; otherwise, they will quickly dry out and become unusable. (Rolled fondant dries especially quickly when exposed to air, so cover any reserve loosely with plastic wrap even when working with it.) When doughs come out of storage after having been there for more than a few days, they may appear somewhat dry or discolored on the surface. Don't get too alarmed. Kneading the dough to a homogenous consistency is usually all that's needed to make it workable again.

MADE WITH MODELING MEDIA

With basic handling tips now behind you, you're ready to roll, so to speak. Here are instructions for making the nine embellishments I call for most frequently in this book and use most often in my day-to-day cookie decorating. *Note:* All of these decorations can be made in any size, so I encourage you to scale them to best suit your particular project. Scaling generally amounts to nothing more than increasing or decreasing the quantity of dough with which you start. And, of course, feel free to make any other decoration you desire. The do-dads here are just a hint of what's possible with modeling media.

1. Cords. (a) Roll a ball of dough between your hands or on your work surface to give it a rough cylindrical shape to start.

(b) Continue rolling the dough on your work surface until it reaches the desired length and width. Apply even pressure along the length of the cord as you roll; otherwise, it will end up looking lumpy. If the dough should slip rather than roll, lightly dampen your surface or try a slightly rougher surface to get more traction.

b.

(c) Trim the ends of the cord to neaten them. If you want the cord to conform to your cookie, secure it to the cookie while the dough is still pliable. Conversely, if you want it to hold another shape, shape it first and let it air-dry until firm enough to move.

c.

2. Ropes (or Twisted Cords). Make two cords of roughly the same length following the instructions on page 55, and place the cords side by side on your work surface.

(a) To get the most uniform twist, it's best not to pick up the rope as you twist. Instead, place the pads of your

a.

fingers on both ends of the rope and roll away from you with one hand and toward you with the other.

(b) Repeat this rolling motion until the rope is twisted all the way into the center. Trim the rope to the desired size. Either apply the rope immediately to cookies or allow it to air-dry if your project requires, such as for the handles for A Tisket, a Tasket (p. 169).

b.

3. Ribbons (Plain, Stitched, and Embossed). *For Plain Ribbons:* Start by rolling a thin sheet of dough, ideally with a pasta machine, as described on page 54. (I usually roll the dough for ribbons about $1/16$ inch thick, or to the #3 setting on an Atlas machine.)

(a) Place the sheet flat on your work surface. Using a ruler as your cutting guide, cut one side of a ribbon with a sharp, clean paring knife.

a.

(b) With the tip of the paring knife or a metal trussing needle, mark off the desired ribbon width, first at one end of the ribbon and then at the other.

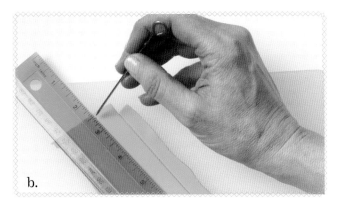

b.

(c) Line up your ruler with the marks made in Step (b) and cut the other side of the ribbon. Do not remove any dough from the work surface until you've finished cutting all the ribbons you can from the sheet. It helps to have dough on either side of the ribbon you're cutting to keep the ribbon from shifting and cutting unevenly. Be sure to clean your knife blade as you go; if dough is left clinging to it, your cuts will look rough. To ensure that the ribbons conform nicely to cookie sides, such as in Come Sail Away (p. 179) and Take the Cake (p. 113), apply them while the dough is still pliable.

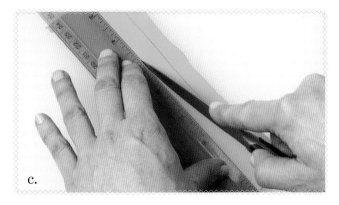

c.

For Stitched Ribbons: Without moving any ribbons cut in Step (c), lay your ruler about $1/8$ inch (or more) away from one of the ribbon's edges. Run a serrated tracing wheel along the ruler edge to create a stitched effect. Repeat to stitch both edges of the ribbon, and the remaining plain ribbons on your work surface.

For Embossed Ribbons (pictured top right): Both textured rolling pins and impression mats (p. 23) can be used to emboss plain ribbons in a variety of patterns. Start as you would to make Plain Ribbons, but roll the sheet of dough a little thicker (i.e., to the #2 setting on an Atlas machine.) You'll need extra thickness to get a good impression. Before cutting the ribbons, run the textured rolling pin over the sheet of dough, or press a mat into the dough by running a plain rolling pin over the mat top. If you cut the ribbons first and then emboss them, you'll distort the ribbons' straight edges.

4. Loop-de-Loop Bows. The dimensions referenced here are for relatively small (about $3/4$-inch) bows, similar to the ones pictured on Take the Cake (p. 113) and Tip-Top Topiary (p. 175). But, remember, these bows can be made any size just by beginning with bigger or smaller ribbons.

(a) Start as you would to make Plain Ribbons, as shown here, or another style, but cut the ribbons about $1/8$ to $3/16$ inch wide and about 12 inches long. Form a loop on one end of a ribbon and gently pinch the bottom of the loop to keep it together. Continue creating loops in this

a.

fashion from the remaining length of ribbon, clustering the loops together as you go to create one big bow.

(b) If one ribbon doesn't make a big enough bow for you, or if the ribbon should break while shaping, add more loops using another ribbon.

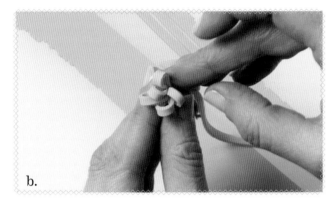

(c) Once you've got a bow with the desired number of loops, gently pinch the bottom again to make sure the loops are stuck to one another. It's easy to misshape soft bows when handling, so I usually air-dry them until firm before attaching to cookies.

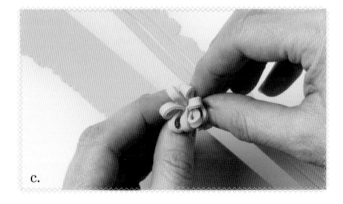

5. Bow Ties. Bow Tie styles can vary from plain to stitched or embossed, as shown here, simply by changing the underlying ribbons that form them. Start by making ribbons of your choice following the instructions on page 56.

(a) For the small ($1^1/4$- to $1^1/2$-inch) Bow Ties atop A Tisket, a Tasket (p. 169), cut ribbons about $1/2$ inch wide and then cut those ribbons into segments about $1^1/4$ to

$1^1/2$ inches long, as pictured here. Or for a different size, just cut segments of bigger or smaller widths and lengths. Work with one segment at a time—and quickly while the dough is still pliable. Pinch the center of the segment from both sides to start a crimp in the middle.

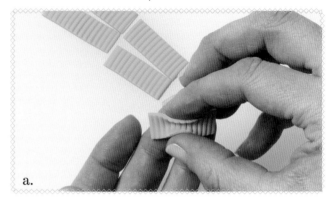

(b) To finish the crimp, turn the segment on its side. Gently press down on the upper edge with the blunt edge of a paring knife or a metal trussing needle until the two edges come together in the center. Repeat to make a Bow Tie from each of the segments. You can also wrap a narrow ribbon around the center of the bow, as pictured on page 168. Let the Bow Ties air-dry until firm before affixing to cookies; otherwise, they can easily misshape.

6. Cutout Flowers and Leaves. *For Cutout Flowers:* Countless cutout flower styles can be made just by changing the cutter you use. Here, I've used a small ($1/2$-inch) daisy cutter, the very one that made the flowers on Take the Cake (p. 113). But go ahead and get creative; the same basic principles apply to all cutout flowers.

(a) Start by rolling your dough into a thin sheet, ideally using a pasta machine (and the #3 setting on an Atlas machine). Cut out as many flowers as you can from the rolled dough. If the cut edges look at all rough, clean your cutter. Any dough clinging to the cutter can cause a rough cut. If the dough sticks in the cutter, no worries. Gently push it out with the bristle-end of a small craft paintbrush to avoid marking the center of the flower. Or, if you intend to mark the center in Step (b), it's okay to use the handle-end, as shown here.

a.

(b) You can leave the flowers flat, in which case they're easy to apply to cookies straight away. Alternatively, you can give them shape by pressing the handle-end of the brush into their centers while the dough is still pliable. (You can also purchase flower plunger cutters that cut and add contour at the same time. See page 268 for sources.) Let contoured flowers air-dry until firm; otherwise, you can

b.

flatten them when applying to cookies.

For Cutout Leaves: Follow Step (a) for Cutout Flowers, left, except use a leaf cutter of your choice. For tiny leaves to match the tiny flowers on Take the Cake (p. 113), use a $3/8 \times 7/8$-inch cutter. Plain, flat leaves are fine, but to give them a little interest, gently score a vein through the center with the blunt edge of a paring knife. For a finishing touch, pinch the bottom of the leaf to add dimension and air-dry before attaching to cookies.

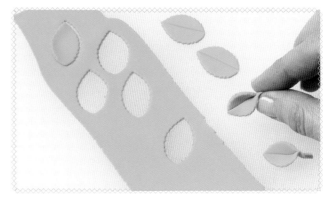

7. Embossed Leaves. Embossed leaves, like those on Jack o' Lanterns (p. 191), are cutout leaves onto which a vein pattern has been imprinted. Embossed leaves can be made two ways. However, in each case, always start by rolling a thin sheet of dough. (Again, the #3 setting on an Atlas machine works best.)

(a) The first method involves the use of a cutter that's specially sized to fit two embossing plates with vein patterns,

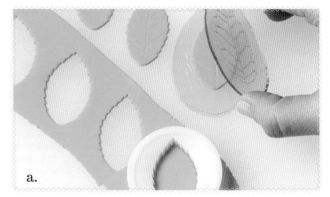
a.

aka veiners. Simply cut the leaf; then set it between the two veiners, taking care to place the imprinted (non-smooth) sides of the veiners against the leaf. Gently press down on the top veiner to emboss the leaf; then remove the dough from between the veiners. Both sides of the leaf should be imprinted.

(b) The second method involves the use of a plunger cutter, basically a combined cutter-and-veiner, as pictured below. Embossed leaves can be made a lot more quickly with this approach; the only tradeoff (and it's minor): this tool only embosses one side of the leaf. To use the tool, apply pressure to the cutter to cut the dough; then, without moving the cutter, press down on the plunger on top to imprint the dough. Lift the cutter. If the leaf does not fall out on its own, then hit the plunger again and it should pop right out.

b.

(c) Add contour to embossed leaves by pinching their bottoms and/or leaning them against the wall of a cookie

c.

sheet until dry. For sources of veiners and plunger cutters, see page 268.

8. Vines. The dimensions referenced here are for the small (1½- to 2-inch) vines on the Jack o' Lanterns (p. 191), but feel free to scale up.

(a) Start by rolling the dough into a tapered cord. That is, follow the instructions for Cords (p. 55), but roll one end so it tapers to a sharp point. For small vines, I usually roll the cords about 4 to 5 inches long and ⅛ inch wide at the nontapered end.

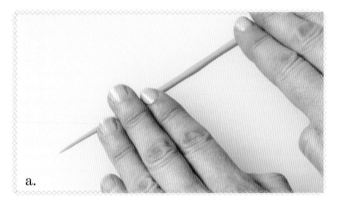

a.

(b) Wrap each cord around a lollypop stick or the handle of a small craft paintbrush (no more than ⅛ inch in diameter, for small vines). Do not press the dough onto the stick, other than to anchor it at the nontapered end of the cord; if you do, you'll have trouble getting the cord off the stick. Lean the lollypop stick or paintbrush against the edge of a cookie sheet to avoid flattening the bottom of the vine.

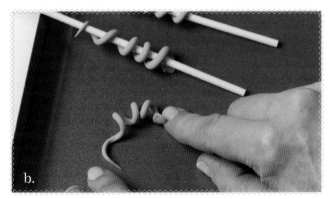

b.

Let the dough air-dry a few minutes, just long enough for the coils to hold their shape when pulled off the sticks. Give the vines a bend for added dimension; then fully air-dry before attaching to cookies.

9. Roses. Small ($1^{1}/_{4}$- to $1^{1}/_{2}$-inch) roses appear on my Open Your Heart Box (p. 165) and can be used on any of my projects that call for small flowers. Just be sure to scale up the dimensions provided here if you want bigger roses. I like to form the rose petals between plastic so their edges can easily be thinned without sticking. Cut along the side seams of a small plastic baggie to create a plastic "folder." This folder will be your workspace in Steps (a) to (c).

(a) Shape the dough into tiny ($^{3}/_{8}$- to $^{1}/_{2}$-inch) spheres, allowing 9 to 10 spheres per small rose, and place them inside the baggie. Close the baggie and use your palm to gently press each sphere into a disk about $^{7}/_{8}$ to 1 inch in diameter.

(b) Rub a bone or ball modeling tool (pictured left) or a smooth object with some heft (such as a lightbulb, shown in action to the right) over the top edge of each disk until the edge is paper-thin.

(c) Shape one of the petals into a cone with the paper-thin edge at the top. Leave the remaining petals covered until you're ready to add them; otherwise, they can quickly dry out.

c.

(d) Wrap the remaining petals, paper-thin edge up, around the central cone so that each one overlaps the next. If the petals haven't overdried, a gentle press on the base of the cone is all that's needed to keep the petals clinging together. As you add petals, use the pads of your thumb and forefinger to turn down some of edges to mimic the unfolding of a real rose. Let the rose partially air-dry and then trim (or twist off) the base of the cone, as desired. Fully air-dry before attaching to cookies.

a.

b.

d.

prelude to the projects

While "Cookie Craft" explains 99 percent of the techniques needed for the following projects, you'll want to peruse these additional must-knows before embarking on your cookie decorating journey.

DE-CODING THE PROJECT KEY

Complexity speaks to the inherent challenge posed by the project and also to the required time, insofar as more complex projects also tend to be more time consuming. Projects range from very simple 2-D cookies to more elaborate 3-D cookie constructions, so there's a project here for everyone.

 Easy enough for novice bakers/decorators; often simple 2-D cookies

 Most home bakers/decorators could make with no trouble; often includes small 3-D cookie construction and/or multi-recipe projects

 Best left to skilled home bakers/decorators or those seeking a challenge; includes large 3-D cookie construction projects and/or multi-recipe projects, though none more complex than a basic gingerbread house

Stand-in indicates simpler design options and/or packaging ideas for certain projects.

Types lists the cookie types that are required, or which can be used, in each project. (Certain rolled cookies are often interchangeable.)

Prep Talk provides storage and make-ahead tips to help you plan how far in advance you can—or should—get started. Additionally, any cookie type preferences (which I sometimes have when types are less interchangeable) and/or special tools or ingredients are noted here.

PROJECT POINTERS

Remember, the best things come in small packages. Expect projects with small yields (typically about 1 to 2 dozen). Cookie decorating is a labor of love, and many of the projects are mini works of art.

Read the recipes, too. Yes, not just the project, but also the recipes used to make it. Each recipe also has make-ahead and storage tips to help you budget—and save—time.

Plan to span. Feel free to break up the projects and tackle them in shorter doses. I often make and freeze the cookie dough up to a month in advance. When I'm ready to go, I'll bake and ice the cookies on one day, let the icing dry overnight, and then finish any decorating or assembly on the next. I rarely bake and freeze cookies, as I prefer them fresh!

Swap cookies if you like. Unless I specify otherwise in "Prep Talk," it's generally okay to substitute rolled cookie doughs for one another. For instance, I often only specify Signature Sugar Cookie Dough, when Shortbread, Straight Up would also work. It's simply that I prefer to reserve the latter for thicker cookies that play up its texture. Likewise, I reserve Construction Gingerbread for only the biggest 3-D projects that truly benefit from its stability.

Swap cookie cutters within reason. In each project, I indicate the exact cutter shapes and sizes that I used to make it, just as it's pictured. I've done this to help you quickly locate the same cutters and achieve the indicated project yields. However, if you can't find a cutter in precisely my dimensions, feel free to substitute others of the same shape in similar size. Just recognize that your yields and results may not match mine. Where cutter size is less critical to a project, I usually refer to it in general terms, such as "small," "large," or "assorted," along with providing a suggested size.

Count on the basics. I've tried to limit the "ingredient" list for each project to those recipes and decorating tools unique to the project. Assume that for every project you'll also need the very basic baking tools: essentially the items in "Tools I Can't Live Without," plus scissors, a cooling rack, a thin-bladed paring knife, and extra powdered sugar for adjusting icing consistency. It's also a good idea to have a hand-cranked pasta machine for projects that call for rolled modeling media.

Avail yourself of a scale, especially for weighing cookie dough. I often call for fractional portions of recipes, and it's usually easier to mix a single recipe, weigh off what you need, and freeze any leftovers for future use, rather than scale down the ingredients. Though I provide both the weight and fractional quantity of dough needed, you'll be much more likely to match my project yields if you weigh the dough rather than eyeball it.

Think big. If a project has especially large pieces, start by cutting them first as I suggest in the project. You'll need a relatively large quantity of dough in order to roll it broadly enough to cut very big pieces, and you'll never have more dough available to you than at the very beginning!

Mix Royal Icing to "glue" consistency (p. 243) to start. Consistency adjustments come in later steps and depend on the decorating task. In addition, always tint before thinning. Food coloring not only affects the icing consistency, but also tends to distribute and dry most evenly when first mixed into thick icing.

Expect icing needs to vary. While it's fairly easy to gauge how much cookie dough a given project will take, icing use is another matter. Not only does Royal Icing volume vary with egg size and beating time, but its consumption is very much a function of decorating skill and exact cookie design, in particular the number of colors and consistencies mixed. For those projects where the colors and decorating techniques are relatively prescribed (as in Jack o' Lanterns, for instance, where a multi-color pumpkin wouldn't make much sense), the icing quantity isn't likely to vary much. But, for projects with more design latitude, treat the indicated icing quantity (as well as the suggested portioning in each step) as a rough guidepost only. As a general rule, it's best to allow no less than $1/4$ to $1/2$ cup Royal Icing per color or consistency for easiest color mixing and handling in parchment pastry cones. For added assistance, I indicate in the ingredient lists when icing use is most likely to vary. And, if you run out of Royal Icing, it's not the end of the world! It mixes in a very brief 5 minutes or less!

Ice with efficiency. To make the decorating go fast, be vigilant about grouping like tasks. For instance, mix all of the icing colors upfront; then, unless a decorating technique (such as marbling) dictates otherwise, apply one icing color at a time to all of the cookies to minimize the swapping out of pastry cones and bags. Alternatively, leave some of the decorating undone and let your guests or family join in the fun.

Handle with care. First, it's smart to assemble projects, especially 3-D ones, on heavy-duty cardboard (see p. 52) so they can easily be moved while drying, or to avoid direct handling. Second, if you're not going to eat a finished project right away, store it as I suggest you store most of my cookie recipes: in airtight containers at room temperature (unless, of course, the project includes a perishable element, such as Ganache or Italian Buttercream). For very big projects, a clean cardboard box wrapped in a garbage bag should be sufficiently airtight. Also make sure that any Royal Icing has dried completely before containing the project; otherwise; the icing will take longer to set up and colors may bleed or spot.

Pictured clockwise from top: *Jewel Box Gem, Fit for a Queen, Ring Leader,* and *Pendant Perfect.*

PARTY GIRL

From sugar bead–studded tiaras to
gilded necklaces and rings, this chapter's
edible bling is every little diva's dream.

Pictured clockwise from upper right: *stenciled necklace with red sugar gem, small cameo necklace, and large cameo necklace.*

pendant perfect

WITH CAMEO APPEARANCE VARIATION

WHAT SWEETER DRESS-UPS FOR YOUR LITTLE PRINCESS than these completely edible necklaces strung on licorice lace? They look ornate, but require nothing more than a cookie stencil (or silicone mold for the Cameo Appearance Variation) and a treasure trove of store-bought dragées and sugar gems.

Makes about 1 dozen (2- to 4-inch) necklaces and 3 to 3½ dozen (⅞- to 1¼-inch) 3-D cookie beads

About 12 ounces (¼ recipe) Cutout Cookie Gingerbread (p. 236) or (½ recipe) Signature Sugar Cookie Dough (p. 234)

Assorted (2- to 4-inch) round, oval, square, and diamond cookie cutters, for pendants

¼-inch round pastry tip (Ateco #10 or #11)

Small (⅞- and 1¼-inch) plain round cookie cutters, for beads

About 3 cups (⅔ recipe) Royal Icing (p. 242), divided; quantity will vary

Brown (optional) and other soft-gel food colorings (p. 14) of your choice

Small craft paintbrush (handle about ¼-inch diameter)

Decorative stencil(s) (p. 24), sized to fit 2- to 4-inch cookie cutters, above

Small offset spatula (p. 14)

Gold and/or silver luster dust or other decorating powder (p. 27, optional)

A few teaspoons clear extract, for painting (optional)

Parchment pastry cones (p. 13)

Stand-in: Stenciled Stack. *Even if you don't string the stenciled cookies onto licorice lace, they'll look regal on a lovely plate.*

TYPES:

Cutout Cookie Gingerbread (p. 236) or Signature

Sugar Cookie Dough (p. 234)

{ pendant perfect, continued }

Readymade ($^3/_8$- to 1-inch) sugar gems (p. 24)

Assorted (3 to 6 mm) dragées
    or sugar beads (p. 26)

1 dozen (2- to 3-foot) pieces licorice
    lace, for stringing pendants

Twizzlers and Lifesavers, for stringing
    with pendants (optional)

PREP TALK:

Either cookie dough in "Types" can be used for this project. However, I prefer Cutout Cookie Gingerbread, because its color complements the rich jewel tones used in the icing. Plus, it's slightly firmer than Signature Sugar Cookie Dough, making it safer to swing around on licorice laces! Be sure to mix and chill the dough as instructed. If packaged in airtight containers at room temperature, this project will stay its best about 1 week.

---

1. Cut and bake the pendants and beads. On a lightly floured surface, roll the dough to a $^1/_8$- to $^3/_{16}$-inch thickness and cut out about 1 dozen (2- to 4-inch) pendants using an assortment of cookie cutter shapes and sizes. Before baking, cut a $^1/_4$-inch hole in the top of each cookie with a round pastry tip. (The opening needs to be big enough to later fit a double strand of licorice lace through.) Roll the remaining dough to the same thickness and cut out about 6 to 7 dozen ($^7/_8$- to $1^1/_4$–inch) rounds for the cookie beads. (You'll need two of each size for each bead.) Cut a $^1/_4$-inch hole through the center of each round, again using the pastry tip. Bake as directed until lightly browned around the edges, or about 9 to 12 minutes for the pendants and 6 to 7 minutes for the beads. If the holes closed during baking, recut them while the cookies are still hot from the oven. Cool completely before icing.

2. Prepare the Royal Icing as instructed on page 242. Reserve about $^1/_2$ cup for stenciling, $^1/_2$ cup for "glue," and another $^1/_2$ cup for beadwork or other borders. *Note:* The quantity of icing will vary with the number of colors and consistencies mixed. It's best to allow no less than $^1/_4$ to $^1/_2$ cup icing per color or consistency for easiest mixing and handling.

3. Top-coat the pendants and beads. Divide the remaining $1^1/_2$ cups icing into as many portions as you want top-coating colors and tint accordingly. (I love rich jewel tones, especially paired with gold dragées and ruby red or emerald green sugar gems on top.) Thin each portion to top-coating consistency (p. 245).

Using the handle-end of a craft paintbrush, apply a smooth coat of icing to each cookie top, including both pendants and beads. Take care to keep the icing from filling the holes. For top-coating technique details, see page 28. Let the cookies dry completely, ideally overnight, before stenciling and applying any sugar gems and/or other decorations.

4. Stencil the pendants. Tint the $^1/_2$ cup icing reserved for stenciling to a color (or colors) that contrasts the top coats on the pendants. (Or leave the icing white, as I have here.) Thin the icing to stenciling consistency (p. 244). Working with one pendant at a time, center a stencil on the cookie top and apply a thin layer of the icing over the stencil openings with a small offset spatula. Do not move the stencil, or the resulting pattern will be blurred. (For more stenciling details, see page 37.) Repeat with the remaining pendants and allow the icing to dry to the touch.

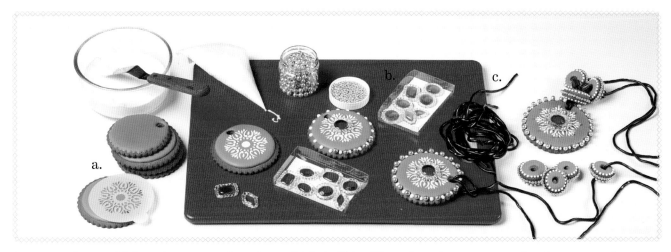

Short and Sweet. *(a) Stencil top-coated pendants. (b) Embellish with readymade sugar gems, dragées or sugar beads, and/or icing borders. (c) Thread a doubled-up strand of licorice lace through the hole in each cookie top, tie a slipknot at the top, and then string the lace with cookie beads and other candies, as desired.*

5. Detail the pendants. If desired, give the icing iridescent highlights (not pictured) by dusting it with gold or silver luster dust, or another decorating powder, or painting it with powder extended with clear extract. (See page 41 for dusting and painting technique details.) Turn the reserved $1/2$ cup icing "glue" into a parchment pastry cone and use it to attach sugar gems, dragées, and/or sugar beads on top of and around the pendants. (The sugar gems used in the projects in this chapter came from fancyflours.com.) The pendant edges can also be accented with Royal Icing beadwork (p. 34) or other borders (p. 46), if desired, using the $1/2$ cup icing reserved for this purpose. *Note:* If you're working with gingerbread, any "glue" used on cookie edges should be tinted brown to match the gingerbread color; otherwise, it will be more likely to show. Also remember to adjust the icing consistency to suit the border you choose. Let the pendants dry completely before stringing in Step 7.

6. Decorate and form the beads. Cookie beads can be decorated any number of ways, but I love to heavily adorn their edges; they look ultra regal this way. But, be warned: applying lots of Royal Icing dots, dragées, and/or sugar beads can take time. If you're in a hurry, feel free to skip these details. Plain cookie beads will look plenty cute, too.

To finish with dots, dragées, and/or sugar beads: Adjust the icing remaining for beadwork to the appropriate consistency, if not already adjusted in Step 5. Fill a parchment pastry cone with the icing and cut a small ($1/16$-inch or more) hole in the tip. Pipe dots around the edge of the top coat on each small ($7/8$- to $1 1/4$-inch) round. Let the icing dry until firm.

(a) Tint the leftover icing "glue" to match the cookie color (in this case, brown). Glue like-size rounds back to back to create single 3-D beads.

b.

(b) Pipe a thin line of "glue" along the seam where the rounds meet.

c.

(c) Place 3 mm dragées or sugar beads on top of the icing seam, all the way around the cookie. Repeat with the remaining cookies. Dry completely before stringing on the necklaces.

7. String the necklaces. Double up a long (2- to 3-foot) piece of licorice lace and thread it through the hole in a pendant. Tie a slipknot at the top, taking care to leave equal lengths of licorice lace on both sides of the pendant. Thread cookie beads (Step 6), Twizzlers (cut crosswise),

VARIATION
{ Cameo Appearance }

Pendants are given greater dimension in this variation by replacing the stenciled patterns with 3-D cameo appliqués, an example of both embossing (p. 44) and appliqué work (p. 45).

Omit the Royal Icing for stenciling, the stencil(s), and the offset spatula listed on page 67, and skip the stenciling in Step 4 on page 68.

Follow the instructions for "Embossing with Molds" (p. 44) to make about 1 dozen (1- to 3-inch) cameo appliqués (1 per pendant) from rolled fondant or another modeling medium. (The silicone molds used to shape the cameos, pictured on page 66, came from firstimpressionsmolds.com.) Using a dry craft paintbrush, dust the tops of the appliqués with cocoa powder to "antique" them and to accentuate the embossed patterns.

The appliqués can be applied either immediately or after they've dried, though they will better conform to the (dry) top-coated pendants if attached while still pliable. Use leftover Royal Icing "glue," thinned to top-coating consistency, to secure them. *Note:* If the appliqués are especially large or thick, use as little "glue" as possible so they can easily be removed before eating. They're entirely edible, but not everyone will want that much sweetness in one bite!

and/or Lifesaver pieces onto the necklace, as desired. (*Note:* I usually work on bubble wrap to avoid messing up the decorated pendants and beads.) Repeat to string the remaining necklaces.

ring leader

LET YOUR PARTY GIRLS LEAD THE LATEST FASHION TREND with these stylish cookies! Make the rings in advance and give them as favors, or supply the components and have the kids design to their hearts' content!

Makes 4 to 5 dozen (³/₄- to 2-inch) single-cookie rings; yield will vary considerably with ring size and configuration

About 3 ounces rolled fondant (p. 53), marzipan, or Chocolate Dough (p. 260), color(s) of your choice, for ring bands

About 6 ounces (¹/₈ recipe) Cutout Cookie Gingerbread (p. 236) or (¹/₄ recipe) Signature Sugar Cookie Dough (p. 234)

Assorted small (³/₄- to 2-inch) cookie cutters, for ring tops

About 1³/₄ cups (¹/₃ recipe) Royal Icing (p. 242), divided; quantity will vary

Brown (optional) and other soft-gel food colorings (p. 14) of your choice

Small craft paintbrush (handle about ¹/₄-inch diameter)

Parchment pastry cones (p. 13)

Readymade (³/₈- to 1-inch) sugar gems (p. 24)

Gumballs or other small (¹/₂- to ³/₄-inch) candies

Small (¹/₂- to ³/₄-inch) cameo appliqués (optional; see "Cameo Appearance," p. 70, for instructions)

Assorted (3 to 6 mm) dragées or sugar beads (p. 26)

Stand-in: Beginner Bling. *Rings made with a single cookie, such as those pictured in the foreground, are the easiest of gems. Add a quick icing border and a readymade jewel on top, and you're done!*

TYPES:

Cutout Cookie Gingerbread (p. 236) or Signature Sugar Cookie Dough (p. 234)

{ ring leader, continued }

Gold and/or silver luster dust or other decorating powder (p. 27, optional)

A few teaspoons clear extract, for painting (optional)

PREP TALK:

Either cookie dough in "Types" works well for this project. Just be sure to mix and chill the dough as instructed. Ring bands made of rolled fondant (or another modeling medium) should be shaped at least a day before ring assembly to give them ample time to air-dry and firm up. Avoid White Chocolate Dough, however, as it is quite heat sensitive and, therefore, less suitable for these delicate pieces. If packaged in airtight containers at room temperature, this project will stay its best about 1 week.

1. Shape the ring bands. As noted in "Prep Talk," ring bands made of modeling media should be shaped ahead. Start by making thin ribbons from the dough following the instructions for Plain, Stitched, or Embossed Ribbons (pp. 56 to 57). I typically cut the ribbons about $1/8$ to $1/4$ inch wide and about 3 to $3^{1}/4$ inches long to start.

Work with one ribbon at a time. Carefully wrap it around your ring finger to size it; then trim to fit your finger, leaving about $1/8$- to $1/4$-inch overlap at the end. Set the ribbon on a cookie sheet lined with parchment paper and turn the ribbon on its side. Bring the ends around to form a perfect circle and seal them together with a dab of water. Repeat to make as many bands as you anticipate rings. (If you make multi-cookie rings, you can get by with less modeling media and fewer than 5 dozen bands.) Let the pieces air-dry until they hold their shape without wilting.

2. Cut and bake the ring tops. On a lightly floured surface, roll the dough to a $1/8$- to $3/16$-inch thickness and cut into various $3/4$- to 2-inch shapes. (I like to cut an assortment of shapes and sizes so that pieces can be stacked into multi-cookie rings.) Bake as directed until lightly browned around the edges, or about 5 to 9 minutes, depending on cookie size. Cool completely before icing.

3. Prepare the Royal Icing as instructed on page 242. Reserve about $1/2$ cup for "glue" and $1/2$ cup for beadwork or other borders. *Note:* The quantity of icing will vary with the number of colors and consistencies mixed. It's best to allow no less than $1/4$ to $1/2$ cup icing per color or consistency for easiest mixing and handling.

4. Top-coat the ring tops. Divide the remaining $3/4$ cup icing into as many portions as you want top-coating colors and tint accordingly. (I typically choose colors that coordinate with the gems and/or candies I'm using on top.) Thin each color to top-coating consistency (p. 245).

Using the handle-end of a craft paintbrush, apply a smooth coat of icing to each cookie top. For top-coating technique details, see page 28. Let the cookies dry completely, ideally overnight, before applying any sugar gems and/or other decorations in Step 5.

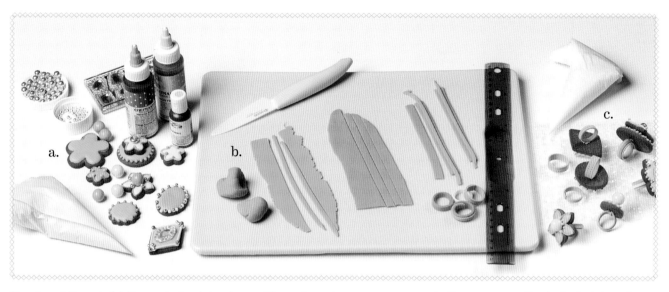

Short and Sweet. *(a) Decorate iced ring tops with readymade sugar gems, gumballs, cameo appliqués (not pictured), dragées, and/or sugar beads. (b) Cut ribbons out of rolled fondant or another modeling medium. Shape into ring bands and let the bands dry until rigid. (c) Attach the bands to the underside of the ring tops with thick Royal Icing.*

5. Decorate and apply borders. Transfer the reserved $^{1}/_{2}$ cup Royal Icing "glue" to a parchment pastry cone and cut a small ($^{1}/_{16}$-inch or more) hole in the tip. Use the "glue" to attach sugar gems, gumballs, cameo appliqués, or other decorative candies to the center of each ring top. Or mount smaller cookies on top of larger ones. (The sugar gems used in the projects in this chapter came from fancyflours. com.) Edge the cookies with smaller sugar gems, dragées, sugar beads, and/or Royal Icing beadwork (p. 34) or other borders (p. 46) using the $^{1}/_{2}$ cup icing reserved for this purpose. If you're working with gingerbread, any "glue" used on the cookie edges should be tinted brown to match the gingerbread color; otherwise, it will be more likely to show. Also remember to adjust the icing consistency to suit the border you choose. Let the cookies dry completely.

6. Paint (optional) and attach the ring bands. As desired, add shimmer to any bands made in Step 1 by painting them with gold or silver luster dust, or another decorating powder, extended with clear extract. (See page 41 for painting technique details.) Affix the bands to the underside of each ring top with leftover Royal Icing "glue." (*Note:* I usually work on bubble wrap to avoid messing up the decorated ring tops.) Let the rings dry completely before moving—or wearing—them!

Froufrou to Fun. *The sophisticated pendants and rings (pictured p. 72) can turn whimsical simply by using splashier colors and fun flower shapes.*

fit for a queen

EVEN IF YOUR DAUGHTER IS TOO YOUNG TO QUALIFY AS A FULL-FLEDGED DIVA, she'll look mighty commanding in this edible headpiece that flaunts the stenciling technique (p. 37).

Makes about 4 (4^{3}4 x 5^{3}4 x 3- to 4-inch-tall) tiaras

Custom template (p. 264), for headband

About 12 ounces (^{1}/4 recipe) Cutout Cookie Gingerbread (p. 236) or (^{1}/2 recipe) Signature Sugar Cookie Dough (p. 234)

8-piece diamond cookie cutter set (Ateco #5259, p. 14)

About 2^3/4 cups (^{2}/3 recipe) Royal Icing (p. 242), divided; quantity will vary

Brown (optional) and other soft-gel food colorings (p. 14) of your choice

Small craft paintbrush (handle about ^{1}/4-inch diameter)

Decorative stencil(s) (p. 24), sized to fit 2 to 2^3/4 x 3- to 4-inch diamond cookie cutters, above

Small offset spatula (p. 14)

Gold and/or silver luster dust or other decorating powder (p. 27, optional)

A few teaspoons clear extract, for painting (optional)

Parchment pastry cones (p. 13)

Readymade (^{3}/8- to 1-inch) sugar gems (p. 24)

Assorted (3 to 6 mm) dragées or sugar beads (p. 26)

TYPES:

Cutout Cookie Gingerbread (p. 236) or Signature Sugar Cookie Dough (p. 234)

PREP TALK:

While either dough can be used for this small-scale 3-D construction project, I prefer Cutout Cookie Gingerbread, because it spreads less and is less vulnerable to humidity. It's also more tender than Construction Gingerbread, which I typically reserve for larger projects. Be sure to mix and chill the dough as instructed. If packaged in airtight containers at room temperature, this project will stay its best about 1 week.

1. Cut and bake the tiara pieces. Start by cutting out a template to fit the headband outline on page 264. (Alternatively, create the outline yourself by tracing halfway around a $5^5/8$ x $7^3/4$-inch oval cake pan on a piece of acetate or cardboard. Slide the pan $1^1/8$ inches away from the top of the arc that you just traced, toward the interior of the arc, and then trace halfway around the pan again. You should end up with a shape identical to that on page 264.) If you plan to make lots of tiaras, consider making a custom cookie cutter; it will save cutting time in the long run. For more information about working with custom templates and cutters, see page 48.

On a lightly floured surface, roll the dough to a $1/8$- to $3/16$-inch thickness and cut out 8 headbands (2 per tiara) using your template (or custom cutter) as a cutting guide. If you don't have a spatula large enough to move these pieces, then cut them directly on prepared cookie sheets to avoid misshaping. Bake these pieces as directed until lightly browned around the edges, or about 6 to 7 minutes. Watch carefully, as the headband tips have a tendency to burn.

Roll the remaining dough to the same thickness as above and cut out 4 large ($2^3/4$ x 4-inch) diamonds (1 per center of each tiara). You may also substitute smaller 2 x 3-inch diamonds here, if desired. Cut out another 8 (2 x 3-inch) diamonds (2 per tiara to flank the large central diamond) and 8 ($1^{11}/16$ x $2^7/16$-inch) diamonds. Cut the 8 smallest diamonds in half to form triangles. These pieces will be used to fill spaces between the large central diamond and the diamonds that immediately flank it. Bake as directed until lightly browned around the edges, or about 6 to 7 minutes for the diamonds and 5 to 6 minutes for the small triangles. Cool completely before decorating.

Short and Sweet. *(a) Make a custom template for the tiara headband by tracing around an oval cake pan (or the outline, p. 264) onto acetate or cardboard. (b) Cut headbands from cookie dough using the template as a cutting guide. Bake along with diamond and triangle cookies. (c) Reinforce the backs of the headbands with Royal Icing of top-coating consistency. Use thick Royal Icing to glue two headbands together, top to bottom, to form a single taller headband; then attach decorated diamond and triangle cookies to the front of the headband with more "glue."*

2. Prepare the Royal Icing as instructed on page 242. Reserve about $1/2$ cup for stenciling, $1/2$ cup for "glue," $1/2$ cup for beadwork or other borders, and another $1/2$ cup for reinforcing the headbands. *Note:* The quantity of icing will vary with the number of colors and consistencies mixed. It's best to allow no less than $1/4$ to $1/2$ cup icing per color or consistency for easiest mixing and handling.

3. Top-coat the diamonds and triangles. Divide the remaining $3/4$ cup icing into as many portions as you want top-coating colors and tint accordingly. (I typically choose colors that coordinate with the gems and/or candies I'm using on top. I also like to top-coat the large diamonds in one color and the smaller triangles in another.) Thin each color to top-coating consistency (p. 245). Using the handle-end of a craft paintbrush, apply a smooth coat of icing to each cookie top. For top-coating technique details, see page 28. Let the cookies dry completely, ideally overnight, before stenciling and applying any sugar gems and/or other decorations.

4. Stencil the diamonds and triangles. Tint the $1/2$ cup icing reserved for stenciling to a color (or colors) that contrasts the top coats on the diamonds. (Or leave the icing white, as I have here.) Thin the icing to stenciling consistency (p. 244). Working with one diamond at a time, place a stencil on the cookie top and apply a thin layer of icing over the stencil openings with a small offset spatula. Take care not to move the stencil, or the resulting pattern will be blurred. (For more stenciling details, see page 37.) Repeat with the remaining diamonds and triangles, as desired, and allow the icing to dry to the touch. You can

also leave these pieces simply top-coated and embellish them as described in the next step.

5. Detail the diamonds and triangles, as desired, by dusting with gold or silver luster dust, or another decorating powder, or by painting with powder extended with clear extract. (See page 41 for dusting and painting technique details.) Transfer the reserved $1/2$ cup Royal Icing "glue" to a parchment pastry cone and cut a small ($1/16$-inch or more) hole in the tip. Use the "glue" to attach small sugar gems, dragées, and/or sugar beads on top of and around the cookies. (The sugar gems used in the projects in this chapter came from fancyflours.com.) If you're working with gingerbread, any "glue" used on the cookie edges should be tinted brown to match the gingerbread color; otherwise, it will be more likely to show. Add beadwork (p. 34) or other borders (p. 46) using the $1/2$ cup icing reserved for this purpose. Remember, adjust the icing consistency to suit the border you choose.

6. Reinforce the headbands. Tint the $1/2$ cup icing reserved for reinforcing the headbands to match the dough color; then adjust it to top-coating consistency. Spread a very thin layer on the back of each headband piece, taking care not to get any icing on the top of the headbands. Allow the icing to dry to the touch. This icing helps strengthen the headbands, especially the tips, making them less likely to bend under humid conditions.

7. Assemble the tiaras. Work on one tiara at a time. Glue 2 headband pieces directly on top of one another with leftover "glue." Make sure that no icing squeezes out the sides.

a.

(a) Glue a small cookie triangle just off-center on the convex side of the headband.

b.

(b) Attach one of the largest (2³/₄ x 4-inch) diamonds in the center, propping the diamond from the back, as needed, to keep it standing straight up.

c.

(c) Glue another triangle to the other side of the central diamond for additional support. Continue to assemble by gluing two of the next largest (2 x 3-inch) diamonds to the headband so that one flanks each triangle on either side of the central diamond. Prop the diamonds again, as necessary. Fit another small triangle next to the bottom of each 2 x 3-inch diamond.

Reinforce the seams between headband and diamonds on the back with additional icing "glue;" then fill in any gaps between the pieces on the front with sugar gems, dragées, or sugar beads.

Repeat Step 7 to make 4 tiaras. Dry completely before moving.

jewel box gem

AFTER GUESTS HAVE MADE NECKLACE AND RING COOKIES, they'll need somewhere to store their trinkets—if they don't gobble them right away, that is. And what more logical place than this gem of a box made with cookies? I've jazzed up the big gingerbread jewelry box (pictured page 82) with wafer paper on the sides and a cookie monogram on top, but small, plain iced boxes (see "Stand-in" below) are charming, too.

Makes about 3 big (5 x 8 x 3⅞-inch-tall) jewelry boxes with lids

Ruler or custom rectangular templates in 4 sizes (see Step 1)

About 3 pounds 7 ounces (1⅙ recipes) Cutout Cookie Gingerbread (p. 236) or Construction Gingerbread (p. 238)

Assorted (3- to 4-inch-long) oval cookie cutters, for monograms

Small (1¼-inch) plain round cookie cutter, for box feet

About 8¾ cups (1¾ to 2 recipes) Royal Icing (p. 242), divided; quantity will vary

Brown and other soft-gel food colorings (p. 14) of your choice

Parchment pastry cones (p. 13)

Small craft paintbrush (handle about ¼-inch diameter)

Small offset spatula (p. 14)

About 9 (8 x 11-inch) sheets printed wafer paper (p. 26), pattern(s) of your choice (optional)

A few tablespoons light corn syrup (optional)

Small sponge brush (optional)

A few (8 x 11-inch) sheets plain wafer paper (p. 26), for printing monograms (optional)

Food-safe marking pens (p. 26, optional)

Stand-in: Think Outside the (Big) Box. *Small iced boxes without any wafer paper on the sides are speedy to make and still look snazzy studded with dragées and a cookie monogram on top! These boxes measure in at about 3½ x 5½ x 3⅜ inches tall.*

TYPES:

Cutout Cookie Gingerbread (p. 236) or Construction Gingerbread (p. 238)

Assorted (3 mm to 6 mm) dragées
or sugar beads (p. 26)

Less than 1 ounce rolled fondant (p.
53) or other modeling medium,
for clasps (optional)

Small (1 1/8-inch) fluted round cookie
cutter, for clasps (optional)

Gold luster dust or other decorating
powder (p. 27), for clasps (optional)

A few teaspoons clear extract,
for painting (optional)

Pastry bag fitted with tip of your
choice, for borders

PREP TALK:

Either cookie dough in "Types" can be used for this relatively large 3-D construction project. I generally avoid Signature Sugar Cookie Dough, except for smaller versions of the box, because of its relative fragility. Be sure to mix and chill the dough as instructed. If packaged in airtight containers at room temperature, this project will stay its best about 1 week.

1. Cut and bake the box pieces. Following the instructions for custom templates (p. 48), make rectangular templates for the box in 4 sizes: 5 x 8 inches for the lid, 4 1/4 x 7 3/8 inches for the bottom, 2 1/2 x 7 1/2 inches for the long sides, and 2 1/2 x 4 1/2 inches for the short sides. Alternatively, you can use a ruler as a cutting guide. Or if you plan to make a lot of boxes, consider making custom cookie cutters; they will save cutting time in the long run. For more information about working with custom templates and cutters, see page 48.

On a lightly floured surface, roll the dough to a 1/8- to 3/16-inch thickness. Since the box pieces are relatively large, it's best to cut them directly on prepared cookie sheets to avoid the misshaping that can occur in transferring from work surface to cookie sheet. For each of 3 boxes, use your templates (or ruler or custom cutters) to cut out the following number of cookies in this order, from big to small: 1 lid, 1 bottom, 2 long sides, and 2 short sides. From the leftover dough, cut out 3 (3- to 4-inch-long) ovals for monograms on the lids and 24 plain (1 1/4-inch) rounds (8 per box) for feet.

Bake the cookies as directed until lightly browned around the edges, or about 9 to 10 minutes for the feet, 12 to 13 minutes for the monograms, and 13 to 15 minutes for the box sides, bottoms, and lids. Trim the box pieces while hot from the oven so that they end up perfectly rectangular. (It's especially important to trim the box bottom to its original size to ensure a good fit with the sides in Step 9.) Cool completely before icing in Step 3.

2. Prepare the Royal Icing as instructed on page 242. Reserve about 1/2 cup for top-coating the monograms, 1/4 cup for reinforcing the box bottoms, 1/4 cup for detailing the monograms, 1 1/4 cups for "glue," and 1 cup for borders on the lids. *Note:* The quantity of icing will vary with the number of colors and consistencies mixed. It's best to allow no less than 1/4 to 1/2 cup icing per color or consistency for easiest mixing and handling.

3. Outline and flood the box sides and lids. I prefer to outline and flood the box sides and lids, as opposed to top-coating without any outlines, in order to get the icing as close to the cookie edges as possible and to ensure a good fit with the wafer paper in Step 5. Divide the remaining $5^1/_2$ cups icing into as many portions as you want colors. I usually limit the colors to two, one for the lid and another for the box sides. Or, if I plan to wafer-paper the pieces in Step 5, I leave all of the icing white so it doesn't interfere with the paper's pattern.

Tint the icing as desired and thin each portion to outlining consistency (p. 244). Transfer each portion to a separate parchment pastry cone and cut a small ($^1/_{16}$-inch or more) hole in each tip. Proceed to outline all of the box sides and lids using colors of your choice and following the outlining instructions on page 29. Thin the leftover icing to flooding consistency (p. 245) and flood the interior of each outlined cookie with the same color of icing used to outline it. For more flooding technique tips, see page 31. Let the icing dry completely before wafer-papering the box sides and lids in Step 5, or otherwise decorating.

4. Top-coat the monograms and reinforce the box bottoms. Tint the $^1/_2$ cup icing reserved for top-coating the monograms to a color (or colors) of your choice and thin to top-coating consistency (p. 245). Again, I usually leave the icing white if I intend to wafer-paper the monograms in Step 6. Using the handle-end of a craft paintbrush, apply a smooth coat of icing to each cookie top. Dry completely before decorating in Step 6.

In the meantime, tint the $^1/_4$ cup icing reserved for reinforcing the box bottoms to match the gingerbread. Adjust the icing to top-coating consistency. Use a small offset spatula to spread a thin layer of icing on the underside of each box bottom. Once dry, this icing will keep the box bottoms from sagging over time, especially under humid conditions.

5. Wafer-paper the box sides and lids (optional). Cut wafer paper to fit the icing on each of your iced box pieces. (For visual interest, I usually wafer-paper the lid with one pattern and the sides with another coordinating pattern.) Work on one cookie at a time. Spread a thin layer of corn syrup on the cookie top coat with a small sponge brush. Affix a matching piece of wafer paper on top. For best results, follow the instructions for wafer-papering on page 38. Let the paper dry at least 1 hour before decorating further in Step 8.

6. Decorate the monograms. Print your guests' monograms onto plain wafer paper. Make sure the monograms fit the top coats on the oval cookies with some room to spare. (*Note:* You can use a dedicated printer with edible ink, p. 24, as I have here. If you don't have one or don't want to make the investment, you can write with food-safe markers on the paper or directly on the cookie top coats, or pipe monograms with extra Royal Icing, again directly on the top coats.) Apply and dry the wafer paper as instructed in Step 5, above.

Finish the monograms with a border of your choice. Tint the $^1/_4$ cup icing reserved for this purpose to the desired color and then thin to the appropriate consistency for your task. (Use icing of beadwork consistency, p. 245, for dots and icing of outlining consistency, p. 244, for more delicate borders such as the Zig Zag Border, pictured on the bigger monogram cookie, p. 82.) Pipe your chosen border following the appropriate technique details on pages 46 to 47. You can also embellish the cookie edges with dragées or sugar beads.

7. Assemble and decorate the box feet. Portion off $^1/_2$ cup icing from the $1^1/_4$ cups icing reserved for "glue."

Short and Sweet. *(a) Cut out box lids, sides, and bottoms using custom templates (or a ruler or custom cutters). Cut out small rounds for box feet and larger ovals for monograms on the lids. Bake and cool. (b) Outline and flood the box lids and sides. Dry completely. Wafer-paper the pieces, as desired. (c) Glue decorated monograms to the lids with thick Royal Icing and pipe a border along the lid edges. Glue box sides to each box bottom, propping as needed. If desired, embellish the box corners, feet, and lids with dragées or sugar beads and/or clasps made of rolled fondant or another modeling medium; then glue the feet to the box bottoms.*

Leave this portion white. Tint the remaining ³/₄ cup to match the gingerbread. Reserve the white "glue" for use in Step 8.

Transfer the brown "glue" to a parchment pastry cone and cut a small (¹/₁₆-inch or more) hole in the tip. Fix the 1¹/₄-inch round cookies back to back using a dab of the "glue" to hold them together. Once the sandwiches have dried, glue 3 mm dragées or sugar beads along their seams following the instructions in Step 6 of Pendant Perfect (p. 69). Save the leftover brown "glue" for use in Steps 8 and 9.

8. Decorate the box lids. Glue a decorated monogram cookie to the center of each decorated lid.

Make clasps (optional): Roll fondant or another modeling medium to a ¹/₈- to ³/₁₆-inch thickness. Cut out 3 rounds (1 per box) using the 1¹/₈-inch fluted round cookie cutter. Cut each round in half and air-dry until no longer tacky to the touch. Paint each half-clasp with gold luster dust or another decorating powder extended with clear extract. (See page 41 for painting technique details.) Let the paint dry and then glue 2 half-clasps to the middle of a long side of each lid, as pictured above. Glue dragées or sugar beads along the seam where the half-clasps come together and on top of the bottom half-clasp, as desired.

Add borders: Tint the 1 cup icing reserved for borders on the lids to a color of your choice, or leave it white. Choose a border style from among those listed in "7 Essential Piping Techniques" (p. 46). Adjust the icing to the proper consistency for your border, transfer to a parchment pastry cone or pastry bag fitted with the right tip, and then pipe away! *Note:* I piped a Trailing Star Border (p. 47) with thick icing and a ¹/₄-inch star tip (Ateco #18 or #27).

As desired, embellish the lid corners and border with dragées or sugar beads using either the reserved white or brown "glue," whichever shows less. (Or tint the white "glue" to match other colors on your box.)

{ jewel box gem, continued }

9. Assemble the boxes. Work on one box at a time. You'll need 2 (2^1/$_2$ x 4^1/$_2$-inch) sides, 2 (2^1/$_2$ x 7^1/$_2$-inch) sides, and 1 (4^1/$_4$ x 7^3/$_8$-inch) bottom per box. To ensure the best possible fit, bevel the edges of the sides with a sharp paring knife following the beveling tips on page 51. Use the leftover brown "glue" from Step 8 to glue the box together at the seams. Prop as needed. Repeat to assemble another 2 boxes.

When the boxes have dried, stud the corners with 5 mm to 6 mm dragées or sugar beads, using the remaining brown "glue" to hold the pieces in place. Lastly, glue 4 feet (from Step 7) onto the bottom of each box, one in each corner. Let the icing dry and then top each box with a decorated lid.

fab bag

FOR A TRULY FASHION-FORWARD PARTY TOUCH, present a grab bag of these fab bags as favors or monogram them all with wafer paper and use them as place cards.

Makes about 14 (1 to 1¼ x 2½ x 2⅜-inch-tall) filled handbags

Less than 2 ounces rolled fondant (p. 53), marzipan, or Chocolate Dough (p. 260), color(s) of your choice, for handles

About 14 ounces (⅓ recipe) Cutout Cookie Gingerbread (p. 236) or (⅔ recipe) Signature Sugar Cookie Dough (p. 234)

2½-inch plain round cookie cutter

About 4 to 5¼ cups (¾ to 1¼ recipes) Royal Icing (p. 242), divided; quantity will vary

Brown (optional) and other soft-gel food colorings (p. 14) of your choice

Parchment pastry cones (p. 13)

A few (8 x 11-inch) sheets plain or printed wafer paper (p. 26), pattern(s) of your choice (optional)

Small sponge brush (optional)

A few tablespoons light corn syrup (optional)

Assorted (3 mm) dragées or sugar beads (p. 26)

Assorted small (½- to 1¼-inch) readymade royal icing embellishments (p. 26), such as flowers, sunglasses, teddy bears, and toy dogs (1 or more per handbag)

About 1¼ cups (½ recipe) Ganache (p. 259) or (¼ to ⅓ recipe) Italian Buttercream (p. 257), for filling handbags (optional)

Pastry bag fitted with ½-inch round tip (Ateco #806)

Stand-in: In the Bag. *If top-coated handbag cookies, as shown on page 88, take more time than you can spare, make tinted sugar cookie or macaron handbags as shown here. For Goofproof Macarons and macaron making tips, see page 249.*

TYPES:

Cutout Cookie Gingerbread (p. 236) or Signature Sugar Cookie Dough (p. 234)

{ fab bag, continued }

PREP TALK:

Either cookie dough in "Types" works well for this project. Just be sure to mix and chill the dough as instructed. Make upright handles from rolled fondant (or another modeling medium) at least a day before handbag assembly to give them ample time to air-dry and firm up. Avoid White Chocolate Dough, as it quite heat sensitive and, therefore, less suitable for these delicate pieces. Handbags filled with Ganache or Italian Buttercream are best eaten immediately after briefly setting up in the fridge. Both fillings are perishable, but extended refrigeration can soften the cookies and lead to spotting of icing colors. If you fill the handbags with Royal Icing, air-dry, and then store in airtight containers, this project will be its best up to 1 week.

1. Shape the upright handles. As noted in "Prep Talk," any upright handles made of modeling media should be shaped ahead. Start by making thin ribbons from the dough following the instructions for Plain, Stitched, or Embossed Ribbons (pp. 56 to 57). I usually cut out strips (1 to 2 per assembled handbag), each about $3/16$ inch wide and $3 1/2$ to 5 inches long. (Floppy handles, like those pictured left, should be made during final assembly in Step 6.) On a parchment paper-lined cookie sheet, bend each strip into a $1 3/4$- to $2 1/2$-inch-tall arc-shaped handle, about $1 1/2$ inches wide at the open end. Let the handles dry until rigid, generally overnight.

2. Cut and bake the cookie handbag pieces. On a lightly floured surface, roll the dough to a $1/8$- to $3/16$-inch thickness. Cut out about 28 rounds (2 per handbag) with the $2 1/2$-inch plain round cookie cutter. As you cut, transfer the cookies to prepared cookie sheets. Trim $1/8$ to $1/4$ inch off the bottom of each round to create a flat edge that spans about $1 1/2$ to $1 5/8$ inches. (This edge will become the bottom of the handbag.) Reroll any dough trimmings, as needed.

Bake the cookies as directed until lightly browned around the edges, or about 9 to 10 minutes. Cool completely before outlining and flooding the cookies in Step 4.

3. Prepare the Royal Icing as instructed on page 242. Reserve about 2 cups for detailing the handbags and $1 1/4$ cups for filling the handbags (optional). *Note:* The quantity of icing will vary with your filling choice and the number of colors and consistencies mixed. Omit the $1 1/4$ cups for filling if you use either Ganache or Italian Buttercream in Step 6 instead. It's also best to allow no less than $1/4$ to $1/2$ cup icing per color or consistency for easiest mixing and handling.

4. Outline and flood the handbags. I like to outline and flood these cookies, as opposed to top-coating without any outlines, in order to get the icing very close to the cookie edges. Divide the remaining 2 cups icing into as many portions as you want colors. Thin each portion to outlining consistency (p. 244) and transfer to separate parchment pastry cones. Cut a small ($1/16$-inch or more) hole in each tip and outline the edge of each handbag in a color of your choice following the outlining instructions on page 29. Thin the leftover icings to flooding consistency (p. 245) and then flood the interior of each outlined cookie with the same color that was used to outline it. For flooding technique tips, see page 31. Let the icing dry to the touch.

{ fab bag, continued }

5. Detail the handbags. As a general rule, I like to decorate the cookies in matched pairs so that the fronts and backs of the assembled handbags look identical.

The quantity of icing for this task will vary widely with your ultimate cookie design(s). For instance, I covered some handbags completely with plain wafer paper custom-printed with monograms; whereas the crisscross pattern (p. 88) requires more icing.

To wafer-paper, simply cut out wafer paper to fit the area that you'd like to cover; use a small sponge brush to spread a thin layer of corn syrup on either the cookie (if covering it completely) or the back of the paper; and fix the paper on top. See page 38 for more wafer-papering details.

Alternatively, skip the wafer-papering and apply icing details more generously on top using the 2 cups icing reserved for this purpose. Just remember to adjust the icing consistency to your detailing task. For thin lines, such as those in the crisscross pattern (p. 88), use icing of outlining consistency (p. 244). And for dots, such as the tiny ones on top of the crisscrosses or on the black handbag, use icing of beadwork consistency (p. 245). Dragées and sugar beads work well as clasps and feet; readymade royal icing flowers also make nice flourishes. Both are best fixed in place with icing "glue" tinted to match what the "glue" is going on (i.e., cookie dough or icing).

6. Fill and assemble the handbags. If you'd rather fill the cookies with Ganache (chilled to piping consistency) or Italian Buttercream instead of Royal Icing, then it's best to assemble the handbags just before serving, as noted in "Prep Talk" (p. 89). Otherwise, tint the remaining $1^1/4$ cups icing reserved for filling to a color (or colors) of your choice and thin to a thick outlining consistency. Transfer the filling(s) to a pastry bag (or bags) fitted with a $^1/2$-inch round tip (Ateco #806).

Assemble one handbag at a time.

a.

(a) (Optional) To make a floppy handle, cut a thin ribbon, matching those cut in Step 1, from the leftover modeling medium.

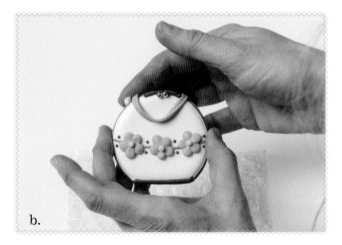

b.

(b) (Optional) Stick both ends of the ribbon to the back of a decorated handbag cookie with a dab of icing; allow the rest of the ribbon to fall into place on the front of the cookie.

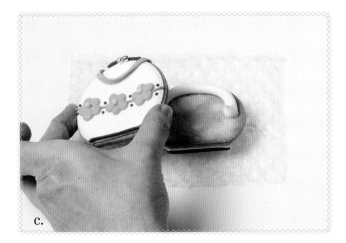

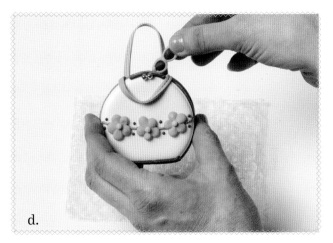

(c) Turn a matching handbag cookie over so its undecorated side faces up. (Work on a small piece of bubble wrap to avoid damaging the decorated side.) Pipe the filling in an arc along the top edge of the handbag; then sandwich the filling by placing the cookie from Step (a), or another matching one without a floppy handle, on top. Do not press on the top edge of the handbag. If you do, the filling will flatten and squeeze out, and the handbag won't appear open.

(d) Insert a predried handle (or two) and another ready-made royal icing trinket, such as sunglasses, a teddy bear, or a toy dog, into the open end. Repeat Steps (a) to (d) to assemble the remaining handbags.

Let the Royal Icing dry completely before standing the handbags straight up, or refrigerate those filled with Ganache or Italian Buttercream just until the filling is set.

Pictured counterclockwise from top: *Lollypalooza; Cream of the Crop, Soft Spot Variation; and Take the Cake, Mothers' Day Cake Variation.*

INCREDIBLE EDIBLES

Proof positive that looks can be deceiving—a menu-full
of cookies artfully disguised as other comely comestibles!
Whether carb-loading for a road race or lingering over
breakfast in bed, you'll be sure to get your sugar fix here.

breakfast in bed

WITH A GOOD EGG, WHAT'S SHAKIN' BACON?, SLICE OF NICE, AND FULL PLATE

BREAKFAST IN BED IS THE ULTIMATE INDULGENCE, especially when the menu consists of nothing but cookies! This cookie collection—comprised of fried eggs, bacon, orange slices, and plates—makes a unique Mothers' Day or housewarming gift, not to mention a convincing April Fool's Day surprise!

Makes about 3 ($10\frac{3}{4}$-inch) plates, plus per plate: 2 ($4\frac{3}{4}$- to 6-inch) fried eggs,
many ($1\frac{1}{8}$ x 6- to 8-inch) pieces of bacon, and 6 ($3\frac{3}{16}$-inch) orange slices

A GOOD EGG

Custom templates (p. 263), for egg white

About 15 ounces ($\frac{2}{3}$ recipe) Signature
Sugar Cookie Dough (p. 234)

$1\frac{7}{8}$-inch plain round cookie
cutter, for egg yolk

About $2\frac{1}{2}$ cups ($\frac{1}{2}$ recipe) Royal
Icing (p. 242), divided

Yellow and orange soft-gel food
colorings (p. 14)

Parchment pastry cones (p. 13, optional)

Stand-in: Too Much on Your Plate? *A plate cookie loaded with a variety of treats is appetizing, there's no doubt. But pairing only egg cookies with a real plate or skillet, as pictured here, will generate plenty of double-takes. Tied with a ribbon and tag, this bundle also makes a cheery housewarming or Mothers' Day gift.*

TYPES:

Signature Sugar Cookie Dough (p. 234) for fried eggs

and orange slices (optional); Traditional Tuiles, Cocoa

Variation (p. 255, optional) for bacon; Construction

Gingerbread (p. 238, optional) for plates

{ breakfast in bed, continued }

PREP TALK:

Because the optional plate cookies are large and weight-bearing, I like to make them out of Construction Gingerbread for added strength. For the smaller cookies, I prefer to use more delicate doughs and to match the color of the dough (or batter) to the food I'm replicating. (So, for instance, I use creamy-white Signature Sugar Cookie Dough for the eggs and orange slices, and cocoa-tinted tuile batter for the bacon.) Be sure to prep the dough and batter as instructed. If packaged in airtight containers at room temperature, this project will stay its best about 1 week.

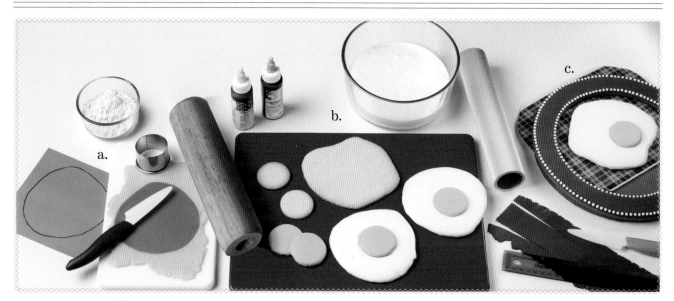

Short and Sweet. *(a) Cut egg white and yolk cookies from Signature Sugar Cookie Dough using a custom template (or custom cutter) for the former and a round cookie cutter for the latter. Bake and cool. (b) Dip (or outline and flood) the egg white cookies in white Royal Icing; then insert a dipped and dried yolk cookie in the center. (c) Assemble the eggs on gingerbread plates (p. 101, optional) decorated with embossed rolled fondant rims and wafer paper. Serve with tuile bacon and orange slice cookies (p. 97 and p. 99, optional).*

1. Cut and bake the whites and yolks. Start by cutting out an egg white template using either (or both) of the outlines on page 263. If you plan to make a lot of eggs, consider making a custom cookie cutter; it will save cutting time in the long run. For more information about working with custom templates and cutters, see page 48.

On a lightly floured surface, roll the dough to a $1/8$- to $3/16$-inch thickness. Since these cookies are relatively large, it's best to cut them directly on prepared cookie sheets to minimize the misshaping that can occur in transferring from work surface to cookie sheet. Cut out about 6 egg whites (2 per plate) using your template (or custom cutter) as a cutting guide. If any of the cut edges appear rough, pat them smooth with your fingertips. Cut out 6 yolks using the $1^7/_8$-inch round cookie cutter. Bake as directed until lightly browned around the edges, or about 11 to 14 minutes for the whites and 8 to 10 minutes for the yolks. Cool completely before decorating.

2. Prepare the Royal Icing as instructed on page 242. Reserve about 2 cups for the egg whites.

3. Decorate the yolks. Tint the remaining $1/_2$ cup Royal Icing to the color of egg yolks using about 5 drops yellow and 2 drops orange food coloring. Thin the icing to dipping consistency (p. 245). Dip the $1^7/_8$-inch rounds following the Nose-Dive Dipping instructions on page 32, taking care to completely cover the cookie edges. Place the cookies on a cooling rack over parchment paper and allow them to drip dry. To keep the cookies from drying to the rack, slide a thin-bladed paring knife under each cookie before the icing dries completely. Let the cookies dry to the touch.

4. Decorate the whites. *For the most realistic egg whites with no visible edges (pictured p. 94):* Thin the 2 cups icing reserved for whites to dipping consistency for large cookies, as described on page 245. Then follow the instructions for Nose Dive-Dipping used in Step 3. (*Note:* Before dipping these cookies, I purposely incorporate air bubbles into the icing by beating it vigorously after it's been loosened. The bubbles will linger and dry on the surface, contributing to a more authentic look.) While the icing is still wet, set a dried cookie yolk in the center of each egg white. *For more stylized egg whites with edges (pictured in "Stand-in," p. 95):* Use the 2 cups icing to outline and flood the egg white cookies following the instructions for outlining and flooding (p. 29 and p. 31, respectively). Remember to adjust the icing to the proper consistency for each task. You will also need parchment pastry cones if you go this route.

WHAT'S SHAKIN' BACON? (optional)

You'll get many more pieces of bacon than can fill 3 plate cookies. However, it's difficult to mix the tuile batter in any smaller quantity, so you'll just have to enjoy the leftovers!

Custom rectangular acetate stencil (see Step 1)

1 recipe Traditional Tuiles, Cocoa
    Variation (p. 255)

About 3 tablespoons powdered sugar

About 3 tablespoons unsweetened cocoa powder

Small offset spatula (p. 14)

Wood grain decorative stencil, for
    bacon texture (p. 24)

Small fine-mesh sieve

Soft-bristled pastry or craft paintbrush

1. Prepare the bacon stencil and batter. For the bacon stencil, cut out a $1^1/_8$ x 6- to 8-inch rectangle in the center of a piece of acetate following the instructions for making custom stencils (p. 49). Mix the Cocoa Variation of Traditional Tuiles as instructed. Combine the powdered sugar and cocoa powder in a separate bowl and set aside.

2. Stencil and bake the bacon. Because the bacon must be shaped quickly while hot from the oven, make just a few pieces at a time.

(a) Set the bacon stencil on a prepared cookie sheet (remember, tuiles require silicone baking mats). Spread a thin layer of tuile batter over the stencil opening using a small offset spatula. The batter need not be any thicker than the thickness of the acetate.

a.

(b) Carefully lift up the stencil and, if possible, stencil a few more pieces of bacon on the cookie sheet, leaving ample space (about 3 inches) between pieces.

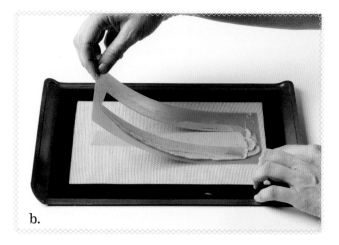

b.

(c) Prop a wood grain stencil directly over one of the stenciled bacon pieces so that it hovers about ⅛ to ¼ inch over the batter. (*Note:* I used the #WT1 wood trim stencil

from victorialarsen.com.) If your stencil is very long, you may have to tape its ends to your tabletop to prevent it from sagging into the batter. Gently sift a small amount of the reserved cocoa mixture over the stencil using the fine-mesh sieve.

c.

(d) Lift the wood grain stencil to reveal the pattern underneath, taking care not to drop any extra cocoa mixture (on the stencil top) onto the pattern. Clean the stencil by shaking off the excess cocoa into a bowl. Repeat Steps (c) and (d) until you've added texture to all of the bacon pieces on the cookie sheet.

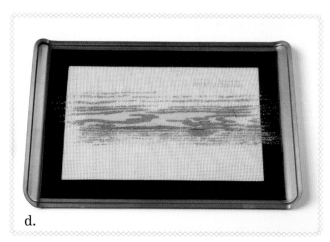

d.

Bake the tuiles as directed until lightly browned around the edges, or about 4 to 5 minutes. Watch them carefully, as they can quickly overcook and burn.

(e) Immediately peel the tuiles off the silicone mat; then gently bend them in a couple of places to add dimension. Work quickly while they are still hot.

e.

Once the tuiles have cooled, dust off any excess cocoa mixture with a soft-bristled brush. (If you brush them when warm, their patterns can smudge.) Immediately transfer the tuiles to airtight containers and keep them there until you're ready to eat. Tuiles are quite vulnerable to humidity and can quickly get soft if not properly contained. Repeat Steps (a) to (e) until all of the batter is used.

SLICE OF NICE (or 3-D wedges, optional)

About 8 ounces ($^1/_3$ recipe) Signature Sugar Cookie Dough (p. 234)

3$^3/_{16}$-inch plain round cookie cutter

About 3$^1/_4$ to 3$^1/_2$ cups ($^2/_3$ to $^3/_4$ recipe) Royal Icing (p. 242), divided; quantity will vary

Orange and yellow soft-gel food colorings (p. 14)

Parchment pastry cones (p. 13)

Small ($^3/_8$- to $^1/_2$-inch) white candies, for seeds

1. Cut and bake the orange slices. On a lightly floured surface, roll the dough to a $^1/_8$- to $^3/_{16}$-inch thickness. Cut out about 8 (3$^3/_{16}$-inch) rounds, transfer the rounds to prepared cookie sheets, and cut each round in half. Slide the halves about $^3/_4$ inch apart, so they don't bake into each other. (*Note:* I cut the halves directly on the cookie sheets to minimize misshaping.) Bake as directed until lightly browned around the edges, or about 9 to 11 minutes. If desired, trim the flat edge of each cookie to straighten it while the cookies are still hot from the oven. Trimming will ensure a better fit of the 3-D wedges in Step 4.

2. Prepare the Royal Icing as instructed on page 242. Reserve about 1$^1/_4$ cups for lines (to mark sections) and the orange pith, $^1/_2$ cup for the rind, and $^1/_4$ cup for gluing wedges. Omit the latter if you don't make wedges.

3. Dip and decorate the orange slices. Tint the remaining 1^1/$_2$ cups icing to the color of orange pulp using about 6 drops orange and 4 to 5 drops yellow food coloring; then thin to dipping consistency (p. 245). Tint the 1^1/$_4$ cups icing reserved for lines and pith to a light yellow using 1 small drop yellow food coloring; then thin to outlining consistency (p. 244). Fill a parchment pastry cone with the yellow icing and cut a very small (^{1}/$_{16}$-inch or less) hole in the tip.

a.

(a) Following the Nose-Dive Dipping technique instructions on page 32, dip each cookie in the orange icing to completely cover the edges. Set the cookies on a cooling rack over parchment paper (to catch the drippings) or a parchment paper-lined cookie sheet.

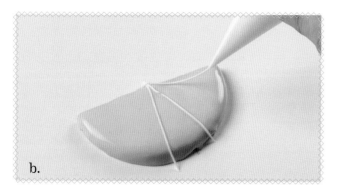

b.

(b) While the icing is still wet, but not runny, pipe thin lines of the light yellow icing on each cookie to mark orange sections. Set 1 to 2 small white candies in the orange icing for seeds. (*Note:* I used candy beads from necklaces made by Ce De Candy and cut the beads in half; Tic Tac mints work, too.) If the yellow lines shift and get wavy when adding the seeds, or if they flow off the orange icing, allow the orange icing to dry a bit longer before adding the lines and seeds. Before the cookies dry completely, gently guide a thin-bladed paring knife under each to sever any icing that may be clinging to the rack or cookie sheet; then dry completely before adding the pith and rind.

Thin the leftover light yellow icing to dipping consistency. Following the Roundabout Dipping technique instructions on page 34, dip the rounded edge of each cookie in the icing by rotating the edge through the icing.

c.

(c) Tint the ^{1}/$_2$ cup icing reserved for rind to a dark orange and thin to dipping consistency. Once the yellow icing is dry to the touch, dip the edges again in the dark orange icing following the procedure just described. Make sure to leave about half of the light yellow pith exposed. Let the orange slices dry completely before serving or forming into wedges in the next step.

d.

4. Assemble the slices into 3-D wedges (optional). To ensure that the straight edges of the slices fit snugly together in 3-D, bevel them with a paring knife following the beveling instructions on page 51.

(d) Secure 2 orange slices together along their beveled edges with a small amount of the $^1/_4$ cup icing reserved for "glue." Be sure to leave a gap between the rounded edges to allow the cookies to stand upright. Prop the pieces so they don't rock or separate at the seam and dry completely before moving. Repeat with the remaining cookies.

FULL PLATE (optional)

$10^3/_4$-inch round custom template
(or cake pan or bowl)

8-inch round custom template
(or cake pan or bowl)

About $3^1/_2$ to 4 pounds ($1^1/_6$ to $1^1/_3$ recipes)
Construction Gingerbread (p. 238)

$4^1/_8$-inch plain round cookie cutter

About $1^1/_4$ cups ($^1/_4$ recipe) Royal
Icing (p. 242), divided

Brown and other soft-gel food colorings
(p. 14) of your choice

Small offset spatula (p. 14)

About 1 pound rolled fondant (p. 53) or
other modeling medium, color(s) of your
choice, for ribbons on plate rims

Parchment pastry cones (p. 13)

Pastry bag fitted with tip of your
choice, for borders

About 3 (8 x 11-inch) sheets printed wafer paper
(p. 26), pattern(s) of your choice (optional)

1. Cut and bake the plate pieces. Following the instructions for custom templates (p. 48), make $10^3/_4$-inch and 8-inch circle templates. Alternatively, you can use cake pans or bowls as cutting guides. If you plan to make a lot of plates, consider making custom cookie cutters; they will save cutting time in the long run. For more information about working with custom templates and cutters, see page 48.

Each plate will be comprised of 3 pieces: a ring for the plate rim, a circular plate base (on which the rim will sit), and a smaller circular foot or pedestal (on which the base will sit). Start by cutting out the rims.

On a lightly floured surface, roll the dough to a $^1/_8$- to $^3/_{16}$-inch thickness. Since these pieces are relatively large, it's best to cut them directly on prepared cookie sheets to avoid the misshaping that can occur in transferring from work surface to cookie sheet. Cut out a $10^3/_4$-inch circle using your template (or pan or bowl) as a cutting guide. Use the other template (or pan or bowl) to cut out an 8-inch circle in the center to leave behind a ring or plate rim. Reroll the leftover dough (including that cut from the center) to make 2 more plate rims (1 per cookie sheet).

Reroll the dough again and cut out another 3 ($10^3/4$-inch) rounds (for the plate bases) and 3 ($4^1/8$-inch) rounds (for the pedestals). Again, cut these pieces directly on prepared cookie sheets. *Note:* You will use closer to $3^1/2$ pounds dough on 3 plates, but the extra is needed to easily roll to the large sizes required for these plates. Leftover dough can always be frozen.

Pat any rough edges flat with your fingertips and bake the cookies as directed until lightly browned around the edges, or about 10 to 15 minutes for the rims, 15 to 19 minutes for the pedestals, and 20 to 22 minutes for the bases. Baking time can vary considerably with dough thickness, so watch closely toward the end of the baking process.

2. Prepare the Royal Icing as instructed on page 242. Reserve about $1/2$ cup for borders around the plate rims and $1/4$ cup for "glue."

3. Reinforce the plate pieces. Tint the remaining $1/2$ cup icing to a brown that matches the gingerbread and thin to top-coating consistency (p. 245). Using a small offset spatula, spread a thin coating of icing on the underside of each rim and plate base, taking care to keep the icing off the top of the cookies. (Once it dries, this icing will keep these cookies from bending if exposed to humidity.) Let the icing dry before further decorating.

4. Make ribbons for the plate rims. Work on one rim at a time. Portion off about 7 to 8 ounces of the rolled fondant or other modeling medium. Follow the instructions for making Plain, Stitched, or Embossed Ribbons (pp. 56 to 57) to make a ribbon wide and long enough to span the plate rim (i.e., about $1^1/2$ to $1^3/4$ inches wide and 32 to 33 inches long). Affix the ribbon to the top of a plate rim with

a small amount of the brown icing left over from Step 3. (*Note:* The ribbon shown on page 94 was embossed with a grosgrain rolling pin. Also, expect to have leftover modeling medium. It's easier to roll ribbons of the size needed here with some extra.) Repeat to cover the remaining plate rims.

5. Add borders to the plate rims. Tint the $1/2$ cup icing reserved for borders to a color of your choice, or leave it white. Choose a border style from among those listed in "7 Essential Piping Techniques" (p. 46). Adjust the icing to the proper consistency for your border, transfer to a parchment pastry cone or pastry bag fitted with the right tip, and then pipe away! *Note:* I piped a Beaded Border (p. 46) around both edges of each ribbon using icing of beadwork consistency (p. 245).

6. Assemble the plates. Turn the plate bases upside down and affix a $4^1/8$-inch cookie (the pedestal) to the center of each plate with the remaining $1/4$ cup Royal Icing "glue." Let the icing dry completely before turning the plates right side up. Glue a rim to the top of each plate. As desired, slip a piece of trimmed wafer paper between the rim and base to add more color and texture. However, it's best to leave the paper loosely inserted between the pieces, as it will buckle over time if glued to the un-iced bases.

lollypalooza

THERE ARE FEW THINGS MORE FUN THAN BEING A KID (OR KID-AT-HEART) IN A CANDY STORE! Fortunately, these jumbo candy cookies make it extra easy to surround yourself with tantalizing sweets, because they use the über-forgiving marbling technique (p. 35).

Makes about 1 dozen (4³⁄8-inch) lollypops

About 11 ounces (¹⁄4 recipe) Cutout Cookie
    Gingerbread (p. 236) or (¹⁄2 recipe)
    Signature Sugar Cookie Dough (p. 234)

4³⁄8-inch plain round cookie cutter or
    other round cutters, as desired

About 5¹⁄2 cups (1¹⁄4 recipes) Royal Icing
    (p. 242), divided; quantity will vary

Soft-gel food colorings (p. 14) of your choice

Parchment pastry cones (p. 13)

Small craft paintbrush (handle
    about ¹⁄4-inch diameter)

Metal trussing needle (p. 15) or toothpicks

About 12 (¹⁄4-inch-diameter) dowel rods
    (cut to desired length) or 12 (11³⁄4-
    inch) cardboard lollypop sticks (p. 268)

Assorted ribbons, for bows (optional)

Gumballs and assorted containers,
    for display (optional)

Clear cellophane bags or sheets (optional)

Stand-in: Eye Candy. *Dainty candy cookies are as eye-catching as lollies—yet even simpler, as they require no mounting on sticks. These cookies use only two marbling patterns—Lollypalooza and Daisy—but by swapping background and foreground colors, I've given the appearance of many more! To replicate the Lollypalooza pattern (bottom left), see Step 5 (p. 105); for the Daisy pattern (bottom right), top-coat a cookie, pipe concentric circles of marbling icing on top, and then draw a metal trussing needle or toothpick in straight lines toward the cookie center.*

TYPES:

Cutout Cookie Gingerbread (p. 236) or Signature
Sugar Cookie Dough (p. 234)

{ lollypalooza, continued }

PREP TALK:

Either cookie dough in "Types" works well for this project. Just be sure to mix and chill the dough as instructed. If packaged in airtight containers at room temperature, this project will stay its best about 1 week.

1. Cut and bake the lollypop tops. On a lightly floured surface, roll the dough to a $1/8$- to $3/16$-inch thickness and cut it into $4 3/8$-inch rounds. (Feel free to vary cookie size, as pictured left.) Bake as directed until lightly browned around the edges, or about 9 to 12 minutes for cookies of this size. To maintain perfectly circular cookie shapes, trim the cookies, while hot from the oven, with the same cutter used to cut them. Cool completely before icing.

2. Prepare the Royal Icing as instructed on page 242. Reserve about 2 cups for marbling and $3/4$ cup for "glue." *Note:* The quantity of icing will vary with the number of colors and consistencies mixed. It's best to allow no less than $1/4$ to $1/2$ cup icing per color or consistency for easiest mixing and handling.

3. Outline the lollypop tops (optional). I like to outline these cookies before applying more icing in Step 5 in order to get the icing very close to the cookie edges. However, if you'd prefer to have more cookie edge showing, skip this step and proceed directly to top-coating in Step 4. Tint the remaining $2 3/4$ cups icing to a color (or colors) of your choice and thin to outlining consistency (p. 244). Transfer each color to a separate parchment pastry cone and cut a small ($1/16$-inch or more) hole in each tip. Proceed to outline each cookie following the techniques on page 29.

4. Prep the icings for top-coating and marbling. Adjust the icing(s) remaining from Step 3 to top-coating consistency (p. 245). *Note:* I prefer to mix the icing(s) to top-coating rather than flooding consistency, because the

marbling colors, below, will be applied to them while wet. Thicker top-coating icing is less likely to result in colors bleeding.

Next, divide the 2 cups icing reserved for marbling into as many portions as you want marbling colors. Tint each portion and then adjust to marbling consistency as described on page 244. (*Note:* Marbling generally looks better, at least to me, when there is a large difference between the intensity of the top-coating color and those used for the marbling. So, in other words, a very light top coat with darker marbling colors, or a dark top coat with lighter marbling colors, shows best.) Turn each of the marbling colors into separate parchment pastry cones and cut a small ($1/16$-inch or more) hole in each tip.

5. Top-coat and marble the lollypop tops. Working with one cookie at a time and the handle-end of a craft paintbrush, apply a smooth coat of icing to the cookie top. (If the cookie was outlined in Step 3, I generally use a top-coating color that matches the outline.) For top-coating technique details, see page 28. From this point forward, it's important to move very quickly. If any of the icing dries even slightly, you'll end up with a rough finish rather than the desired smooth one.

For the Lollypalooza pattern (pictured left): (a) Start by piping alternating colors of marbling icing in straight lines through the cookie center. Place the lines of marbling icing very close together, less than $1/8$ inch apart, if you want an intensely swirly pattern. To see more top-coating color, simply place the lines further apart. Or, for a bolder

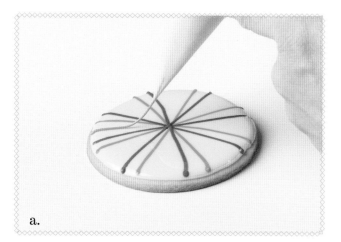

a.

pattern, cut slightly larger holes in the tips of your cones. Don't worry if your lines aren't perfectly straight. If you draw through any imperfections in the next step, you can mask most errors. (I told you marbling was forgiving, didn't I?)

(b) Using a metal trussing needle or toothpick, draw a circle around the outer edge of the icing in one continuous motion.

b.

(c) Lift the trussing needle and draw another circle closer to the center, about $1/2$ inch from the first, but move in the opposite direction this time. Lift the trussing needle

again and draw another circle about $1/2$ inch from the second one, this time drawing in the original direction. Lastly, draw a small circle in the very center to soften the point where all the marbling colors intersect—and voilà!

c.

Note: Myriad other patterns can be created by playing with the variables described in "Marbling" (p. 35). Let your imagination run wild! Or try the Daisy pattern in "Stand-in" (p. 103) or the Starburst pattern (p. 36). Repeat with the remaining cookies. Allow the cookies to dry thoroughly.

6. **Mount and serve or display (optional).** Affix a decorated lollypop top to the end of each dowel rod or lollypop stick with the reserved $3/4$ cup Royal Icing "glue." Let the "glue" dry completely before attempting to move the lollypops. Tie ribbons around the dowel rods or lollypop sticks, as desired. Serve as-is, display in gumball-filled containers as shown on page 104, or wrap the cookie tops in cellophane for gift giving.

cream of the crop
WITH SOFT SPOT VARIATION

PUT EVERYONE IN GOOD HUMOR WITH THESE ICE CREAM CONES made of not one, but three goodies: tuiles, macarons, and a creamy buttercream or ganache filling!

Makes about 2½ dozen (2 x 8-inch-tall) triple-scoop ice cream cones

12-piece plain round cookie cutter set (Ateco #5457, p. 14)

3 recipes Goofproof Macarons (p. 249), mixed 1 recipe at a time

Yellow, brown, and other soft-gel food colorings (p. 14) of your choice

Pastry bag(s) fitted with $1/2$-inch round tip (Ateco #806)

A few tablespoons multi-color jimmies and/ or sugar confetti (p. 26, optional)

About $5^1/4$ cups (2 to $2^1/3$ recipes) Ganache (p. 259) or ($1^1/4$ to $1^1/3$ recipes) Italian Buttercream (p. 257), divided

About $2^1/2$ dozen (6-inch) cardboard lollypop sticks (p. 268)

Custom triangular acetate stencil, for cones (see Step 3)

1 recipe Traditional Tuiles (p. 255)

Medium offset spatula (p. 14, blade about $1^1/4$ x $6^1/2$ inches)

1 or more ($1^7/8$ x $4^3/8$-inch-tall) metal pastry horn molds, for shaping cones

Stand-in: We All Scream for Ice Cream. *Especially when shortcuts can be found! Feel free to simplify this project by replacing the triple-decker macaron ice cream scoops with double or single soft-swirls made with meringue rosettes. (See Soft Spot Variation, p. 112.) You can also skip the waffle cone stenciling in Step 3 (p. 110); plain tuile cones (bottom right) look very realistic, too.*

TYPES:

Goofproof Macarons (p. 249) for ice cream scoops;

Traditional Tuiles (p. 255) for cones

Pictured: *Cream of the Crop with Soft Spot Variation (bottom right).*

{ cream of the crop, continued }

For waffle cone pattern (optional):

About 6 tablespoons powdered sugar

About 2 tablespoons unsweetened cocoa powder

Diamond grid decorative stencil (p. 24)

Small fine-mesh sieve

Soft-bristled pastry or craft paintbrush

---

1. Bake the macaron ice cream scoops. Prepare 2 cookie sheets by tracing about 20 ($1^7/_8$-inch), 20 ($1^1/_2$-inch), and 20 ($^7/_8$-inch) circles on pieces of parchment paper sized to fit the sheets. Use plain round cookie cutters from the cutter set as your tracing guides. Leave no less than $^3/_4$ inch between circles and put like sizes on the same cookie sheet(s). You'll need 6 cookie sheets in total for 3 batches of Goofproof Macarons. Turn over the papers and secure them to the cookie sheets with a dab of shortening or butter in each corner. *Note:* Turning over the paper keeps the tracing marks from being transferred onto the cookies during baking.

Mix the Goofproof Macarons a batch at a time, even if you don't intend to tint each batch a different color, as pictured left. You'll have better control over batter consistency and be less likely to overfold (which can result in lopsided macarons). To tint the batter, add soft-gel food coloring of your choice at the end of Step 3 (p. 250). I usually add no more than 20 to 25 drops coloring; if you add more, you defeat the purpose of dehydrating the egg whites at the start. Transfer the batter to a pastry bag fitted with a $^1/_2$-inch round tip (Ateco #806) and pipe it into the outlines just traced, leaving a little room to spare to allow for spreading. If desired, sprinkle jimmies and/or sugar

PREP TALK:

The egg whites for Goofproof Macarons must be dehydrated for 20 to 24 hours before baking. Once baked, the macarons may be filled with Ganache or Italian Buttercream up to a few days prior to final ice cream cone assembly. Since both fillings are perishable, be sure to refrigerate the filled macarons until you're ready to serve. However, for best flavor and texture, bring them to room temperature before serving.

Tuiles are always their crispest and tastiest on the day they're made, which is why I prefer to bake the tuile cones just before filling. However, if you're pressed for time, the cones can be made up to 1 week ahead provided they're stored in airtight containers at room temperature. Because tuiles soften quickly when exposed to humidity, it's best to fill the cones immediately before serving.

---

confetti on the top edge of each round while the batter is still tacky. Air-dry the macarons as instructed (p. 251). To minimize discoloration of these cookies, bake all sizes about 10 minutes at 300°F; then drop the oven temperature to 275°F and bake until set, or about 8 to 10 minutes longer for the largest ($1^7/_8$-inch) rounds and closer to 5 to 7 minutes more for the smaller rounds. (Whatever you do, watch the macarons closely as they can brown in a flash!) Repeat to mix and bake the remaining batches.

2. Make the filling and assemble the triple-decker scoops. Prepare either Ganache to piping consistency or Italian Buttercream. Portion off about $2^3/_4$ cups. If you've made buttercream (or White Chocolate Ganache) and multi-color macarons, divide the filling and tint each portion to match your macaron colors. Or to save time, leave the filling untinted. Transfer the filling to a pastry bag (or bags, if more than one color) fitted with a $^1/_2$-inch round tip (Ateco #806). *Note:* Reserve the remaining 2$^1/_2$ cups filling for use in Step 4. If you plan to assemble the cones on a different day than the scoops, then refrigerate this filling until needed.

Assemble one triple-decker scoop at a time. Turn a 1$^7/_8$-inch, 1$^1/_2$-inch, and $^7/_8$-inch macaron flat side up on your work surface. (I like to mix up the macaron colors.) Line them up end to end so that the largest macaron is on the bottom and the smallest is on the top. Pipe a small mound of filling (of matching color, if desired) in the center of each macaron; then place a lollypop stick along the center of the cookies. Only the bottom end of the stick should extend beyond the macarons. Pipe a small amount of additional filling on top of each macaron to cover the stick and then top with macarons of matching size and color. Repeat to make a total of 30 (3-macaron) sticks. Refrigerate the macaron sticks in airtight containers until ready for further assembly in Step 4.

3. Make the tuile cones. Cut out a 5$^1/_4$ x 3$^1/_2$-inch-tall triangle in the center of a piece of acetate following the instructions for making custom stencils (p. 49). Prepare Traditional Tuiles as instructed. At the end of Step 4 (p. 256), mix in 1 drop yellow and 1 drop brown food coloring for a truer ice cream cone color. Because the tuiles must be shaped quickly while hot from the oven, make just a few pieces at a time.

Short and Sweet. *(a) Use Ganache or Italian Buttercream to sandwich three different sizes of decorated Goofproof Macarons around lollypop sticks. Refrigerate the macaron sticks to set the icing. (b) Spread batter for Traditional Tuiles through a custom triangular stencil onto prepared cookie sheets. Stencil with a grid pattern using a mixture of cocoa powder and powdered sugar, as desired. Bake the tuiles and wrap around pastry horn molds to shape into cones. (c) Fill the cones with leftover Ganache or Italian Buttercream and insert a trimmed macaron stick in the top of each cone.*

(a) Set the stencil on a prepared cookie sheet (remember, tuiles require silicone baking mats). Spread a thin layer of tuile batter over the stencil opening using a medium offset spatula. The batter need not be any thicker than the thickness of the acetate. (*Note:* I use a medium spatula rather than a small one in order to evenly fill this relatively large stencil in the fewest possible swipes.) Repeat to add a few more triangles to the cookie sheet, if possible.

a.

(b) *(Optional)* If desired, add a waffle cone pattern to each triangle. Combine the powdered sugar and cocoa powder. Set a diamond grid stencil on pieces of cardboard so it hovers over one of the triangles, but does not touch the

b.

batter. (*Note:* The stencil pictured here is a plastic paint grid from a hardware store.) Sift the cocoa mixture evenly over the stencil using the fine-mesh sieve.

(c) *(Optional)* Carefully lift the stencil to reveal the pattern underneath, taking care not to drop any extra cocoa mixture (on the stencil top) onto the pattern. Clean the stencil by shaking off the excess cocoa into a bowl. Repeat Steps (b) and (c) for each triangle on the cookie sheet, as desired.

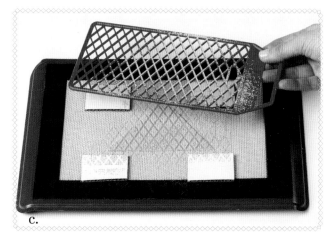

c.

(d) Bake the tuiles as directed, until set and barely, if at all, discolored, or about 3 to 5 minutes. While the tuiles are still hot from the oven, lift them off the cookie sheet and

d.

wrap them around metal pastry horn molds to make mini ice cream cones.

(e) *(Optional)* Once the tuiles have cooled, dust off any excess cocoa mixture with a soft-bristled brush. (If you brush them when warm, their patterns can smudge.) Store the tuiles as instructed in "Prep Talk" as soon as they've cooled.

e.

Repeat Steps (a) to (e) until all of the tuile batter is used.

4. Assemble the ice cream cones. As noted in "Prep Talk," it's best to assemble the ice cream cones just before serving, so the tuiles stay crispy. About 30 minutes before assembling, take the macaron sticks out of the refrigerator to allow their filling to soften.

Bring the $2^1/2$ cups filling reserved in Step 2 to room temperature if it was refrigerated. Transfer to a pastry bag fitted with a $1/2$-inch round tip (Ateco #806). Pipe enough filling into each cone to reach the top; then insert one of the macaron sticks into the filling. (You'll need to trim the sticks to fit the cones.) Serve immediately.

VARIATION
{ Soft Spot }

Makes about 2 to $2^1/2$ dozen ($1^3/4$ x $5^3/4$-inch-tall) double soft-swirl ice cream cones; yield will vary with egg size and beating time.

Omit the Goofproof Macarons in Step 1 (p. 109) and make 1 recipe Meringues (p. 253) instead. Transfer the meringue to a pastry bag fitted with a $1/2$-inch star tip (Ateco #826) and pipe into $1^1/2$-inch rosettes, as described on page 254. Bake the rosettes as instructed until dry but not discolored, or about 1 hour at 225^0F and another $1/2$ hour or more at 200^0F. (Feel free to reduce the oven temperature earlier if you see any meringues starting to crack.) Since meringues bake a relatively long time, any sugar pieces applied before baking can bleed or melt in the heat of the oven. So in this case, I prefer to attach jimmies and sugar confetti with Royal Icing "glue" after the meringues have cooled. (You'll need less than $1/4$ cup additional icing for this task.)

Prepare closer to $2^1/2$ cups (1 recipe) Ganache (chilled to piping consistency) or ($1/2$ to $2/3$ recipe) Italian Buttercream. Also prepare Traditional Tuiles as instructed in Step 3 (p. 110). To assemble double soft-swirl cones, simply fill the cones with Ganache or Italian Buttercream and stick one meringue upside down in the top of each cone; then pipe a small amount of filling on the bottom of the meringue and set another meringue right side up on top. Single soft-swirl cones can also be made by setting one meringue right side up on each filled cone.

take the cake

WITH MOTHERS' DAY, CHRISTMAS, AND BIRTHDAY CAKE VARIATIONS

YOU MAY HAVE SEEN MY MINI WEDDING CAKES IN *COOKIE SWAP,* but here I take the cake with cookie cakes for all occasions—Mothers' Day, Christmas, that special birthday, you name it. Plus, I've elevated the presentation (pun intended) by giving you the option to turn single-layer cakes (1 cookie per tier) into taller double-layer cakes (2 cookies per tier), or to serve the cakes on cookie pedestals as shown on page 114.

Makes about 7 (2¼ x 2⅞-inch-tall) 3-tier double-layer cakes,
3 (3³⁄₁₆ x 4⅛-inch-tall) 4-tier double-layer cakes, or twice as many single-layer cakes

About 1 pound 6 ounces (1 recipe) Shortbread, Straight Up (p. 240)

12-piece plain round cookie cutter set (Ateco #5457, p. 14)

About 2 to 2½ cups (⅓ to ½ recipe) Royal Icing (p. 242), divided; quantity will vary

Soft-gel food colorings (p. 14) of your choice

Small craft paintbrush (handle about ¼-inch diameter)

Parchment pastry cones (p. 13)

About 3 ounces rolled fondant (p. 53) or other modeling medium, color(s) of your choice, for wide cake ribbons (optional for single-layer cakes)

About 2 ounces rolled fondant or other modeling medium, color(s) of your choice, for thin ribbons and Loop-de-Loop Bows (p. 57)

Assorted tier-top decorations, per Variations (p. 117)

Stand-in: A Saucy Setup. *Mini cake stands can be made by gluing together decorated cookie rounds (as pictured p. 114), but if time is of the essence, they can also be constructed by setting teacup saucers atop candlesticks or salt cellars, as pictured under these wintry Christmas cakes.*

TYPE:

Shortbread, Straight Up (p. 240)

Pictured: *Take the Cake, Mothers' Day Variation (top and middle) and Birthday Variation (far left and right).*

PREP TALK:

Because shortbread retains its shape better than most rolled doughs when cut thick, Shortbread, Straight Up is the dough of choice for these chunky cake tiers. Be sure to mix and chill the dough as instructed. All cake decorations made of modeling media, excluding ribbons and bows, should be shaped at least a day ahead to give them ample time to air-dry and firm up. If packaged in airtight containers at room temperature, this project will stay its best about 1 week.

1. Cut and bake the cake tiers. On a lightly floured surface, roll the dough to a ³/₈-inch thickness. *For 3-tier cakes:* Cut out equal numbers of 2¹/₄-inch, 1¹/₂-inch, and ⁷/₈-inch plain rounds and arrange like sizes on the same cookie sheet. You should end up with about 15 cookies of each size. *For 4-tier cakes (i.e., yellow cake, pictured top right, p. 114):* Cut out 3³/₁₆-inch rounds as well. In this case, you'll end up with about 6 cookies in each of the 4 sizes.

Bake the cookies until lightly browned on the bottom, or about 25 to 30 minutes. The smaller cookies will bake closer to 25 to 27 minutes. *For extra tall, double-layer cakes (i.e., green, yellow, and pink cakes, pictured top and right, p. 114):* Be sure to trim the cookies while hot from the oven with the cookie cutters originally used to cut them. Trimming will lead to straighter, better fitting tiers in Step 5. For trimming tips, see page 51.

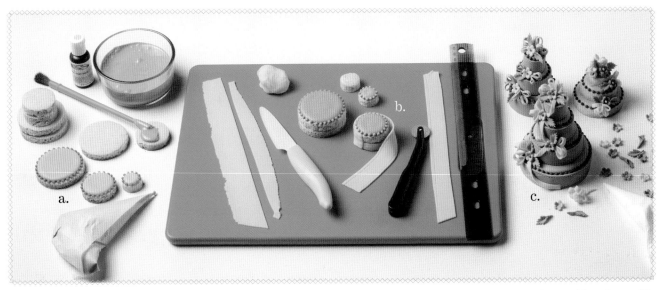

Short and Sweet. *(a) Top-coat graduated sizes of shortbread rounds with Royal Icing. Add dots to the cookie edges with icing of beadwork consistency. (b) As desired, cover the sides of each cake tier with ribbons made of rolled fondant or another modeling medium. Add texture to the ribbons by drawing along the edges with a serrated tracing wheel. (c) Stack into 3- or 4-tier cakes by securing the tiers with thick Royal Icing. Finish by gluing tiny bows, flowers, and other decorations to the tops of each tier.*

2. Prepare the Royal Icing as instructed on page 242. Reserve about $1/2$ cup for beadwork on the cake edges, $1/2$ cup for "glue," and $1/4$ cup for applying wide ribbons (optional) in Step 6. *Note:* The quantity of icing will vary with cake configuration and the number of colors and consistencies mixed. You'll need closer to $2 1/2$ cups (total) for single-layer cakes and only 2 cups (total) for double-layer cakes. It's also best to allow no less than $1/4$ to $1/2$ cup icing per color or consistency for easiest mixing and handling.

3. Top-coat the cake tiers. Tint the remaining $3/4$ to $1 1/4$ cups icing to a color (or colors) of your choice; then thin to top-coating consistency (p. 245). (Again, the larger quantity is only needed for single-layer cakes, where all of the cookies are top-coated.) *For single-layer cakes:* Using the handle-end of a craft paintbrush, apply a smooth coat of icing to each cookie top. For more top-coating instructions, see page 28. *For double-layer cakes:* Top-coat half of the cookies in each size. Let the icing dry to the touch before proceeding to the next step.

4. Apply beadwork to the cake borders. Tint the $1/2$ cup icing reserved for beadwork to a color that contrasts the cookie top coats and adjust to the consistency for beadwork (p. 245). Transfer the icing to a parchment pastry cone and cut a small ($1/16$-inch or more) hole in the tip. Apply dots to the edges of each top-coated cookie following the instructions for beadwork on page 34. Dry completely before assembling.

5. Assemble the cakes. *For single-layer cakes:* Stack the iced cookies 3 (or 4) tiers high, starting with the largest round on the bottom and ending with the smallest on the top. Use a dab of the reserved $1/2$ cup icing "glue" to secure the tiers to one another. *For double-layer cakes:* As above, start with the largest rounds, but stack one iced cookie atop another un-iced one of like size to create a double-layer tier. Repeat this double-decking process with the remaining tiers; then glue the tiers together from largest on the bottom to smallest on the top. Allow the "glue" to set 20 to 30 minutes before proceeding to Step 6.

6. Add wide ribbons to the cake sides (optional for single-layer cakes). Wide ribbons, made of rolled fondant or another modeling medium, are entirely optional for single-layer cakes, since their untrimmed cookie edges look clean and tidy. However, for double-layer cakes, I like to cover the trimmed cookie edges and the seam where the cookies meet in each tier, as pictured center on page 115. Thin the $1/4$ cup icing reserved for applying ribbons to top-coating consistency.

Work on one cake at a time. (If ribbons are exposed to the air too long, they will get brittle and crack when wrapped around the tiers.) Follow the instructions for making Plain, Stitched, or Embossed Ribbons (pp. 56 to 57) to cut thin (about $1/4$-inch-wide for single-layer cakes; $3/4$-inch-wide for double-layer cakes) ribbons long enough to wrap around each tier. (*Note:* The ribbons, pictured on page 114, have been stitched.) Secure the ribbons to the sides of each tier with a thin coating of icing. Repeat to cover as many cakes as desired.

7. Add thin ribbons, Loop-de-Loop Bows, and other tier-top decorations. Again, work on one cake at a time. Start by cutting out thin (about $3/16$- to $1/8$-inch-wide) ribbons of modeling medium in a color that contrasts your other tier-top decorations (i.e., flowers, leaves, etc., depending on the decorating variation.) Drape the ribbons between tiers, as desired, using a small amount of leftover Royal Icing "glue" to hold the ends in place. Shape ribbons of the same size into tiny bows (about 1 per tier) following the instructions for Loop-de-Loop Bows on page 57. Affix the bows to the tier tops, between any draped ribbons, using more "glue." Immediately glue your other tier-top decorations next to each bow to cover its ends. Repeat to decorate the remaining cakes. Store as directed until ready to serve.

VARIATIONS

Listed below are the tier-top decorations used for the Take the Cake Variations, pictured on pages 113 and 114.

{ Mothers' Day Cake }

Small (about $1/2$-inch) tinted Cutout Flowers (p. 58), colors of your choice (1 per tier)

Small (about $3/8$ x $7/8$-inch) green Cutout Leaves (p. 59, 1 to 2 per tier)

{ Christmas Cake }

Small ($1/2$- to $7/8$-inch) readymade royal icing embellishments (p. 26), such as poinsettias, holly, and/or candles (1 per tier)

Note: The royal icing embellishments pictured on the cakes in "Stand-in" (p. 113) came from fancyflours.com.

{Birthday Cake }

Small ($1/2$- to $3/4$-inch) rolled fondant (or other modeling medium) birthday candles (below, 1 or more per tier, or about 25 to surround a 3-tier double-layer cake)

Note: The rolled fondant candles used in this variation look best on double-layer cakes.

Crafting Birthday Candles

(a) Push the rolled fondant (or another modeling medium) through a garlic press. Cut off 1/2- to 3/4-inch lengths of dough from the press.

(b) Gently roll the candles on a flat surface to straighten them out; then line them up and trim to a uniform length. Dry until firm enough to handle without misshaping.

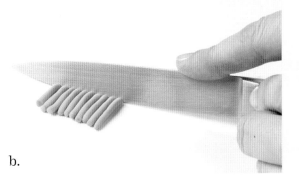

b.

(c) Pipe a tiny flame on top of each candle using yellow or orange Royal Icing of top-coating or thin outlining consistency (p. 244). Set the candles in bubble wrap to keep them from rolling while the flames dry.

c.

a.

chow bella

YES, PRETTY INDEED, especially when you consider that everything you see—from place mat to spaghetti and meatballs—is some form of cookie or icing. I've made these place settings on the small side, unlike the life-size portions in Breakfast in Bed (p. 95), but you can always scale them up if you please. Alternatively, skip the pasta on top and use the mats and plates to present Take the Cake (p. 113) or other cookie treats.

Makes 8 (5½ x 7¾-inch) pasta dinner and place mat cookies

Ruler or custom rectangular template, for place mats (see Step 1)

About 3 pounds 5 ounces (1 to 1¹/₆ recipes) Cutout Cookie Gingerbread (p. 236) or (2 to 2¹/₃ recipes) Signature Sugar Cookie Dough (p. 234)

4³/₈-inch fluted round cookie cutter, for plate rims

2⁷/₈-inch and 3¹/₂-inch plain round cookie cutters, for plate rims and bases

About 9¹/₂ to 9³/₄ cups (2 recipes) Royal Icing (p. 242), divided; quantity will vary

Brown, yellow, red, and other soft-gel food colorings (p. 14) of your choice

Parchment pastry cones (p. 13)

Small craft paintbrush (handle about ¹/₄-inch diameter)

About 4 (8 x 11-inch) sheets printed wafer paper (p. 26), pattern(s) of your choice (optional)

Small sponge brush (optional)

A few tablespoons light corn syrup (optional)

9 to 10 ounces rolled fondant (p. 53) or other modeling medium, color(s) of your choice, for place mat fringe and napkins

Stand-in: Blue Plate Special. *Cut corners, but not style, by replacing the macaron meatballs with chocolate-covered malt balls, brown M&Ms, or Tootsie Rolls shaped into tiny balls. Rolled fondant or another modeling medium can be cut into broad sheets to replace the iced place mat cookies, too.*

TYPES:

Cutout Cookie Gingerbread (p. 236) or Signature Sugar Cookie Dough (p. 234) for place mats and plates;

Goofproof Macarons (p. 249) for meatballs

{ chow bella, continued }

1/2 recipe Goofproof Macarons (p. 249)

Pastry bag fitted with 1/4-inch round tip (Ateco #10 or #11)

About 1/4 cup Ganache (p. 259) or Italian Buttercream (p. 257), Chocolate Variation (optional)

Pastry bag fitted with 3/8-inch grass tip (Ateco #133)

Wax candy soda bottles, for garnish (optional)

PREP TALK:

Either cookie dough in "Types" works well for the place mats and plates for this project. Just be sure to mix and chill the dough as instructed.

The egg whites for Goofproof Macarons (for the meatballs) must be dehydrated for 20 to 24 hours before baking. Once baked, the macarons may be filled with Ganache or Italian Buttercream up to a few days prior to serving. Since both fillings are perishable, be sure to refrigerate the filled macarons until you're ready to eat. Alternatively, the macarons can be filled with Royal Icing to avoid refrigeration. Plates topped with Royal Icing-filled macarons will be their best up to 1 week, if stored in airtight containers.

1. Cut and bake the place mat and plate rims and bases. Each of the 8 pasta dinner and place mat cookies will be comprised of 1 place mat cookie and 1 dinner plate cookie composed of a fluted ring for the rim and a plain round base.

Start by making a 5 1/2 x 7 1/8-inch rectangular template for the place mat following the instructions for custom templates (p. 48). Alternatively, use a ruler as a cutting guide, or if you're planning to make lots of these cookies, consider making a custom cookie cutter; it will save cutting time in the long run. For more information about working with custom templates and cutters, see page 48.

On a lightly floured surface, roll the dough to a 1/8- to 3/16-inch thickness. Since the mats are relatively large, it's best to cut them directly on prepared cookie sheets to minimize the misshaping that can occur in transferring

from work surface to cookie sheet. Cut out 8 place mats using the rectangular template (or ruler or custom cutter) as a cutting guide. Reroll the dough to the same thickness and cut out 8 (4 3/8-inch) fluted rounds for the plate rims. As you cut, transfer these cookies to prepared cookie sheets and cut out a 2 7/8-inch plain round in the center of each to complete the rim. (*Note:* Again, it's best to cut out the centers directly on the cookie sheets to minimize misshaping.) Once again, reroll the leftover dough, including the centers just cut from the rims, and cut out 8 (3 1/2-inch) plain rounds for the plate bases.

Bake the cookies as directed until lightly browned around the edges, or about 11 to 13 minutes for the place mats and bases and closer to 9 to 10 minutes for the rims. If needed, trim the place mat edges while hot from the oven to straighten. Cool completely before decorating in Step 3.

2. Prepare the Royal Icing as instructed on page 242. Reserve about 1 1/2 cups for outlining and flooding the plate rims and bases, 1/4 cup for "glue," 1 cup for detailing the place mats and plate rims, 1/4 cup for meatballs (optional), 1 1/4 cups for spaghetti, and 1/4 cup for sauce. *Note:* The quantity of icing will vary with your filling choice and the number of colors and consistencies mixed. Omit the 1/4 cup for meatballs if you plan to fill the macarons with Italian Buttercream or Ganache instead. It's also best to allow no less than 1/4 to 1/2 cup icing per color or consistency for easiest mixing and handling.

3. Outline and flood the place mats. I prefer to outline and flood the place mat cookies, as opposed to top-coating without any outlines, in order to get the icing as close to the edges as possible. Divide the remaining 5 1/4 cups icing into as many portions as you want colors on your place mats. If wafer-papering the mats in Step 5, I usually limit the mat color to white so it doesn't interfere with the paper's pattern.

Tint the icing as desired and thin each portion to outlining consistency (p. 244). Transfer each portion to a separate parchment pastry cone and cut a small (1/16-inch or more) hole in each tip. Outline all of the mats using colors of your choice and following the outlining instructions on page 29. Thin the leftover icing to flooding consistency (p. 245) and flood the interior of each outlined cookie with the same color of icing used to outline it. Let the icing dry completely before wafer-papering or otherwise decorating the cookies in Step 5.

Short and Sweet. *Outline and flood (or top-coat) the place mat, plate rim, and plate base cookies with Royal Icing. (a) Once the icing is dry, wafer-paper the mats, as desired. (b) Finish the plate rims with beadwork, and the mats with fringe made of rolled fondant or another modeling medium and/or other icing details. Make tiny Goofproof Macarons for meatballs. Glue a plate rim on top of each base and use a pastry bag fitted with a grass tip to pipe Royal Icing spaghetti on top. (c) Drizzle the spaghetti with red Royal Icing sauce, glue the plates to the mats, and garnish with macaron meatballs, rolled fondant napkins, and wax candy soda bottles, as desired.*

4. Top-coat the plate rims and bases. Tint the $1^1/2$ cups icing reserved for the plate rims and bases to a color (or colors) of your choice; then thin to top-coating consistency (p. 245). Using the handle-end of a craft paintbrush, apply a smooth coat of icing to each of the plate rims and bases. For top-coating technique details, see page 28.

5. Wafer-paper the place mats (optional) and detail the mats, plate rims, and plate bases. Wafer-papering the place mats is completely optional, but I often like to use a red-checked pattern to resemble a real mat or tablecloth. *To wafer-paper the mats:* Simply cut printed wafer paper to fit the icing on top of the mats. Work on one mat at a time. Use a small sponge brush to spread a thin layer of corn syrup on the cookie top coat; then fix a wafer paper cutout on top. Repeat to paper the remaining mats. Let the paper dry for at least 1 hour before applying fringe on the edges (below) or other details on top, as the paper can lift if details are added while it is still wet. For more information about the wafer-papering technique, see page 38.

For fringe on the mats: Thin a small portion of the $1/4$ cup icing reserved for "glue" to top-coating consistency (p. 245) and set aside. Work on a few mats at a time. Follow the instructions for cutting Plain Ribbons (p. 56) to make several strips out of rolled fondant, or another modeling medium, that fit the ends of each place mat. (Allow 1 to 2 strips for each end; cut strips about $1/2$ inch wide and $5^5/8$ inches long.) Before the strips dry, make a series of cuts at $1/16$-inch intervals along one of the long sides of each strip (to make the fringe); then glue the uncut edge of a strip (or 2 stacked strips) to the end of a place mat using a thin coating of the loosened "glue." As the fringe is drying, use the tip of a paring knife to separate and lift the fringe ends to add dimension. Repeat to add fringe to the remaining mats.

For details on the mats and plate rims: Tint the 1 cup icing reserved for detailing the mats and plates to a color (or colors) of your choice. For dots around the plate rims, such as those pictured on page 118, thin the icing to the consistency for beadwork (p. 245). For the Trailing Beaded Border (p. 46) along the edge of the place mat fringe, thin the icing to outlining consistency (p. 244). Transfer the icing(s) to separate parchment pastry cones, cut a small ($1/16$-inch or more) hole in each tip, and add details to whatever extent! (There's no need to detail the plate bases, since they won't show in the final construction.) Let the icing dry before assembling the plates in Step 7.

6. Make and fill the macaron meatballs. Prepare $1/2$ recipe Goofproof Macarons as instructed, but tint the batter at the end of Step 3 (p. 250) by adding about 15 drops brown food coloring. Transfer the batter to a pastry bag fitted with a $1/4$-inch round tip (Ateco #10 or #11) and pipe into tiny ($1/2$-inch) rounds. Air-dry as instructed (p. 251); then bake until set, but minimally discolored, or about 10 minutes. *Note:* $1/2$ recipe will make many more macarons than you'll need, but it's difficult to mix the batter in any smaller quantity. Save any extra macarons for snacking!

The macarons may be filled with the $1/4$ cup Royal Icing reserved for meatballs, Ganache (chilled to piping consistency), or Italian Buttercream, Chocolate Variation. The Royal Icing will set to a firm, crunchy texture and require no refrigeration, whereas the other fillings will stay soft. They are also perishable and must be refrigerated. To fill the meatballs, transfer your filling of choice to a pastry bag fitted with a $1/4$-inch round tip (Ateco #10 or #11). Pipe a small dollop of filling on the flat side of half of the macarons and then sandwich with another macaron on top. Store as directed in "Prep Talk" until ready to assemble.

7. Assemble the dinner plates. As noted in "Prep Talk," it's best to assemble these cookies close to serving time if you've filled the macarons with Ganache or Italian Buttercream.

Start by tinting the $1^1/_4$ cups icing reserved for spaghetti to a very pale yellow; then tint the $^1/_4$ cup icing reserved for sauce to a tomato red. Thin the yellow icing just slightly until it pushes easily out of a pastry bag fitted with a $^3/_8$-inch grass tip (Ateco #133), but still holds its shape. Thin the red icing to top-coating consistency.

Work on one cookie at a time. Using the remaining icing "glue," attach a plate rim to a plate base. Pipe squiggles of yellow icing on top of the plate; then dribble a small amount of red icing on top. Before the icing sets up, insert a few macaron meatballs into the top of the pasta and sauce. Repeat to decorate a total of 8 plates.

Glue the plates to the place mats, as desired. You can also roll out thin sheets of rolled fondant or another modeling medium, cut them into small squares, and then fold them into napkins to glue plateside, along with wax candy soda bottles! Mangia!

move over, cupcake!

DON'T GET ME WRONG, I LOVE THE CUPCAKE TREND as much as the next baker, but somehow I feel like the cookie has gotten the short end of the stick. Heck, cookies are arguably easier to make, certainly more portable, and just as tasty and chameleon-like as cupcakes. Any doubts? Then take a closer look at these treats (pictured below and on page 2).

Makes about 8 ($2^3/_4$ x 3- to $3^1/_8$-inch-tall, 3- to 4-cookie) cupcakes

About 11 ounces ($^1/_4$ recipe) Cutout Cookie Gingerbread (p. 236) or ($^1/_2$ recipe) Signature Sugar Cookie Dough (p. 234)

$2^1/_4$-inch and $1^7/_8$-inch plain round cookie cutters

About $1^1/_2$ to $1^3/_4$ cups ($^1/_3$ recipe) Royal Icing (p. 242), divided; quantity will vary

Brown (optional) and other soft-gel food colorings (p. 14) of your choice

Small craft paintbrush (handle about $^1/_4$-inch diameter)

Assorted small (about 1-inch) letter or other decorative stencils (p. 24, optional)

Small offset spatula (p. 14, optional)

Parchment pastry cones (p. 13)

Sugar confetti (p. 26, optional)

$^1/_2$ recipe Meringues (p. 253)

Pastry bag fitted with $^1/_2$-inch star tip (Ateco #826)

About 8 paper cupcake liners (with no more than a $2^1/_4$-inch opening) or No Finer Liners (p. 127, optional)

Stand-in: Lose the Letters. *I've monogrammed the cookies inside these cupcakes using the stenciling technique (p. 37); then tucked them into chocolate cupcake liners (aka No Finer Liners, p. 127). But to save time, skip the monograms and use regular paper liners.*

TYPES:

Cutout Cookie Gingerbread (p. 236) or Signature Sugar Cookie Dough (p. 234) for cookies inside; Meringues (p. 253) for frosting on top

Either cookie dough in "Types" works well for this project. Just be sure to mix and chill the dough as instructed. If stored in airtight containers, both meringues and cookies will be their best for about 1 week. Meringues are especially vulnerable to humidity, so they should be contained as soon as they've cooled. If No Finer Liners are used instead of paper liners, they are best stored separately in the fridge until ready to assemble.

1. Cut and bake the cookies for the cupcake insides. Each cupcake will be comprised of 1 meringue cupcake topper and 3 to 4 round cookies—specifically, 1 ($2\frac{1}{4}$-inch) round and 2 to 3 ($1\frac{7}{8}$-inch) rounds stacked inside a cupcake liner.

On a lightly floured surface, roll the dough to a $\frac{1}{8}$- to $\frac{3}{16}$-inch thickness. Cut out about 8 ($2\frac{1}{4}$-inch) rounds and another 24 ($1\frac{7}{8}$-inch) rounds (3 per cupcake). Bake as directed until lightly browned around the edges, or about 7 to 8 minutes for the $1\frac{7}{8}$-inch cookies and 8 to 10 minutes for the $2\frac{1}{4}$-inch cookies. Trim the $1\frac{7}{8}$-inch cookies while hot from the oven using the $1\frac{7}{8}$-inch cookie cutter. (Trimming will ensure a better fit in the cupcake liners in Step 7.) Cool completely before decorating.

2. Prepare the Royal Icing as instructed on page 242. Reserve about $\frac{1}{4}$ cup for stenciling (optional) and $\frac{1}{2}$ cup for "glue" or cookie borders. *Note:* The quantity of icing will vary with the number of colors and consistencies mixed, especially for borders, and whether you stencil in Step 4. It's best to allow no less than $\frac{1}{4}$ to $\frac{1}{2}$ cup icing per color or consistency for easiest mixing and handling.

3. Top-coat the cookies. Tint the remaining 1 cup icing to a color (or colors) of your choice and thin to top-coating consistency (p. 245). Using the handle-end of a craft paintbrush, apply a smooth coat of icing to each cookie top. For top-coating technique details, see page 28. Let the icing dry completely, ideally overnight, if you intend to stencil the smaller $1\frac{7}{8}$-inch cookies.

4. Stencil the small cookies (optional). I like to leave the larger $2\frac{1}{4}$-inch cookies simply top-coated to ensure that the meringue cupcake toppers sit flush against them once the cupcakes are fully assembled. But you can decorate the $1\frac{7}{8}$-inch cookies in just about any way. I've chosen to stencil mine with the initials of my party guests. To replicate my cookies, tint the $\frac{1}{4}$ cup icing reserved for stenciling to contrast the top-coating color; then thin to stenciling consistency (p. 244). Work on one cookie at a time. Set a small letter stencil on the cookie top and apply a thin layer of icing over the stencil openings using a small offset spatula. See page 37 for stenciling technique details. Repeat with the remaining $1\frac{7}{8}$-inch cookies.

5. Add borders to the cookies. Tint the remaining $\frac{1}{2}$ cup icing reserved for "glue" to a color that matches your cookie dough (i.e., brown if gingerbread), transfer to a parchment pastry cone, and cut a small ($\frac{1}{16}$-inch or more) hole in the tip. Use the "glue" to attach sugar confetti to the cookie edges, as pictured left. Alternatively, tint the icing to a color of your choice, adjust its consistency, and use it to apply delicate Beaded, Trailing Beaded, or Zig Zag Borders, as described in "7 Essential Piping Techniques" (p. 46). I generally avoid large textured borders piped with

Short and Sweet. *(a) Paint silicone cupcake liners with melted chocolate. Place in the freezer to set and then pop out the chocolate liners. (Or use paper cupcake liners.) (b) Prepare Meringues. Pipe into large rosettes for cupcake toppers and bake. (c) Stencil small top-coated cookies and embellish their edges with sugar confetti or other borders, as desired. Assemble cupcakes by stacking a few cookies and a meringue topper in each cupcake liner.*

pastry tips, simply because the cookies won't stack as tightly in Step 7. Let the borders dry completely.

6. Prepare the meringue cupcake toppers. Mix Meringues as described on page 253, but for $1/2$ recipe, beat closer to 5 to 7 minutes after all the sugar is added. (The meringue should still be very stiff, but not so stiff that it doesn't form wispy peaks.) Once the meringue is at the right consistency, beat in food coloring, as desired.

Fit a pastry bag with a $1/2$-inch star tip (Ateco #826) and fill the bag with meringue. Pipe large ($1^7/8$- to 2-inch) rosettes on a parchment paper-lined cookie sheet following the instructions on page 254. Bake as directed until the meringues are dry to the touch but not at all brown, or about $1^1/2$ to 2 hours. (Humidity can greatly affect baking time.) As soon as the meringues have cooled, contain them as directed in "Prep Talk." *Note:* $1/2$ recipe Meringues makes more cupcake toppers than you will need, but it is difficult to mix this recipe in any smaller quantity. Store any extra meringues as directed and snack on them later!

7. Assemble the cupcakes. Just before serving, stack 2 to 3 ($1^7/8$-inch) cookies in each paper or chocolate cupcake liner. (*Note:* You may only be able to fit 2 cookies in each chocolate liner, unless you paint the chocolate very thin.) Cap off each stack with a $2^1/4$-inch round and then with a meringue topper, and enjoy!

NO FINER LINERS (optional)

8 ounces chocolate makes about
8 (2^3_4 x 1^3_8-inch-tall) chocolate cupcake liners

(a) Use a small offset spatula to apply a thin coating of melted (coating or premium) chocolate to the inside of a silicone cupcake liner (p. 268), taking care to cover the sides and bottom completely. (I used tinted coating chocolate for these liners. For more about the difference between coating and premium chocolate, see "Definitions," p. 258.) Spread any excess chocolate that pools into the corners onto the sides and/or gently shake it into a bowl. It's important to have as thin and uniform a coating as possible if you want to fit the cookies from Move Over, Cupcake! (p. 124) inside. Smooth the chocolate along the top edge of the liner.

b.

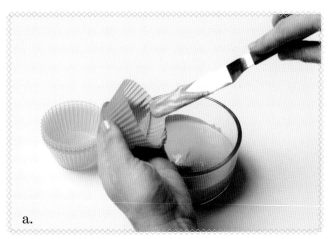

a.

(b) Invert the liner onto a parchment paper-lined cookie sheet. Inverting prevents excess chocolate from settling back into the corners of the liner.

(c) Repeat Steps (a) and (b) to prepare as many liners as fit on the cookie sheet. Place the pan in the freezer to quickly set the chocolate. Once the chocolate is firm, gently peel back the silicone liners and pop out the chocolate ones inside. Store in airtight containers in the fridge until ready to use.

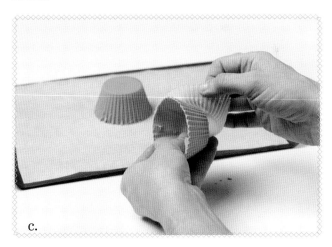

c.

Pictured clockwise from top: *Mam-moth Stand-in (small 2-D butterflies), Beetlemania, Caterpillar Caper, and Mam-moth (giant 3-D butterfly).*

WHERE THE WILD THINGS ARE

Whether they fly, leap, slither, wiggle, or crawl, the whimsical creatures in this animal kingdom are sure to find their way into your heart—and stomach. Ideal for little and big adventurers who prefer a walk on the wild side!

caterpillar caper

KIDS WILL DELIGHT IN EVERY INCH OF THESE PLAYFUL CRAWLERS, from the very top of their gumball heads down to their cookie bodies and licorice legs. Shape the cookies into straight or wavy lines for caterpillars or into 3-D arcs for inchworms. Or leave them in pieces and make a game of assembling them with your youngsters.

Makes 7 to 8 (6- to 6½-inch) caterpillars or (5 x 1¾- to 2½-inch-tall) inchworms

About 6 ounces (¹/₈ recipe) Cutout Cookie Gingerbread (p. 236) or (¹/₄ recipe) Signature Sugar Cookie Dough (p. 234)

Small (⁷/₈-inch) plain round cookie cutter

About 2³/₄ cups (²/₃ recipe) Royal Icing (p. 242), divided; quantity will vary

Soft-gel food colorings (p. 14) of your choice

Parchment pastry cones (p. 13)

7 to 8 (³/₄-inch) gumballs (1 per caterpillar), for heads

7 to 8 wire stamens normally used for gumpaste flowers (p. 268), for antennae (optional; *Note:* Must remove before eating.)

7 to 8 (¹/₂-inch) gumballs (1 per caterpillar), for tails

About 3 (1³/₄-inch) wheels licorice lace (such as Haribo Wheels), for legs

Sugar confetti (p. 26), for eyeballs

Ground chocolate cookies, for dirt (optional)

Brownie rocks, for display (optional; see Step 7)

TYPES:

Cutout Cookie Gingerbread (p. 236) or Signature Sugar Cookie Dough (p. 234)

PREP TALK:

While either dough, above, can be used for this project, I think these crawlers' colors pop more against gingerbread. Be sure to mix and chill the dough as instructed. If packaged in airtight containers at room temperature, this project will stay its best about 1 week.

1. Cut and bake the bodies. On a lightly floured surface, roll the dough to a $1/8$- to $3/16$-inch thickness. Cut out 7 to 8 dozen ($7/8$-inch) rounds and bake as directed until lightly browned around the edges, or about 7 to 9 minutes. Cool completely before decorating in Step 3.

2. Prepare the Royal Icing as instructed on page 242. Reserve about $3/4$ cup for filling, $1/2$ cup for "glue," and another $1/2$ cup for eyes and dots. *Note:* The quantity of icing will vary with the number of colors and consistencies mixed. It's best to allow no less than $1/4$ to $1/2$ cup icing per color or consistency for easiest mixing and handling.

3. Top-coat the bodies. Divide the remaining 1 cup icing into as many portions as you want top-coating colors and tint as desired. Adjust the icing to thick top-coating consistency (p. 245). Transfer each portion to a separate parchment pastry cone and cut a relatively large ($1/8$-inch or more) hole in each tip. *Note:* You can also apply the icing with the handle-end of a craft paintbrush, as I usually do when top-coating, but it's a little easier to control the distribution of icing on very small cookies with a pastry cone.

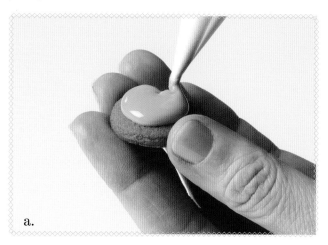

a.

(a) Pipe enough icing on the top of each round cookie to smoothly top-coat it. Since each caterpillar body will be comprised 10 to 12 rounds, assembled into 5 or 6 sandwiches or segments, I like to ice cookies in sets of 10 to 12, with each set in a single color.

b.

(b) While the icing is still wet, set a large ($3/4$-inch) gumball on top of 7 to 8 cookies to make heads; then, as desired, fold gumpaste flower stamens in half and slip one behind each gumball to make antennae. Also stick smaller ($1/2$-inch) gumballs into another 7 to 8 cookies to create tails. Let the icing dry completely before proceeding to the next step.

4. Fill the bodies to make segments. Start by prepping the licorice legs by unwinding the licorice rolls and cutting them into $3/4$- to 1-inch lengths. You'll need 2 pieces for each caterpillar segment or about 10 to 12 pieces for each caterpillar. Tint the $3/4$ cup icing reserved for filling to a color (or colors) of your choice. Thin to thick top-coating consistency. Transfer each color to a separate parchment pastry cone and cut a relatively large ($1/8$-inch or more) hole in each tip.

c.

d.

(c) Turn over half of the cookies in each set and pipe a small mound of icing on the back of each one. Insert 2 pieces of licorice on either side of the icing so they stick out beyond the sides of the cookies; then quickly cap each icing mound with one of the remaining cookies in the set to make a sandwich, pressing just until the icing squeezes to the cookie edges but no further. (If the icing runs over the cookie edges, thicken it to outlining consistency with powdered sugar.) Dry completely.

5. Assemble the segments into caterpillars (and inchworms). I typically like to assemble my crawlers 5- to 6-segments long, including a segment with a gumball head and another with a gumball tail. But feel free to make them as long or short as you like.

(d) Simply stick the top-coated sides of the sandwich cookies together end to end using the $^1/_2$ cup icing reserved for "glue." Since the "glue" will ultimately be visible, it's best to tint it to color-coordinate with the top coats. For caterpillars, assemble the segments in a flat "walking position" with feet pointed down, as pictured above. For inchworms, assemble the segments on their sides into an arc shape. (Once dry, the inchworms can be propped into

walking position.) As needed, prop segments with gumballs with other cookies or small objects. (These segments are top heavy and tend to flop off until the icing is dry.)

6. Add eyes and other details. While the crawlers are drying, affix sugar confetti to each head for eyeballs using the leftover "glue." Tint the remaining $^1/_2$ cup icing to a color (or colors) of your choice and thin to beadwork consistency (p. 245). Use it to pipe pupils on the eyeballs and dots on the crawlers' backs and feet. Any leftover icing from Steps 3 and 4 can also be used for this purpose.

Do not move the crawlers until completely dry, and always handle carefully using a large spatula underneath for support.

7. Display (optional) and serve. Present on ground cookie crumb dirt with brownie rocks, as desired. *Note:* Inchworms are most easily propped with crumbs. A (14$^1/_2$-ounce) box chocolate cookies makes about 3$^1/_2$ cups crumbs. For rocks, bake Basic or Blonde Brownies (p. 247) in 8 x 8 x 2-inch pans and cut into small chunks. Also, don't forget: tell guests to remove any wire antennae before eating.

mam-moth

LAND ONE OF THESE SUPERSIZED TREATS IN YOUR TUMMY, and you'll be flying high for quite some time. I traced the outline of a large butterfly cookie cutter and then blew it up 150 percent to make the templates for the giant marbled wings on these lovely creatures.

Makes about 6 (4¾ to 5¾ x 5⅝-inch) butterflies or moths

Custom template (p. 266), for wings

About 14 ounces (¹⁄₃ recipe) Cutout Cookie Gingerbread (p. 236) or (²⁄₃ recipe) Signature Sugar Cookie Dough (p. 234)

Small (¹⁄₂- to ³⁄₄-inch) plain round cookie cutter (or pastry tip)

About 4¼ cups (³⁄₄ to 1 recipe) Royal Icing (p. 242), divided; quantity will vary

Soft-gel food colorings (p. 14) of your choice

Parchment pastry cones (p. 13)

Metal trussing needle (p. 15) or toothpicks

About 6 (¹⁄₂-inch) gumballs (1 per butterfly), for heads

About 6 wire stamens normally used for gumpaste flowers (p. 268), for antennae (optional; *Note: Must remove before eating.*)

Stand-in: Tony in 2-D, Too. *If time is of the essence, make flat butterflies using a standard size butterfly cookie cutter; then substitute store-bought candies for the iced and filled cookies used for the butterfly bodies pictured left. For instance, I used a combination of Skittles and mini M&Ms on these beauties.*

TYPES:

Cutout Cookie Gingerbread (p. 236) or Signature Sugar Cookie Dough (p. 234)

{ mam-moth, continued }

PREP TALK:

While either dough in "Types" can be used for this small-scale 3-D construction project, I prefer Cutout Cookie Gingerbread, because it's a little less vulnerable to humidity. It's also more tender than Construction Gingerbread, which I typically reserve for larger, weight-bearing 3-D projects. Be sure to mix and chill the dough as instructed. If packaged in airtight containers at room temperature, this project will stay its best about 1 week.

1. Cut and bake the wings. First, decide on the shape of the wings. You can use the outline on page 266. Or you can trace the wing from your favorite butterfly cookie cutter and then blow it up so that the wing spans $5^{1}/_2$ to $5^{3}/_4$ inches from top to bottom, the size shown on page 134. To make a template from the outline, follow the instructions on page 48. Alternatively, if you plan to make a lot of butterflies, consider making a custom cookie cutter; it will save cutting time in the long run. For more information about working with custom templates and cutters, see page 48.

Set aside 1 to 2 ounces of the dough for use in Step 2. On a lightly floured surface, roll the remaining dough to a $1/_8$- to $3/_{16}$-inch thickness. Cut out about 6 wings using your template (or custom cutter) as a cutting guide. Turn over the template (or cutter) and cut out another 6 wings in mirror images of the ones just cut. You should end up with 6 sets of matched pairs. Bake as directed until lightly browned around the edges, or about 9 to 11 minutes.

2. Cut and bake the bodies. On a lightly floured surface, roll out the reserved dough to a $1/_8$- to $3/_{16}$-inch thickness. Using a $1/_2$- to $3/_4$-inch round cookie cutter (or pastry tip), cut out about 6 rounds per butterfly. Bake as directed, but only about 5 to 7 minutes for these smaller cookies.

3. Prepare the Royal Icing as instructed on page 242. Reserve about $2^{1}/_2$ cups for marbling the wings, $3/_4$ cup for top-coating and filling the bodies, and $1/_2$ cup for

"glue." *Note:* The quantity of icing will vary with the number of colors and consistencies mixed. It's best to allow no less than $1/_4$ to $1/_2$ cup icing per color or consistency for easiest mixing and handling.

4. Outline the wings. Though I don't always outline cookies before marbling, I like to outline when marbling with many colors, since the relatively large amount of icing on top is more likely to flow off—and if the icing flows off, the marbled pattern will distort in the process. Tint the remaining $1/_2$ cup icing to a dark color. (*Note:* I love black for high contrast.) Thin to outlining consistency (p. 244), transfer to a parchment pastry cone, and cut a small ($1/_{16}$-inch or more) hole in the tip. Proceed to outline each wing following the technique instructions on page 29. Since these cookies are relatively large, I also divide the top and bottom of the wings with the outline so that each area can be marbled separately in the next step. Marbling icings will be less likely to set up while you're working if you apply them in smaller areas, an area at a time.

5. Marble and detail the wings. Divide the $2^{1}/_2$ cups icing reserved for marbling into as many portions as you want marbling colors; tint as desired and then thin each portion to marbling consistency (p. 244). (Remember, high-contrast colors work best for marbling.) Transfer each portion to a separate parchment pastry cone and cut a relatively large ($1/_8$-inch or more) hole in each tip. *Note:* In case you're wondering why I don't call for any top-coating icing, it's

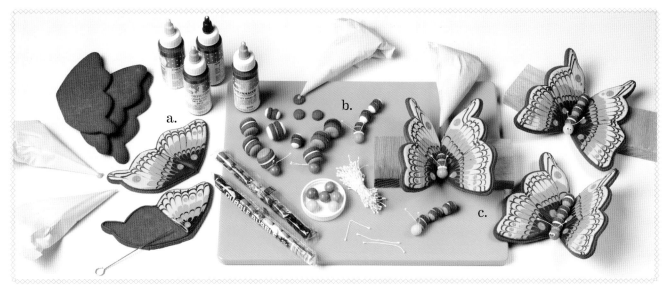

Short and Sweet. *(a) Outline and then marble pairs of wings. (b) For the segments of the butterfly bodies, top-coat small cookie rounds. Insert gumballs into some of the wet top coats to make heads. Antennae can also be inserted, if desired. Let the rounds dry; then sandwich them with Royal Icing. (c) Prop the wings so they sit at an angle to one another. Glue them together in the center with thick Royal Icing; then glue cookie sandwiches along each seam to complete the bodies. Add eyes using Royal Icing of beadwork consistency.*

because none is used in this marbling application! Instead, marbling colors are piped side by side to fully top-coat the cookies, as described below.

Work on one wing per matched pair at a time.

(a) Start with the upper (or lower) half of the wing. Apply colors in wide bands so that they completely fill the interior of this portion of the wing. Then pipe thinner lines of a contrasting marbling color (i.e., black) on top. The surface of the icing should end up very smooth, as if it had been simply top-coated.

(b) Immediately run a metal trussing needle or toothpick through all of the colors to create a marbled pattern of your choice. In this case, I drew several lines starting at the outer edge of the wing and ending in the center. Remember to move quickly before any of the icing colors set up.

a.

b.

c.

(c) While the icing is still wet, pipe on dots of different sizes and colors, as desired.

Follow Steps (a) to (c) to marble and detail the other half of the wing. Repeat this process on the other wing in the matched pair to create a mirror image. Repeat with the remaining wings to create 6 matched sets. Let the wings dry completely before assembling in Step 7.

Note: Myriad other wing patterns can be created by playing with the variables described in "Marbling" (p. 35). Feel free to depart from the pattern shown here.

6. Top-coat and fill the bodies. Divide the $3/4$ cup icing reserved for top-coating and filling the bodies into 2 or more portions and tint each portion to color-coordinate with the wings just piped. Thin each portion to a thick top-coating consistency (p. 245). Transfer each portion to a separate parchment pastry cone and cut a relatively large ($1/8$-inch or more) hole in each tip. *Note:* You can also apply the icing with the handle-end of a craft paintbrush, as I usually do when top-coating, but it's a little easier to control the distribution of icing on very small cookies with a pastry cone.

Pipe enough icing onto each cookie round to smoothly top-coat it. Since each body will be comprised of 6 rounds, turned into 3 sandwiches or segments, I like to top-coat cookies in sets of 6, with each set in a single color. While the icing is still wet, set a gumball on top of 1 cookie per set to make the butterflies' heads; then, as desired, fold gumpaste flower stamens in half and slip them behind the gumballs to make antennae, as pictured on page 132. Let the icing dry until the cookies can be turned over without disrupting the top coats.

To fill: Turn half of the cookies in each set upside down and pipe a small mound of icing in the center of each. (Choose a color that contrasts the top coats in that set.) Quickly cap each icing mound with one of the remaining cookies in the set to make a sandwich, pressing just until the icing squeezes to the cookie edges but no further. (If the icing runs over the cookie edges, thicken it to outlining consistency with powdered sugar.) Let the icing dry until firm.

7. Assemble the butterflies. Work on one butterfly at a time. Place matched wings together so they meet in the center. Prop the wings at an angle to each other using crumpled paper towels or another lightweight object; then glue them together at the seam using the $1/2$ cup icing reserved for this purpose. (Be certain that the icing "glue" makes contact with the Royal Icing on each wing; if you glue naked cookie to naked cookie, the wings may later break apart at the seam.) Glue a sandwich containing a gumball head to the topmost part of the seam and then glue 2 more matching sandwiches just beneath it, touching back to back. Pipe eyes on the gumball using leftover Royal Icing thinned to beadwork consistency (p. 245). Repeat to make about 6 butterflies.

Do not move the butterflies until completely dry, and always handle carefully using a large spatula underneath for support. Remind guests to remove any wire antennae before eating.

lounge lizards

DON'T BE STARTLED IF YOU FIND THESE CHARACTERS LOUNGING ABOUT YOUR KITCHEN or dining room. Constructed from cookies from horned heads to hind haunches, they're thoroughly delectable.

Makes about 3 (5 x 10¼ x 6⅜-inch-tall) lizards

Custom templates (pp. 264 to 265), for lizard body, feet, haunches, and tail

About 2 lb 3 ounces (³/₄ recipe) Cutout Cookie or Construction Gingerbread (p. 236 or p. 238) or (1¹/₂ recipes) Signature Sugar Cookie Dough (p. 234)

8-piece diamond cookie cutter set (Ateco #5259, p. 14), for lizard horns

About 7¹/₄ cups (1¹/₂ to 1²/₃ recipes) Royal Icing (p. 242)

Soft-gel food colorings (p. 14) of your choice

Parchment pastry cones (p. 13)

3 dozen blanched slivered almonds (1 dozen per lizard), for claws

Less than 1 ounce rolled fondant (p. 53) or other modeling medium, color(s) of your choice, for eyelids

2-inch plain round cookie cutter

6 (³/₄-inch) gumballs (2 per lizard), for eyeballs

About 4 dozen (³/₈- to ¹/₂-inch) round candies (such as mini M&Ms and Skittles), for pupils and spots

Ground graham crackers, for sand (optional)

Fondant rocks and brownie ledges, for display (optional; see Step 6)

TYPES:

Cutout Cookie Gingerbread (p. 236), Construction Gingerbread (p. 238), or Signature Sugar Cookie Dough (p. 234)

PREP TALK:

Any of the doughs, above, can be used for this relatively large 3-D construction project. But because none of the individual pieces is very large and weight-bearing, Construction Gingerbread isn't a necessity and even more delicate Signature Sugar Cookie Dough works just fine. Be sure to mix and chill the dough as instructed. If packaged in airtight containers at room temperature, this project will stay its best about 1 week.

{ lounge lizards, continued }

1. Cut and bake the lizard parts. Start by cutting out templates to fit the outlines for the lizard body, feet, haunches, and tail on pages 264 to 265. If you plan to make a lot of lizards, consider making custom cookie cutters; they will save cutting time in the long run. For more information about working with custom templates and cutters, see page 48.

On a lightly floured surface, roll the dough to a $1/8$- to $3/16$-inch thickness. It's best to cut the bodies and feet directly on prepared cookie sheets, as these pieces are rather large and can distort in the process of transferring from work surface to cookie sheet. Start by cutting out 3 bodies using your template (or custom cutter) as a cutting guide. Flip over the template (or cutter) and cut out 3 more bodies in mirror images of the first set. (These pieces will form the back sides of the lizards.) Reroll the leftover dough and cut out the following lizard parts in this order, from big to small: 3 back feet, 3 front feet, 3 back haunches, 3 more back haunches (mirror images of the first), 3 front haunches, 3 more front haunches (mirror images of the first), and 3 tails.

Lastly, for the lizards' horns, use the cookie cutter set to cut out the following number of diamonds for each of the 3 lizards: 1 ($2^3/4$ x 4-inch or $2^1/4$ x $3^1/2$-inch), 2 (2 x 3-inch), 2 ($1^5/8$ x $2^1/2$-inch), 3 ($1^3/8$ x 2-inch), 4 (1 x $1^1/2$-inch), and 1 ($5/8$ x 1-inch) diamonds. Then cut the diamonds in half into triangles. (You should end up with about 26 triangles per lizard, about 23 of which will ultimately get used.) I usually trim the triangles cut with the 2 largest cutters so their bases measure $1^1/2$ to $1^3/4$ inches. Trimmed, these triangles appear taller and fit better on the lizards in Step 5.

Group like-size cookies on the same cookie sheet and bake as directed until lightly browned around the edges, or about 10 to 13 minutes for larger body parts and closer to 7 to 8 minutes for the smaller triangles.

2. Prepare the Royal Icing as instructed on page 242. Reserve about $1^1/4$ cups for outlining and flooding the triangles, 1 cup for outlining the triangles (a second time), and another 1 cup for "glue."

3. Outline and flood the lizard pieces. I prefer to outline all of the cookies before flooding, as opposed to top-coating without any outlines, in order to get the icing as close to the cookie edges as possible. Tint the remaining 4 cups icing to a dark color. (I usually use dark green.) Thin to outlining consistency (p. 244), transfer to a parchment pastry cone, and cut a small ($1/16$-inch or more) hole in the tip. Outline all of the lizard parts, except for the triangles. Thin the leftover icing to flooding consistency (p. 245) and fill in all of the outlined cookies following the flooding techniques on page 31. Before the icing dries, gently press slivered almonds (for claws) into the tops of the front and back feet. Allow about 3 almonds per foot, or 12 per lizard.

Tint the $1^1/4$ cups reserved for outlining and flooding the triangles to another color of your choice. (I usually mix lime green by combining green and yellow food coloring.) Thin to outlining consistency; then outline and flood all of the triangles following the steps described for the other body parts, above.

Let the cookies dry before detailing in the next step.

4. Detail the lizard pieces. Tint the 1 cup icing remaining for outlining the triangles (a second time) to a dark color that contrasts the triangles just iced. (I usually use the same color as on the bodies, i.e., dark green.) Thin to outlining consistency, transfer to a parchment pastry cone,

{ lounge lizards, continued }

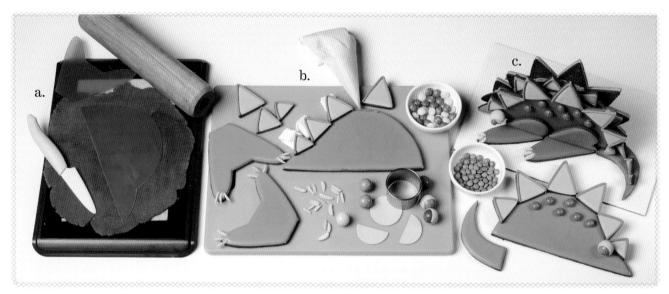

Short and Sweet. *(a) Use custom templates (or custom cutters) to cut the lizard body parts, and a diamond cutter set (not pictured) to cut triangles for the lizards' horns. Bake and cool the pieces; then outline and top-coat with Royal Icing. Before the icing on the feet dries, insert slivered almonds to mimic claws. (b) Glue decorated horns on the lizards' heads and backs with thick Royal Icing; also glue on candies (for spots) and gumballs covered with rolled fondant or another modeling medium (for eyes and eyelids). Dry completely. (c) Assemble the various lizard pieces using thick Royal Icing.*

and cut a relatively large ($1/8$-inch or more) hole in the tip. Pipe a thick outline around the edge of each triangle.

To save time, you need only decorate the front-facing side of each lizard; however, the candy quantities indicated on page 139 allow for both sides to be decorated.

For eyeballs with eyelids: Thin a small amount of the 1 cup icing reserved for "glue" to top-coating consistency (p. 245). Roll the rolled fondant or other modeling medium into a thin ($1/16$-inch) sheet. Cut the sheet into 3 (2-inch) circles and then cut each circle in half. Wrap each gumball with a half-circle to create an eyelid. (Use the thinned "glue" to keep the half-circles in place.) Pinch any excess modeling medium off the back of the eyeballs; then top each eyeball with a small candy, such as a mini M&M

pictured on page 140, to create a pupil. Glue an eyeball onto each lizard head with the remaining thick "glue." *For spots:* Glue other small candies, such as Skittles shown above, to the lizards' backs. *Note:* Tint the "glue" to match the color of the object to which you're applying the "glue," i.e., the lizard body or the gumball. That way, the "glue" will be less likely to show.

Let the "glue" dry completely before assembling the lizards in the next step.

5. Assemble the lizards. If not already done, tint the remaining "glue" to match the color of the lizards' bodies; then adjust the consistency, if needed, so that the "glue" is very stiff.

Start by gluing triangles along the top of each lizard body. (Lay the lizard bodies flat on your work surface for this task.) Begin about mid-head with a triangle cut from a $1^3/8$ x 2-inch diamond and then add successively bigger triangles so that one of the biggest triangles sits at the top-center of each lizard's back. From the top of the lizard to its rear end, simply reverse the order of the triangles to end with a triangle cut from a 1 x $1^1/2$-inch or smaller diamond. (All in, I typically use 7 triangles along the head and back of each lizard body.) As you add triangles, prop their tips to keep them level. Let the icing dry completely before proceeding.

Work on one lizard at a time. Choose 2 bodies that are mirror images of one another and glue them back to back. Prop upright and dry, as needed, until both pieces can easily be picked up as a unit. Glue the unit on top of a set of front and back feet. Glue front and back haunches on both sides of the body so they align with the feet. (The haunches should provide enough support to keep the lizard standing on its own, but, if not, prop until the "glue" is completely dry.) Carefully slip a tail under the back end of the lizard and glue it in place. Repeat to construct the beginnings of 2 more lizards.

Once the "glue" on the bodies is dry, add smaller triangles along the seam where the bodies come together on each lizard. I usually use about 6 triangles (per lizard), one peeking out between each of the triangles mounted on the front-facing body. Glue 3 more triangles (in the 2 smallest sizes) upright on top of each tail.

Do not move the lizards until the "glue" is completely dry. Carefully slide them onto their final destination or support from underneath with a large offset spatula.

6. Display (optional). Present on ground graham cracker sand with fondant rocks and brownie ledges, as desired. *Note:* A ($14^1/2$-ounce) box graham crackers makes about $3^1/2$ cups crumbs. For brownie ledges, bake Basic or Blonde Brownies (p. 247) in shallow pans and cut into big slabs.

beetlemania

THIS TREAT IS SURE TO DRAW GROUPIES IN DROVES. Not only is it cute as a bug's ear, but it also surprises the taste buds with a rich-and-chewy brownie hidden under its crunchy icing shell. What's more, it's a cinch to decorate with the oh-so-speedy dipping technique (p. 32).

Makes about 2½ dozen (1¾-inch) or 1 dozen (2¼-inch) beetles

¹/₂ recipe Basic or Blonde Brownies (p. 247)

Silicone (1³/₄- to 2¹/₄-inch) hemisphere baking molds (p. 24)

About 4¹/₂ cups (1 recipe) Royal Icing (p. 242), divided

Soft-gel food colorings (p. 14) of your choice

Parchment pastry cones (p. 13)

2 to 4 (1³/₄-inch) wheels licorice lace (such as Haribo Wheels), for legs and antennae; quantity will vary with beetle size

Decorated cookie leaves, for display (optional)

TYPES:

Basic or Blonde Brownies (p. 247)

PREP TALK:

While either brownie, above, can be used in this project, I prefer less sweet Basic Brownies to complement the Royal Icing that goes on top. If packaged in airtight containers at room temperature, this project will stay its best about 1 week.

Silicone hemisphere baking molds are needed to give the beetles their perfectly round shapes. While on the pricey side, these molds are definitely worth the investment if you plan to make beetles frequently or en masse.

1. Bake the brownie bodies. Prepare the brownies as instructed and turn the batter into silicone hemisphere baking mold(s). Place the baking mold(s) on a cookie sheet (or sheets) for stability. Bake until a cake tester inserted in the center brownie comes out with damp crumbs on it, or about 20 minutes for 1³/₄-inch molds or closer to 25 to 30 minutes for 2¹/₄-inch molds. Let the brownies cool until you can handle them and then carefully pop them out of the molds, domed sides up, onto cooling racks. Cool completely. Gently press out any divots on the domed sides with your fingertips. *Note:* The 2¹/₄-inch brownies will rise more than their smaller counterparts. It's best to trim any domes off the flat side of the brownies, so the legs and antennae are easier to attach in Step 5. The beetles will also sit flatter if trimmed.

2. Prepare the Royal Icing as instructed on page 242. Reserve about 1 cup icing for body details, 1¹/₄ cups for beetle heads, and ¹/₄ cup for eyes. *Note:* While you can use coating or premium chocolate (p. 258) for dipping the beetles, I much prefer Royal Icing. It's easier to control the consistency of Royal Icing, in turn making it easier to

Short and Sweet. *(a) Bake the brownies in silicone hemisphere baking molds. (b) Dip each brownie in Royal Icing to completely coat its domed side and immediately add contrasting Royal Icing details (i.e., a line down the center and dots). Dry fully; then dip the ends in more contrasting Royal icing to make heads. Dry again. (c) Glue licorice lace segments (antennae and legs) to the bottoms with thick Royal Icing. Flip over and add small Royal Icing dots for eyes.*

smoothly coat the beetles. Food coloring also translates much more vibrantly into Royal Icing than white chocolate. (And I have yet to find a red coating chocolate that isn't dull.)

3. Coat and detail the bodies. Tint the remaining 2 cups icing to a color of your choice. (I often use red or dark green.) Thin to dipping consistency (p. 245) and transfer to a small bowl so the icing sits at least 2 inches deep.

Tint the 1 cup icing reserved for body details to a color of your choice. (Black naturally goes with red, and yellow with green!) Divide this icing in half and thin one half to outlining consistency (p. 244) and the other to beadwork consistency (p. 245). Transfer the icings to separate parchment pastry cones. Cut a barely perceptible hole in the tip of the cone that contains the outlining icing. Cut a small ($1/16$-inch or more) hole in the other tip.

Work on one beetle at a time.

(a) Following the Nose-Dive Dipping instructions on page 32, submerge each body (dome side down) in the dipping icing, taking care to completely coat the top. Wipe the excess icing off the brownie bottom on the edge of the bowl and place the body (dome side up) on a parchment paper-lined cookie sheet or rack. Fill in any fingerprints from holding the beetle with extra icing.

While the icing is still wet, use the outlining icing to pipe a thin line down the center to demarcate the wings.

b.

(b) Immediately add 4 to 5 dots to each wing using the icing of beadwork consistency. Start just off center of the beetle top with a big dot and gradually make the dots smaller and smaller as you move down each wing. (Leave the other end free of dots, as the head will go there in Step 4.) For the roundest dots, hold your cone perpendicular to the beetle. You can also add the dots after the dipping coat dries, but the dots will stick out and be slightly less realistic that way. Repeat with the remaining bodies.

Before the icing dries completely, slide a thin-bladed paring knife under each body to sever the icing and to neaten the icing along the bottom edge. Dry completely, or until you can handle without messing up the icing. *Note:* You will have dipping icing left over, but the extra icing is needed to provide enough depth for dipping.

4. Add the heads. Tint the $1^1/4$ cups icing reserved for the heads to a color that matches or complements the body details; then thin to a thick dipping consistency (p. 245). Transfer the icing to a small bowl so the icing sits at least 2 inches deep.

Work on one beetle at a time. Dip the dot-free end into the icing to cover about one-quarter to one-third of the body. Wipe the excess icing off the brownie bottom and set the beetle on a clean parchment paper-lined cookie sheet or rack. Repeat to add heads to all of the beetles. While the icing is wet, once again use a paring knife to move each beetle and neaten its bottom edge. Dry completely. *Note:* You will again have some dipping icing left over.

5. Add antennae, legs, and eyes. Thicken the leftover icing from Step 4 to "glue" consistency (p. 243). Turn the beetles upside down and attach small pieces of licorice lace to their undersides to create antennae and legs. (Work on bubble wrap to avoid messing up the beetle tops.) On large ($2^1/4$-inch) beetles, I typically use 2 antennae and 4 ($1^1/2$- to $1^3/4$-inch) legs, whereas on small ($1^3/4$-inch) beetles, I use 4 ($3/4$- to 1-inch) legs or just antennae. That said, 2 wheels licorice is usually enough for small beetles.

Lastly, tint the $1/4$ cup icing reserved for eyes to contrast the heads (or leave it white) and thin to the consistency for beadwork. Transfer the icing to a parchment pastry cone and cut a very small ($1/16$-inch or less) hole in the tip. Once the licorice has dried in place, turn the beetles right side up and pipe a pair of tiny dots close to the point where the antennae meet.

6. Display (optional). Serve the beetles as-is or present on an arrangement of oversized decorated cookie leaves, as shown on page 144.

Pictured left to right: *Snake Charmer and King of the Hill Variation. Cactus cookie made from custom template (p. 267) with flower from fancyflours.com.*

snake charmer

WITH KING OF THE HILL VARIATION

CRAFTED AS IT IS FROM COOKIE DISKS AND LICORICE LACE, THIS CREATURE IS ONE TO LOVE, **not fear!** Let it wind its way along your table, or give it additional support and charm it into a king cobra (p. 152).

Makes about 3 (23- to 25-inch) snakes

Custom templates (p. 267), for head and tail, or 1⅞ x 2¾-inch teardrop cookie cutter, for tail

About 1 lb 7 ounces (½ recipe) Cutout Cookie Gingerbread (p. 236) or (1 recipe) Signature Sugar Cookie Dough (p. 234)

12-piece plain round cookie cutter set (Ateco #5457, p. 14)

¼-inch round pastry tip (Ateco #10 or #11)

About 2¾ cups (⅔ recipe) Royal Icing (p. 242), divided; quantity will vary

Soft-gel food colorings (p. 14) of your choice

Small craft paintbrush (handle about ¼-inch diameter)

Parchment pastry cones (p. 13)

A few ounces rolled fondant (p. 53) or other modeling medium, including red for tongues and white for fangs

About 6 pieces small (⅜-inch) round candies (such as mini M&Ms), for eyes

Small (⅝ x 1-inch) diamond cookie cutter, for head details (optional)

3 (3-foot) pieces licorice lace, for stringing snakes

Ground graham crackers, for sand (optional)

Large cookie cactus, for display (optional; see Step 6)

Stand-in: Unpainted Pythons. *Looking for a shortcut? Skip the cookie top-coating (right snake) and mix food coloring directly into Signature Sugar Cookie Dough to make multi-colored cookie disks (left snake). Looking for another? These generously sized slitherers are perfect centerpiece material. But for quicker assembly and more personalized portions, make smaller snakes by scaling down the templates and cookie cutters used for the body parts.*

TYPES:

Cutout Cookie Gingerbread (p. 236) or Signature Sugar Cookie Dough (p. 234)

{ snake charmer, continued }

PREP TALK:

Either dough in "Types" can be used for this project. If you'd rather tint the dough than ice it as described in "Stand-in" (p. 149), then use Signature Sugar Cookie Dough. Be sure to mix and chill the dough as instructed. If packaged in airtight containers at room temperature, this project will stay its best about 1 week.

1. Cut and bake the snake pieces. Start by cutting out templates to fit the snake head and tail outlines on page 267. Alternatively, the tails can be cut with a $1^7/8$ x $2^3/4$-inch teardrop cutter, as described below. If you plan to make a lot of snakes, consider making a custom cookie cutter for the head; it will save cutting time in the long run. For more information about working with custom templates and cutters, see page 48.

On a lightly floured surface, roll the dough to a $1/8$- to $3/16$-inch thickness. Using your snake head and tail templates (or cutters) as cutting guides, cut out 6 pieces of each shape, or 2 heads and 2 tails per snake. To cut tails with the teardrop cutter, first cut out a teardrop; then move over the cutter about $3/4$ inch and cut again to create a narrower teardrop that measures about 1 inch at its widest part.

For the snake bodies, cut out 60 round cookies in each of the following sizes: $1^1/2$ inches, $1^1/4$ inches, and $7/8$ inch. (You should have about 20 rounds of each size for each of 3 snakes.) Place the cookies on prepared cookie sheets and cut $1/4$-inch holes in the center of each round. Use a $1/4$-inch round pastry tip (Ateco #10 or #11) if you can't find a cutter of this size.

Bake the cookies as directed until lightly browned around the edges, or about 7 to 11 minutes, depending on cookie size. Cool completely before decorating.

2. Prepare the Royal Icing as instructed on page 242. Reserve about $3/4$ cup for detailing the snake heads and tails and $1/4$ cup for "glue." *Note:* The quantity of icing will vary with the number of colors and consistencies mixed. It's best to allow no less than $1/4$ to $1/2$ cup icing per color or consistency for easiest mixing and handling.

3. Top-coat the snake pieces. Divide the remaining $1^3/4$ cups icing reserved for top-coating into as many portions as you want colors on your snakes; then tint each portion accordingly. (I generally like to top-coat the heads and tails in the same color and the rounds in 2 to 3 contrasting colors, most often red, yellow, and black to mimic coral snakes.) Adjust each portion to top-coating consistency (p. 245).

Using the handle-end of a craft paintbrush, apply a smooth coat of icing to each cookie top. (Be sure to keep icing out of the holes of the round cookies.) For top-coating technique details, see page 28. You may also outline and flood the pieces to get a little closer to the cookie edges; however, this two-step process will take more time. Let the icing dry to the touch.

4. Detail the heads and tails. Divide the $3/4$ cup icing reserved for detailing into as many portions as you want colors; then tint accordingly. Adjust the icings to the proper consistency for your detailing task and transfer each icing to a separate parchment pastry cone. Here, I've used icing of beadwork consistency (p. 245) for dots on the eyes (see "For eyes," below) and the snake tails, and icing of outlining consistency (p. 244) for the stripes on both the heads and tails. *Note:* It's only necessary to detail half of the heads, just the ones that face up.

For eyes: Roll the modeling medium into thin ($1/16$-inch) sheets and cut out small half-circles from the sheet. Cover small candies halfway with the half-circles to create eyelids; then glue these pieces onto the heads with the remaining $1/4$ cup icing reserved for "glue." Add dots for pupils as described immediately above.

For tongues and fangs: While White Chocolate Dough (p. 260) will work for tongues and fangs, I prefer to use rolled fondant for these delicate pieces, since it holds up better in heat and humidity. Roll red fondant into a thin ($1/16$-inch) sheet and cut out 3 small (about $1/8$ x 3-inch) strips from the sheet; then cut a fork or "V" in one end of each strip (aka tongue). Glue the un-forked end of a tongue to the bottom of each undecorated snake head; that is, to the heads that will be facing down. Bend the tongues to add dimension. Shape fangs from white rolled fondant and glue them onto the bottom of the heads that will be facing up. Let the rolled fondant dry until rigid before moving the heads.

As desired, roll any leftover modeling medium into thin sheets and cut out small ($5/8$ x 1-inch) diamonds, as pictured on page 148, or other shapes for decorating the tops of the heads.

5. Assemble the snakes. Work on one snake at a time.

(a) Using the leftover "glue," attach 2 snake tail cookies back-to-back to one end of a 3-foot piece of licorice lace. Dry until set.

a.

String about 60 round cookies on the licorice. (*Note:* Tinted sugar cookie rounds are shown below.) Start with the smallest ($7/8$-inch) rounds and gradually move to the largest ($1 1/2$-inch) rounds at the midpoint of the snake; then move from largest to smallest rounds toward the head. I like to group like-cookie colors in small sets and to alternate the sets to create a striped effect.

(b, c) Trim the licorice, leaving about 1 to 2 inches at the "free" end. Glue an undecorated snake head (with tongue) under the free end; then sandwich the end with a decorated snake head cookie (with fangs) on top.

b.

c.

Repeat to make another 2 snakes. Let the "glue" on the heads and tails dry completely before moving the snakes. Be sure to support the snakes from underneath when moving, as the licorice lace can stretch, leaving more slack in the snakes than desirable.

6. Display (optional). Present on ground graham cracker sand with a large cookie cactus, as desired. *Note:* A (14^1/$_2$-ounce) box graham crackers makes about 3^1/$_2$ cups crumbs. For the cactus template, see page 267.

VARIATION
{ King of the Hill }

About 4 ounces Cutout Cookie
    Gingerbread (p. 236) or Signature
    Sugar Cookie Dough (p. 234)

3^1/$_4$ x 4-inch heart cookie cutter

About ^{3}/$_4$ cup Royal Icing (p. 242)

3 (11^3/$_4$-inch) cardboard lollypop sticks (p. 268)

Ground graham crackers, for sand to
    support hood-ends of cobras

1. Follow the instructions for Snake Charmer (p. 149), but in Step 1, roll out another 4 ounces dough and cut out 3 (3^1/$_4$ x 4-inch) heart cookies. Cut the hearts in half and bake as directed. These pieces will become the flared hoods on the cobras.

2. Prepare an additional ^{3}/$_4$ cup Royal Icing (p. 242). Reserve ^{1}/$_4$ cup for "glue."

3. Top-coat the hoods. Tint the remaining ^{1}/$_2$ cup Royal Icing to a color that coordinates with the rest of your snake pieces; then thin the icing to top-coating consistency (p. 245). Top-coat the half-hearts and dry completely. (You can also outline and flood the cookies to get closer to the edges, if desired.)

4. Assemble the cobras. Work on one cobra at a time. After gluing the tail pieces to the licorice lace (Step 5, p. 151), string on just the rounds (about 40) that make up the last two-thirds of the snake. Trim the licorice lace at the other end and fix the last round in place (so it won't fall off the lace) with the reserved Royal Icing "glue." Repeat to make the back ends of 2 more cobras. Let the "glue" dry completely.

In the meantime, assemble the front hooded portions of the cobras. Again, work on one cobra at a time.

(a) Bend over one end of a (11³/₄-inch) lollypop stick about 1¹/₂ to 1³/₄ inches; then glue one of the smallest remaining cookie rounds in place at the bend in the stick.

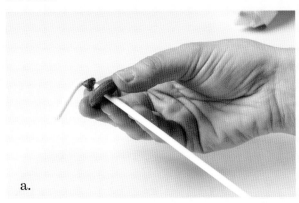

a.

(b) Thread the remaining third of the snake (about 20 rounds) on the stick. Push the pieces close together and fix the last round in place with more "glue." Repeat to make 2 more threaded sticks. Let the "glue" dry.

b.

(c) Lay 2 half-hearts (for a hood) on your work surface and line them up so they meet at their cut edges. Prop them at an angle to each other. Glue the threaded portion of a lollypop stick on top so that the heart pieces stick to the cookie rounds and extend beyond the rounds about 1¹/₂ inches on either side.

Repeat to mount the 2 remaining threaded sticks on hearts. Again, let the "glue" dry completely.

c.

(d) Lastly, glue a decorated snake head (with fangs, Step 4, p. 150) to the top of the bent end of each stick. (The cobras look best with only 1 snake head rather than 2 heads placed back to back.) Prop the heads as needed until the icing is completely dry.

d.

5. Display. Plunge the exposed lollypop stick on the front portion of a cobra into a small hill of graham cracker crumb sand (to stand straight up). Lay a back portion on more sand, right next to the stick, to give the appearance of a single connected snake. Repeat to connect 2 more cobras.

proud as a peacock
WITH TURKEY IN THE STRAW VARIATION

YOU'LL BE PROUD AS A PEACOCK AS YOU SERVE UP THIS SHOWY TREAT. The intricate feathered fans on these birds look complicated, but, as with most marbled cookies, their looks are deceiving—the marbling technique (p. 35) is inherently quick and easy!

Makes 7 ($3^1/4$ to $4^1/4$ x $6^1/4$ x $5^5$8-inch-tall) peacocks

Custom templates (p. 266), for peacock fan (of feathers), body, and wings

About 1 pound 9 ounces ($^1/2$ recipe) Cutout Cookie Gingerbread (p. 236) or (1 recipe) Signature Sugar Cookie Dough (p. 234)

$2^1/2$-inch fluted round cookie cutter, for peacock base

About $9^1/4$ cups (2 recipes) Royal Icing (p. 242), divided; quantity will vary

Green, blue, purple, yellow, orange, black, or other soft-gel food colorings (p. 14) of your choice

Small craft paintbrush (handle about $^1/4$-inch diameter)

Parchment pastry cones (p. 13)

Metal trussing needle (p. 15) or toothpicks

About $1^1/2$ dozen wire stamens normally used for gumpaste flowers (p. 268), for peacock crowns (optional; *Note:* Must remove before eating.)

Pastry bag fitted with $^1/4$-inch leaf tip (Ateco #352)

TYPES:

Cutout Cookie Gingerbread (p. 236) or Signature Sugar Cookie Dough (p. 234)

PREP TALK:

Either dough, above, can be used for this small-scale 3-D construction project. Be sure to mix and chill the dough as instructed. If packaged in airtight containers at room temperature, this project will stay its best about 1 week.

{ proud as a peacock, continued }

1. Cut and bake the peacock pieces. Start by cutting out templates to fit the peacock fan, body, and wing outlines on page 266. If you plan to make lots of peacocks, consider making custom cutters; they will save cutting time in the long run. For more information about working with custom templates and cutters, see page 48.

On a lightly floured surface, roll the dough to a 1/8- to 3/16-inch thickness. It's best to cut the large and/or delicate pieces, such as the fans and bodies, directly on prepared cookie sheets to avoid the misshaping that can occur in transferring from work surface to cookie sheet. Using your templates (or custom cutters) as cutting guides, cut out 7 fans, 7 bodies, and 14 wings.

Roll out the remaining dough to the same thickness and cut out 7 (2 1/2-inch) fluted rounds for the peacock bases.

Bake the cookies as directed until lightly browned around the edges, or about 10 to 12 minutes for the fans and closer to 7 to 10 minutes for the smaller parts. Watch the bodies carefully as narrow areas, like the necks and beaks, will brown more quickly. Cool completely before decorating.

2. Prepare the Royal Icing as instructed on page 242. Reserve about 2 1/2 cups for outlining and flooding the fans, 1/2 cup for marbling the fans, 2 1/2 cups for detailing the fans and bodies, and 1 1/4 cups for feather details and "glue." *Note:* The quantity of icing will vary with the number of colors and consistencies mixed. It's best to allow no less than 1/4 to 1/2 cup icing per color or consistency for easiest mixing and handling.

3. Top-coat the bases, and outline and flood the bodies and wings. *For the bases:* Portion off about 1 cup of the remaining 2 1/2 cups icing. Set aside the other 1 1/2 cups for the bodies and wings. Tint the 1-cup portion to a dark green or another color of your choice; then thin to

top-coating consistency (p. 245). Using the handle-end of a craft paintbrush, apply a smooth coat of icing to each cookie base. For top-coating technique details, see page 28. Save the remaining icing (dark green) for use on the fans in Step 4.

For the bodies and wings: I prefer to outline and flood these cookies, as opposed to top-coating without any outlines, in order to get the icing as close to the cookie edges as possible. Tint the reserved 1 1/2 cups icing to a peacock blue using a mixture of blue and purple food coloring. Thin the icing to outlining consistency (p. 244) and transfer to a parchment pastry cone. Cut a small (1/16-inch or more) hole in the tip; then outline the bodies and wings following the techniques on page 29. Thin the leftover blue icing to flooding consistency (p. 245) and fill the interiors of the bodies and wings using the techniques described on page 31.

Note: You can also marble the wings, as pictured on page 154. Simply pipe a contrasting icing color, borrowed from the icing reserved for marbling and detailing (Steps 4 and 5), in 2 lines along the edge of the wing; then draw a metal trussing needle or toothpick in straight lines from the outer edge of the wing to the other side. Work quickly while the icings remain wet.

4. Outline, flood, and marble the fans. Thicken the leftover icing from Step 3 (dark green) to outlining consistency and outline a 2 x 2 3/4-inch half-oval area in the center of each fan. (The bodies and fans will eventually be joined in these areas.) Loosen the remaining icing to flooding consistency and then flood the half-oval areas. Let the icing dry to the touch.

Tint the 2 1/2 cups icing reserved for outlining and flooding the fans to a lime green (a mixture of green and yellow) or another color of your choice. Thin to outlining consistency

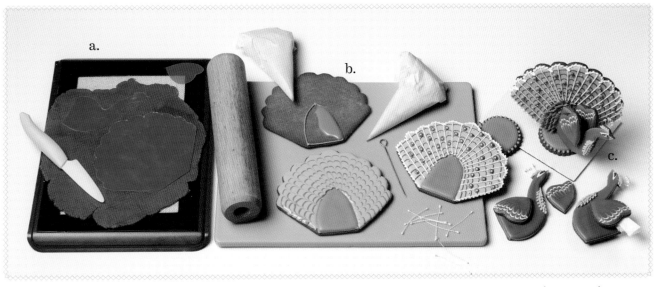

Short and Sweet. *(a) Cut out peacock fans, bodies, wings, and round bases using custom templates (or cutters). Bake and cool. (b) Outline and flood the fans with Royal Icing; then marble to mimic feathers. Add details, such as dots, outlines, and a Trailing Beaded Border around the edges. Ice and detail the bodies, wings, and bases. Use Royal Icing "glue" to attach crowns to the heads, as desired. (c) Assemble the peacocks atop the bases with more "glue."*

and outline the edge of each fan per the instructions on page 29. Thin the leftover outlining icing to flooding consistency, transfer to a new parchment pastry cone, and cut a relatively large ($1/8$-inch or more) hole in the tip. Tint the $1/2$ cup icing reserved for marbling the fans to a dark green or another color that contrasts the fan color. Thin to marbling consistency, transfer to a parchment pastry cone, and cut a small ($1/16$-inch or more) hole in the tip.

Work on one fan cookie at a time.

(a) Flood the area surrounding the half-oval with the lime green (or other) icing. You can marble the interior of the fans in myriad ways, but for this pattern, (b) immediately

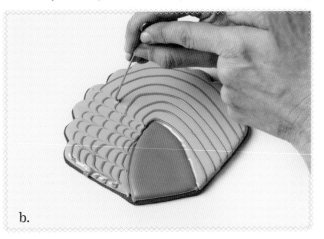

apply the marbling (dark green) icing in arcs that span the width of the fan; then quickly draw a trussing needle or toothpick through the icing in about 20 straight lines that start at the outer edge of the fan and finish at the edge of the half-oval in the center. Allow the fans to dry to the touch.

5. Detail the fans. Again, the fans can be detailed any number of ways using the 2¹/₂ cups icing reserved for this purpose. Just remember to adjust the icing consistency to your specific detailing task. For my pattern, (c) start by cov-

c.

ering the toothpick tracks from marbling with white icing of outlining consistency. Use the same icing to pipe a Trailing Beaded Border (p. 46) around the edges of the fans.

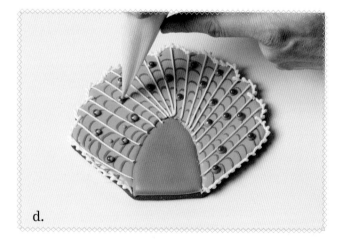

d.

(d) Lastly, use icing of beadwork consistency (p. 245) to add orange, dark blue, and light blue (or other color) dots on top of each other to mimic the spots on peacock feathers. Avoid detailing the 2 x 2³/₄-inch half-oval areas in the center of the fans, as you'll be applying icing feathers there during assembly in Step 8.

6. Detail the peacock bodies and bases. Use the leftover icing from Steps 4 and 5 to dress up the peacock bodies and bases. To replicate my birds, mix leftover lime green icing to outlining consistency and use the Trailing Beaded Border technique (p. 46) to apply feather details to the crown and breast of each bird. Apply white and black details around the birds' eyes using icing of top-coating consistency (p. 245). Use leftover orange icing from the fans for dots around the bases; then thicken to outlining consistency (p. 244) and pipe beaks on the birds. No matter how you detail these pieces, let the icing dry completely before proceeding to Step 7 or 8.

7. Add crowns (optional). Cut 1¹/₂ dozen wire stamens in half and trim each half to ¹/₂ to ³/₄ inch in length. Flip over a peacock body onto a small piece of bubble wrap (to avoid damaging the front of the cookie) and attach 5 half-stamen pieces to the top of the head with a dab of the 1¹/₄ cups icing reserved for "glue." Repeat to add crowns to all of the birds. Let the "glue" dry before moving.

8. Assemble the peacocks. Tint the remaining 1¹/₄ cups icing for feather details and "glue" to a dark green or another color that coordinates with the peacock bodies. Use the icing to glue a wing to the front and back of each peacock body, taking care to keep the icing from showing. To give the front wings more lift, prop them away from the bodies with small pieces of paper towel or other light-weight objects. The back wings should peek over the top of the peacock bodies, as pictured on page 154. Let the wings dry in place.

Fill a pastry bag fitted with a ¹/₄-inch leaf tip (Ateco #352) with the remaining "glue" and pipe feathers in the half-oval in the center of a fan. (Some of the feathers will show in the final construction; those that get hidden behind the body will act as "glue.") Stand the fan up; then insert the back end of a peacock body (now with wings) into the icing feathers at a 45-degree angle to the fan. Prop as needed to keep the fan and body standing up. Repeat to make the beginnings of 6 more peacocks.

When the icing is dry, carefully set each body-fan piece on top of a cookie base. Reinforce the seams between fan and base, and body and base, with more "glue" applied from the back. Again, prop as needed and don't move until the "glue" is completely dry. Also, very important: remember to tell guests to remove the wire crowns before eating.

VARIATION
{ Turkey in the Straw }

Proceed as directed in Proud as a Peacock (p. 155), except use turkey body and wing cutters instead of the peacock body and wing templates in Step 1. (I used a 3-D cookie cutter set from fancyflours. com, for all but the fan.) Outline and flood the body and wings with brown icing and use fall hues, such as red and orange, for the marbling and detailing icings in Steps 4 to 6. Omit the wire stamens in Step 7 and instead pipe a waddle and crest on each turkey using red icing of outlining consistency (p. 244) and the Trailing Beaded Border technique (p. 46). Assemble into turkeys as instructed in Step 8 and present with pieces of Shredded Wheat biscuits for hay.

Halloween projects pictured clockwise from top: *A suspended spider from Along Came a Spider, the Witch Craft Variation of What a Hoot, and Jack o' Lanterns.*

SO THIS SEASON

Why do we so often reserve cookies for the winter holidays when we should use the excuse of any occasion to enjoy them throughout the year? After all, what sweeter gift is there than a cookie lovingly baked and decorated by hand?! Yes, cookies—whether dressed as presents, favors, or décor—are always in vogue, as you'll see in this spectacular show of the seasons.

love letters

WITH OPEN YOUR HEART BOX

WHEN A BOX OF RUSSELL STOVER'S NO LONGER REGISTERS APPRECIATIVE OOHS AND AHHS, offer this Valentine's project as a token of your undying love. Whether or not you craft the accompanying gingerbread box, the project makes a very special statement—literally and figuratively!

Makes 4 dozen (1¾- to 2-inch) letter or heart cookies and 1 (8¼ x 10¼ x 2½-inch-tall) box

LOVE LETTERS

About 10 ounces (¼ recipe) Cutout Cookie
   Gingerbread (p. 236) or (½ recipe)
   Signature Sugar Cookie Dough (p. 234)

Assorted (1¾- to 2-inch) letter
   and heart cookie cutters

About 2½ cups (½ recipe) Royal Icing
   (p. 242), divided; quantity will vary

Soft-gel food colorings (p. 14) of your choice

Small craft paintbrush (handle
   about ¼-inch diameter)

Parchment pastry cones (p. 13)

1 Open Your Heart Box (p. 165, optional)
   or other container(s), for display

Stand-in: Message in a Bottle. *No time to make the gingerbread box to house your message? No worries. Tumble the cookie letters and hearts into a clear jar and tie a color-coordinated ribbon around the lid. Easy for you; plus, guests will have the added fun of unscrambling your message!*

TYPES:

Cutout Cookie Gingerbread (p. 236) or Signature

Sugar Cookie Dough (p. 234) for letters and hearts;

Construction Gingerbread (p. 238, optional) for boxes

{ love letters, continued }

PREP TALK:

I prefer the delicacy of either Cutout Cookie Gingerbread or Signature Sugar Cookie Dough for the letters and hearts; however, because of its strength advantage, Construction Gingerbread is the safest choice for the box, which has a very large lid and weight-bearing bottom. Be sure to mix and chill the doughs as instructed. If packaged in airtight containers at room temperature, this project will stay its best about 1 week.

1. Cut and bake the letters and hearts. First, decide on the cookie message to spell out within your box (or other container). My Open Your Heart Box, pictured right, has 12 compartments that conveniently fit the words "I LUV YOU" interspersed among small heart cookies.

On a lightly floured surface, roll the dough to a $1/8$- to $3/16$-inch thickness and cut out the letters needed to spell your message, along with hearts for filler. You'll need about 4 dozen cookies (4 per compartment), to fill one of my Open Your Heart Boxes. The cookies should also be no more than $1 3/4$ to 2 inches in order to fit.

Bake the cookies as directed until lightly browned around the edges, or about 6 to 8 minutes for cookies of this size. Cool completely before icing.

2. Prepare the Royal Icing as instructed on page 242. Reserve about $1 1/2$ cups for beadwork or other borders. *Note:* The quantity of icing will vary with the number of colors and consistencies mixed. It's best to allow no less than $1/4$ to $1/2$ cup icing per color or consistency for easiest mixing and handling.

3. Top-coat the letters and hearts. Divide the remaining 1 cup icing into as many portions as you want top-coating colors and tint accordingly; then thin each portion to top-coating consistency (p. 245). Using the handle-end of a craft paintbrush, apply a smooth coat of icing to each cookie top. For top-coating technique details, see page 28. Let the icing dry to the touch.

4. Detail the letters and hearts. Divide the $1 1/2$ cups icing reserved for beadwork (p. 34) or other borders into as many portions as you want colors; then tint accordingly. Adjust the icing to the proper consistency for your chosen detailing task(s). For cookies as small as these, I generally avoid large textured borders piped with pastry tips and stick to delicate lines and dots, using icing of outlining and beadwork consistency (p. 244 and p. 245, respectively). Once the icings are mixed, transfer each to a separate parchment pastry cone and cut a small ($1/16$-inch or more) hole in each tip; then detail to your heart's content! Let the icing dry completely before packaging the cookies in Open Your Heart Box or some other container.

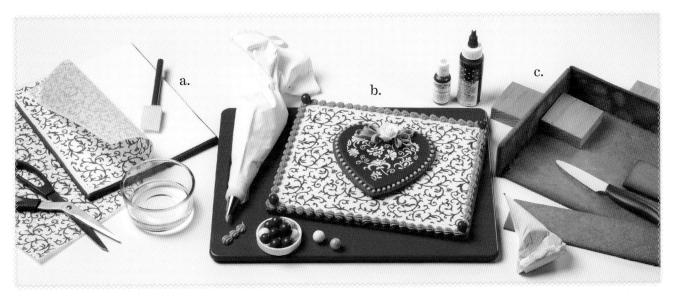

Short and Sweet. *(a) Use a small sponge brush to spread a thin layer of corn syrup on an iced (and completely dry) gingerbread box lid; then affix a trimmed piece of wafer paper to the top. (b) Finish the edges of the lid with a Royal Icing border, embellish the corners with gumballs, and glue a decorated heart cookie on top. (c) Assemble the box sides and bottom with thick Royal Icing "glue," and prop as needed. Top with the lid only after the "glue" is completely dry.*

OPEN YOUR HEART BOX (optional)

Ruler or custom rectangular templates in 4 sizes (see Step 1)

About 2 pounds (2/3 recipe) Construction Gingerbread (p. 238)

Large (4 1/4 x 5 1/4-inch) heart cookie cutter

About 3 3/4 cups (3/4 recipe) Royal Icing (p. 242), divided

Parchment pastry cones (p. 13)

Brown and other soft-gel food colorings (p. 14) of your choice

Small craft paintbrush (handle about 1/4-inch diameter)

Heart-shaped decorative stencil (p. 24), sized to fit large heart cookie cutter, above

Small offset spatula (p. 14)

2 (3/4-inch) Loop-de-Loop Bows (p. 57), color of your choice (optional)

1 small (1 1/4- to 1 1/2-inch) Rose (p. 61), color of your choice (optional)

1 (8 x 11-inch) sheet printed wafer paper (p. 26), pattern of your choice

A few tablespoons light corn syrup

Small sponge brush

Pastry bag fitted with tip of your choice, for borders

4 (1/2-inch) gumballs, color(s) of your choice, for decorating box corners (optional)

1 (8 x 11-inch) piece corrugated cardboard, for box dividers (optional)

{ love letters, continued }

1. Cut and bake the box pieces. Following the instructions for custom templates (p. 48), make rectangular templates for the box in 4 sizes: $8^{1}/_{4}$ x $10^{1}/_{4}$ inches for the lid, $7^{3}/_{8}$ x $9^{3}/_{8}$ inches for the bottom, 2 x $9^{1}/_{2}$ inches for the long sides, and 2 x $7^{1}/_{2}$ inches for the short sides. Alternatively, you can use a ruler as a cutting guide. Or if you plan to make a lot of boxes, consider making custom cookie cutters; they will save cutting time in the long run. For more information about working with custom templates and cutters, see page 48.

On a lightly floured surface, roll the dough to a $^{1}/_{8}$- to $^{3}/_{16}$-inch thickness. Since the box pieces are relatively large, it's best to cut them directly on prepared cookie sheets to avoid the misshaping that can occur in transferring from work surface to cookie sheet. Use your templates (or ruler or custom cutters) to cut out the following number of cookies in this order, from big to small: 1 lid, 1 bottom, 2 long sides, and 2 short sides. From the leftover dough, cut out a large ($4^{1}/_{4}$ x $5^{1}/_{4}$-inch) heart for decorating the box top.

Bake the cookies as directed until lightly browned around the edges, or about 20 to 23 minutes for the bottom and lid, 15 to 20 minutes for the box sides, and closer to 11 to 12 minutes for the heart. Trim the box pieces while hot from the oven so they end up perfectly rectangular. (It's especially important to trim the box bottom to its original size to ensure a good fit with the sides in Step 6.) Cool completely.

2. Prepare the Royal Icing as instructed on page 242. Reserve about $^{1}/_{4}$ cup for top-coating the heart, $^{1}/_{2}$ cup for stenciling and detailing the heart, $^{1}/_{2}$ cup for lid borders, and 1 cup for assembling and detailing the box.

3. Outline and flood the lid. I prefer to outline and flood the lid, as opposed to top-coating without any outlines,

in order to get the icing as close to the cookie edges as possible and to ensure a good fit with the wafer paper in Step 5. Thin the remaining $1^{1}/_{2}$ cups icing to outlining consistency (p. 244). Leave this icing white, unless you want some color to show through the wafer paper that will be applied in Step 5. Transfer the icing to a parchment pastry cone and cut a small ($^{1}/_{16}$-inch or more) hole in the tip. Pipe an outline around the lid following the outlining technique instructions on page 29. Thin the leftover icing to flooding consistency (p. 245) and proceed to flood the lid interior. For more flooding technique tips, see page 31. Let the lid dry completely, ideally overnight, before wafer-papering in Step 5. You can also ice the box sides if you'd like, though you'll need more icing.

4. Top-coat, stencil, and detail the heart cookie. Tint the $^{1}/_{4}$ cup icing reserved for top-coating the heart to a color of your choice; then thin to the proper consistency (p. 245). Using the handle-end of a craft paintbrush, apply a smooth coat of icing to the cookie top. Let the icing dry completely, ideally overnight, before stenciling, below.

Thin the $^{1}/_{2}$ cup icing reserved for stenciling to the appropriate consistency (p. 244). Leave the icing white or tint it to complement the heart's top coat. Center the heart–shaped stencil on the cookie top and apply a thin layer of the icing over the stencil openings with a small offset spatula. Do not move the stencil, or the resulting pattern will be blurred. Let the icing dry to the touch. *Note:* The stencil used here came from designerstencils.com. For more stenciling details, see page 37.

As desired, attach 2 Loop-de-Loop Bows (p. 57) to either side of the "V" in the heart with a dab of leftover stenciling icing thickened to "glue" consistency. Glue a small Rose (p. 61) in the center of the bows to conceal their ends.

Thin the leftover icing from this step to the consistency

for beadwork (p. 245) and pipe dots around the edge of the heart. Set the heart aside for use in the next step.

5. Wafer-paper and decorate the lid. Cut the wafer paper to fit the icing on the lid. (*Note:* The wafer paper pictured below came from fancyflours.com.) Spread a thin layer of corn syrup on the cookie top coat with a small sponge brush. Anchor the paper to one end of the lid and gradually press down the rest of paper. Avoid laying down the paper in one fell swoop, as you can trap air bubbles that can be hard to work out. Trim away any excess paper from the edges and let the paper dry at least 1 hour before applying a border, below. For more wafer-papering instructions, see page 38.

Tint the 1/2 cup icing reserved for lid borders to a color that complements the wafer paper and choose a decorative border from among those in "7 Essential Piping Techniques" (p. 46). Adjust the icing to the proper consistency for your border, transfer to a parchment pastry cone or pastry bag fitted with the right tip, and then pipe away! *Note:* The lid, pictured below, has a Trailing Star Border (p. 47) piped with thick icing and a 1/4-inch star tip (Ateco #18 or #27).

Embellish the box corners with gumballs, as desired, while the icing is still wet. As a finishing touch, attach the heart cookie from Step 4 to the center of the lid with a dab of leftover icing.

6. Assemble the box. Portion off 3/4 cup of the 1 cup icing reserved for assembling the box. Tint it to a brown that matches the gingerbread. Leave the remaining 1/4 cup white and set it aside.

Thin 1/4 cup of the brown icing to top-coating consistency. Use a small offset spatula to spread a thin layer of the icing on the underside of the box bottom. Once dry, this icing will keep the box bottom from sagging due to humidity and minimize the risk of cracking under the weight of Valentine's cookies! Let the icing dry.

Make sure the remaining 1/2 cup brown icing is a thick "glue" consistency. Thicken, as needed, with powdered sugar. Bevel the edges of the box sides to ensure a tight fit. (See beveling tips on page 51.) Glue a short side and long side of the box to one another and also to the bottom of the box, propping until the "glue" is dry. Be sure to wipe off any excess "glue" that squeezes into the box; you want to see as little of it as possible. Affix the remaining sides in a similar fashion.

Detail the 4 outer seams with beadwork (p. 34) using the reserved 1/4 cup white icing. (Remember to adjust the icing consistency for this task as instructed on p. 245.) Let the box dry completely before moving and/or filling. It's safest to slide it onto its final destination (a plate or platter) before filling and to keep it supported from underneath despite its reinforcement. *Note:* I made dividers for the box by interlocking strips of corrugated cardboard, but this step is completely optional.

Pictured: *Tapered May Day Baskets.*

a tisket, a tasket

WITH MAY DAY AND EASTER BASKET VARIATIONS

A GREEN AND YELLOW BASKET! OR ANY BASKET FOR THAT MATTER . . . in fact, this one basket can be morphed into two shapes, tapered or straight, and two equally colorful styles, one with flowers for May Day or another with eggs and bunny cookies for Easter.

Makes about 9 tapered (3^3⁄$_{16}$ x 2^1⁄$_4$-inch-tall) or 6 straight (3^3⁄$_8$ x 2^1⁄$_4$-inch-tall) baskets (with cookies to fill the latter)

3 to 5 (6-inch) chocolate licorice twists (such as Twizzlers) or 2 to 3 ounces brown rolled fondant (p. 53) or other modeling medium, for basket handles

About 1 pound 10 ounces (^{1}⁄$_2$ recipe) Cutout Cookie Gingerbread (p. 236)

12-piece plain round cookie cutter set (Ateco #5457, p. 14)

12-piece fluted round cookie cutter set (Ateco #5407, p. 14)

About 2^1⁄$_2$ to 5^1⁄$_2$ cups (^{1}⁄$_2$ to 1^1⁄$_4$ recipes) Royal Icing (p. 242), divided; quantity will vary

Brown and other soft-gel food colorings (p. 14) of your choice

Small craft paintbrush (handle about ^{1}⁄$_4$-inch diameter)

Pastry bag fitted with ^{3}⁄$_8$-inch basketweave tip (Ateco #47, optional)

Sugar confetti (p. 26), for decorating basket bases

6 to 9 small (1^1⁄$_4$- to 1^1⁄$_2$-inch) Bow Ties (p. 58, 1 per basket)

Additional Royal Icing and decorations for May Day Baskets or Easter Baskets (p. 173)

TYPE:

Cutout Cookie Gingerbread (p. 236)

PREP TALK:

While Signature Sugar Cookie Dough can certainly be used for this project, I much prefer Cutout Cookie Gingerbread. Not because of texture or flavor, but because the brown dough is, well, more basket-like! It also coordinates better with handles made of chocolate licorice twists or Chocolate Dough. Be sure to mix and chill the cookie dough as instructed.

Handles, whether made of modeling media or licorice, should be prepared at least a few days prior to basket assembly to give them ample time to air-dry and firm up. Avoid White Chocolate Dough, as it is relatively heat sensitive and, therefore, less suitable for these slender pieces. If packaged in airtight containers at room temperature, this project will stay its best about 1 week.

{ a tisket, a tasket, continued }

1. Shape the basket handles. Start this step at least a few days ahead of cookie baking to allow the handles adequate time to air-dry. Chocolate Dough (even the dark variety) is more susceptible to heat than other modeling media, so it may require more drying time. The licorice will remain flexible even after drying, but the other doughs will become quite rigid.

For licorice handles: Simply cut licorice twists in half lengthwise and lie flat on a parchment paper-lined cookie sheet. You'll need 1 half-twist per handle.

For handles made of rolled fondant or another modeling medium: Follow the instructions for Ropes (p. 56) to shape the fondant or other modeling medium into 6 to 9 ropes (1 per basket), each about 10 to 11 inches long and $^1/_8$ inch in diameter. Shape each rope into an arc (about 4 to 4$^1/_2$

inches tall and 2$^1/_4$ to 2$^1/_2$ inches wide at the open end) on a parchment paper-lined cookie sheet. Handles of this size and shape should fit comfortably in the opening in the top ring cookie on each basket. Dry as instructed in "Prep Talk."

2. Cut the basket pieces. On a lightly floured surface, roll the dough to a $^1/_8$- to $^3/_{16}$-inch thickness. Feel free to cut either tapered or straight baskets, below, but note that both types require the cutting of rings. Rings are best cut directly on prepared cookie sheets to prevent the misshaping that can occur in transferring from work surface to cookie sheet. The dough cut from the center of the rings will also need to be rerolled to get the proper number of cookies.

For tapered baskets: Each of the 9 baskets will be comprised of 1 fluted round cookie for the basket base, plus 3 solid round cookies and 3 ring cookies that together

Short and Sweet. *(a) Top-coat the cookie disks and rings that form the sides of the baskets and dry completely.*
(b) Stack the disks and rings, securing each piece with thick Royal Icing. Glue sugar confetti to the basket bases for color.
(c) Add handles made of licorice twists or a modeling medium and fill each basket with other decorative elements, such as readymade royal icing roses (above), real crystallized mini roses (p. 168), or Easter cookies and mini candy eggs (p. 173).

form the basket sides. Start by cutting out approximately 9 rounds in each of the following 6 sizes: $3^3/_{16}$ inches, $2^7/_8$ inches, $2^1/_2$ inches, $2^1/_4$ inches, $1^7/_8$ inches, and $1^1/_2$ inches. As you go, cut holes out of the centers of the $3^3/_{16}$-inch, $2^7/_8$-inch, and $2^1/_2$-inch rounds, using smaller round cutters, to leave behind rings about $1/_2$ inch wide. Once all the rounds and rings have been cut for the basket sides, cut out about 9 ($2^1/_2$-inch) fluted rounds for the basket bases.

For straight baskets: Each of these baskets will also be comprised of 1 fluted round base, 3 solid round cookies, and 3 ring cookies, but because these baskets aren't tapered, you'll only end up with pieces for 6 baskets. Cut out approximately 3 dozen ($2^7/_8$-inch) rounds (6 per basket). As you go, cut holes in the centers of half of the rounds, using the $2^3/_{16}$-inch round cutter, to leave behind rings about $1/_4$ to $3/_8$ inch wide. Once all of the rounds and rings have been cut, cut out about 6 ($3^3/_8$-inch) fluted rounds for the basket bases. You will have some leftover dough in this case, which can be used to make small cookies to fill the baskets, such as the bunnies in the Easter Baskets (p. 173).

3. Bake the cookies as directed until lightly browned around the edges, or about 9 to 10 minutes for the solid rounds and closer to 7 to 9 minutes for the rings. The rings have a tendency to shrink a bit during baking. To ensure that they end up the same size as the solid rounds, stretch any shrunken ones back to full size while the cookies are still hot from the oven. Simply push evenly on the inside of the rings until they reach the desired size, but be careful to avoid overstretching and breaking. Cool completely before icing.

4. Prepare the Royal Icing as instructed on page 242. Reserve about 1 cup for "glue" and 3 cups (optional) for basketweave on straight baskets. *Note:* The quantity of icing will vary with the number of colors and consistencies mixed, and whether you add basketweave in Step 7. If you skip the basketweave, allow closer to $2^1/_2$ cups (total) icing. It's also best to allow no less than $1/_4$ to $1/_2$ cup icing per color or consistency for easiest mixing and handling.

5. Top-coat the basket pieces. Tint the remaining $1^1/_2$ cups icing to a color (or colors) of your choice; then thin to top-coating consistency (p. 245). Set aside the fluted round bases and the 9 ($3^3/_{16}$-inch) rings if making tapered baskets, or 6 ($2^7/_8$-inch) rings if making straight baskets. These cookies will be left un-iced. Using the handle-end of a craft paintbrush, apply a smooth coat of icing to the remaining cookie tops. Take care to push the icing as close to the cookie edges as possible so it can be seen once the cookies are stacked. For top-coating technique details, see page 28. Allow the cookies to dry thoroughly, ideally overnight, before assembling them into baskets.

6. Assemble the baskets. Tint the 1 cup icing reserved for "glue" to a brown that matches the gingerbread. Test the icing to make sure it's still very thick and adjust the consistency as needed. Remember, each basket will be comprised of 1 fluted base cookie, 3 solid round cookies, and 3 rings.

For tapered baskets: Work on one basket at a time. Set 1 ($2^1/_2$-inch) un-iced fluted cookie base on your work surface. Using the reserved "glue," secure 1 each of the following cookies on top, in this order: $1^1/_2$-inch, $1^7/_8$-inch, $2^1/_4$-inch, $2^1/_2$-inch, $2^7/_8$-inch, and $3^3/_{16}$-inch rounds. (The last 3 cookies will be rings; the $3^3/_{16}$-inch ring should also be un-iced.) Take care to center the cookies on top of one another; otherwise the basket will be lopsided. Also apply as little "glue" as possible, just enough to keep the cookies together. This will make it easier for

{ a tisket, a tasket, continued }

eaters to separate the cookies later if they'd rather have smaller portions. Repeat with the remaining cookies to make about 9 baskets.

For straight baskets: Again, work on one basket at a time. Start by setting 1 (3^3/$_8$-inch) un-iced fluted cookie base on your work surface. Then glue 3 solid (2^7/$_8$-inch) cookies on top (all iced), followed by 2 iced (2^7/$_8$-inch) rings and, lastly, 1 un-iced (2^7/$_8$-inch) ring. Repeat to make 6 baskets.

7. Apply basketweave (pictured below, optional) to straight baskets only. If you prefer maximum color showing on the sides of your baskets, then, by all means, skip this step. But if you'd like added texture on straight baskets, read on! (Basketweave is difficult to apply to tapered baskets due to their shape. I wouldn't attempt it.)

Tint the 3 cups Royal Icing reserved for basketweave to match the gingerbread. Test the icing to make sure it's still thick enough to hold its texture when piped through a pastry bag fitted with a ^{3}/$_8$-inch basketweave tip (Ateco #47). Adjust the consistency as needed.

Work on one basket at a time. Starting in the back of the basket at the top, pipe a basket slat that spans the first and second cookie. Jump down a cookie and pipe another slat directly underneath the first, spanning the third and fourth cookies. Jump to the fifth cookie and pipe a third and final slat spanning the fifth and sixth cookies, again directly underneath the slat above it. Move the pastry bag to the right (or left) and pipe another two slats in vertical alignment, but this time starting with the second cookie from the top. (So, connect the second and third cookies, and the fourth and the fifth cookies.) Move to the right (or left) again and start at the first cookie, repeating the process until you've piped completely around the basket. Let the icing dry before handling the basket sides. *Note:* You will likely have icing left over, but a relatively full pastry bag is needed to provide adequate hand clearance and visibility.

8. Decorate the basket bases. Use leftover Royal Icing "glue" to affix sugar confetti to the edge of each basket base. You can also use leftover icing to apply other borders or details, as desired.

9. Apply the handles and bows. *For licorice handles:* Use leftover Royal Icing "glue" to fix the ends of a licorice twist to opposing sides of the top ring cookie on each basket. Attach the twists to the very top of the rings, rather than inside them. The handles will be longer and more appropriately sized to the baskets this way.

For handles made of rolled fondant or another modeling medium: Attach the handles by gluing the ends to the inside of the top ring of each basket. These handles are taller than the licorice ones, so they needn't be mounted on the very top of the rings.

Prop the handles as needed until they have dried in place; then glue small Bow Ties on top.

10. Fill the baskets. Follow the decorating instructions for May Day or Easter Baskets (p. 173) and then serve up these tiny totes to your favorite friends!

VARIATIONS

Note: Because either styling variation can be used with either basket type, tapered or straight, the icing quantities listed below are for the maximum number (9) of baskets.

{ May Day Baskets }

Tint about $1/2$ cup Royal Icing to a brown that matches the gingerbread; then use it to glue mini crystallized roses and leaves (or royal icing roses) to the top edge of each basket. Fill the insides of the baskets by tucking a loose rose in the center, or by gluing a rose onto a chocolate-covered candy stick (or lollypop stick) and inserting the stick in the center. *Note:* The crystallized roses, pictured on page 168, came from crystallizedflowerco.com, and the royal icing roses, pictured on page 170, came from fancyflours.com.

If working with royal icing roses (optional): Tint $3/4$ cup Royal Icing to a leaf green. Adjust the icing, as needed. It should be very thick and hold its shape when piped through a pastry bag fitted with a $1/4$-inch leaf tip (Ateco #352). Pipe icing leaves around the flowers to fill any gaps.

{ Easter Baskets }

Tint about $2^1/4$ cups Royal Icing to a grass green using a mixture of green and yellow soft-gel food coloring. Adjust the consistency, as needed, so that the icing is very thick. Transfer the icing to a pastry bag fitted with a $3/8$-inch grass tip (Ateco #133). Seat a small bunny cookie (pictured right), chick cookie, or marshmallow chick in the top of each basket. (You may need to break off the bottoms to fit.) Pipe green icing grass around the bunnies (chicks) to keep them in place; then add more grass around the top of each basket. While the icing is still wet, arrange readymade royal icing or candy Easter eggs in it. *Note:* The royal icing eggs, pictured right, came from fancyflours.com.

Basket Bonanza. *Straight baskets, such as these styled as Easter Baskets, can be simply stacked (top and right baskets) or textured with a basketweave pattern using thick Royal Icing (left basket). See Step 7 (p. 172) for basketweave details.*

tip-top topiary

A CHARMING ADDITION TO ANY SPRINGTIME PARTY, these topiaries tempt with two cookie types—iced cookies on top and brownies nestled in the pots. My take, below, stands 6 to 7 inches tall—a perfect size for a place card or favor. But you can also scale these trees up or down to suit your fancy.

Makes about 8 ($1^3/4$ x $2^1/8$ x $6^7/8$-inch-tall) topiaries

About 11 ounces ($1/4$ recipe) Cutout Cookie
   Gingerbread (p. 236) or ($1/2$ recipe)
   Signature Sugar Cookie Dough (p. 234)

12-piece fluted round cookie cutter
   set (Ateco #5407, p. 14)

About $2^1/4$ cups ($1/3$ to $1/2$ recipe)
   Royal Icing (p. 242), divided

Green and other soft-gel food colorings
   (p. 14) of your choice

Small craft paintbrush (handle
   about $1/4$-inch diameter)

Pastry bag fitted with $1/4$-inch
   leaf tip (Ateco #352)

About 4 dozen small ($3/8$- to $3/4$-inch)
   readymade royal icing daisies or
   roses (p. 26, 6 flowers per topiary)

Parchment pastry cones (p. 13)

8 (8-inch) cardboard lollypop sticks
   (p. 268, 1 per topiary)

16 small ($1/2$- to $3/4$-inch) Loop-de-Loop
   Bows (p. 57, 2 per topiary, optional)

$1/2$ recipe Basic or Blonde Brownies (p. 247)

Silicone brownie pop or other baking
   mold (p. 24; see Step 6)

About 8 ounces rolled fondant (p. 53) or
   other modeling medium, color(s) of
   your choice, for wrapping flower pots

Stand-in: Macaron Mania. *French macaroons (aka macarons) are all the rage. And there's no reason you, too, can't jump on the bandwagon—and save some time—with this project! Skip the iced cookies, pictured on page 174, and simply sandwich pairs of green-tinted Goofproof Macarons with Ganache or Italian Buttercream around lollypop sticks. Tied with real ribbons and name tags, they make pretty favors sans brownie pots. Note: To firm up the buttercream and keep the sandwiches in place, briefly chill the macaron sticks before serving.*

TYPES:

Cutout Cookie Gingerbread (p. 236) or Signature
Sugar Cookie Dough (p. 234) for topiary rounds;

Basic or Blonde Brownies (p. 247) for flower pots

{ tip-top topiary, continued }

PREP TALK:

Either cookie dough in "Types" can be used for this project, as can either brownie recipe. Be sure to mix and chill the dough as instructed. The brownies are best baked in small but relatively deep (2-inch) silicone baking molds, as specified in Step 6, in order to give the topiary tops sufficient support. If packaged in airtight containers at room temperature, this project will stay its best about 1 week.

1. Cut and bake the topiary rounds. On a lightly floured surface, roll the dough to a $1/8$- to $3/16$-inch thickness. Cut out about 16 ($2^1/8$-inch) fluted rounds (2 per topiary), 16 ($1^1/2$-inch) fluted rounds, and another 16 ($1^1/8$-inch) fluted rounds. You should end up with about 8 sets of 6 cookies, 2 in each of the 3 cookie sizes. Group like-size cookies on the same cookie sheet. Bake as directed until lightly browned around the edges, or about 7 to 8 minutes for the smallest cookies and closer to 9 to 10 minutes for the largest cookies. Cool completely before decorating.

2. Prepare the Royal Icing as instructed on page 242. Reserve about $3/4$ cup for leaves and beadwork, $1/2$ cup for "glue" for the topiary tops, and $1/4$ cup for "glue" for the pots.

3. Top-coat the topiary rounds. Tint the remaining $3/4$ cup icing to a dark (or light) green and thin to top-coating consistency (p. 245). Using the handle-end of a craft paintbrush, apply a smooth coat of icing to each cookie top. For top-coating technique details, see page 28. Let the icing dry to the touch.

4. Detail the rounds. Tint the $3/4$ cup icing reserved for leaves and beadwork to a slightly lighter (or darker) green than the one used for top-coating. Transfer the icing to a pastry bag fitted with a $1/4$-inch leaf tip (Ateco #352) and pipe small leaves on half of the cookies in each size. Before the icing sets, arrange readymade mini royal icing daisies or roses on top of the leaves. *Note:* It's best to decorate half of the cookies as just described—that is, one side of each topiary. The topiaries will be easier to assemble in Step 5 without bulky decorations on the back.

Thin the leftover icing to the consistency for beadwork (p. 245) and transfer to a parchment pastry cone. Cut a small ($1/16$-inch or more) hole in the tip and pipe dots around all of the cookie edges using the beadwork technique (p. 34). Dry completely before assembling in the next step.

5. Assemble the topiary rounds on sticks. Tint the $1/2$ cup icing reserved for gluing the topiary tops to the same green color used for top-coating and transfer to a parchment pastry cone. Work on one topiary at a time. Place a set of 3 cookies (without flowers), in each of the 3 sizes, top down on your work surface so that the cookies touch end to end and are ordered large to small. Apply "glue" in the center of all 3 cookies and then set a lollypop stick on top. (The end of the stick should not extend beyond the edge of the small cookie at the top.) Pipe more "glue" on top of the cookies and place like-size rounds (with flowers) face up on top to sandwich the stick. Repeat to make 8 sticks. Dry completely before moving. While the topiary sticks are drying, glue small Loop-de-Loop Bows, as desired, between cookie rounds. Store the topiary sticks in airtight containers if you don't plan to make the brownies immediately.

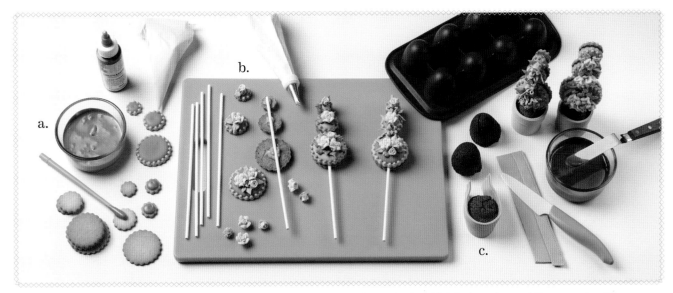

Short and Sweet. *(a) Top-coat round cookies in three sizes for the topiaries. Finish the edges of the rounds with beadwork. (b) Pipe Royal Icing leaves on half of the rounds in each size; then immediately set readymade royal icing flowers on top. Use icing "glue" to mount like-size cookies back to back on lollypop sticks, starting with the largest rounds and ending with the smallest rounds at the top. (c) Wrap small brownies with rolled fondant or another modeling medium to make flower pots; then insert an assembled topiary stick into each pot.*

6. Bake the brownies. Prepare $1/2$ recipe Basic or Blonde Brownies. *Note:* You will only need about $1/4$ recipe for 8 topiaries, but it's easier to mix $1/2$ or 1 recipe and portion off what you need. Any extra brownies can be eaten or frozen for later!

Turn the batter into the brownie pop or other baking mold. (*Note:* I use an 8-compartment Wilton mold with $1\,3/4$-inch-diameter chambers, about 2 inches deep. You can also use small, greased muffin tins, though they won't provide as much support.) Bake until a cake tester inserted in the center of each brownie comes out with damp crumbs on it, or about 30 minutes. Brownies baked in shallower muffin tins will take less time. Cool completely.

7. Wrap the brownies and assemble the flower pots. Tint the $1/4$ cup icing reserved for gluing the pots to a color (or colors) that match(es) the tinted rolled fondant or other modeling medium; then thin to top-coating consistency (p. 245).

Work on a few pots at a time. Follow the instructions for making Plain Ribbons (p. 56) to cut the modeling medium into ribbons, each about $1\,1/2$ inches wide and $5\,1/4$ inches long (or wide and long enough to completely cover the sides of your brownies). Cut the same number of thinner Stitched Ribbons (p. 57), each about $1/2$ inch wide and the same length as the ones just cut. Affix a thin ribbon to the top of each wide one with a small amount of loosened "glue." Spread more "glue" on the back of each double-ribbon and then wrap one around each brownie so that the thin ribbon is at the top, mimicking the lip of a garden pot. Insert a trimmed topiary stick into the center of each pot using a dab of leftover thick "glue" (Step 5) to hold the stick in place. Prop, as needed, until the icing is dry. Repeat to wrap and assemble the remaining pots.

come sail away

ANY SAILBOAT COOKIE WOULD SEEM MAGICAL adrift a sea with brownie islands underneath a sunny cookie sky. But these 3-D sail boats are doubly dreamy, crafted as they are with not one, but two types of cookies!

Makes about 11 (2¼ x 4 x 4- to 4½-inch-tall) sailboats

About 9 to 10 ounces rolled fondant (p. 53) or other modeling medium, color(s) of your choice, divided, for masts, cleats, flags, and boat wraps (optional for masts and wraps; if skipped, allow about 1 to 2 ounces)

12 (6-inch) cardboard lollypop sticks (p. 268; 1 for shaping sails, others optional for masts)

About 3¼ cups (⅔ to ¾ recipe) Royal Icing (p. 242), divided

Custom template (p. 264), for boat hull

About 12 ounces (½ recipe) Shortbread, Straight Up (p. 240), for boat hulls

Soft-gel food colorings (p. 14) of your choice

Parchment pastry cones (p. 13)

Custom triangular acetate stencil, for sail (see Step 7)

1 recipe Traditional Tuiles (p. 255)

Medium offset spatula (p. 14, blade about 1¼ x 6½ inches)

About 2 dozen Lifesavers candies (2 per sailboat), for mast supports and lifesavers

Brownie islands, for display (optional; see Step 9)

Meringue (p. 253) clouds and decorated cookies in the nautical theme, for display (optional)

Stand-in: A Breezier Boat. *If you're worried about going overboard, don't be. Take this project down a notch by skipping the brownie islands, meringue clouds, and cookie sun, and just making 3-D boats. Or go a step further and replace these 3-D boats with simple 2-D iced sugar cookies (not pictured).*

TYPES:

Shortbread, Straight Up (p. 240) for boat hulls;

Traditional Tuiles (p. 255) for sails

{ come sail away, continued }

PREP TALK:

Because shortbread retains its shape better than most rolled doughs when cut thick, Shortbread, Straight Up is the dough of choice for the chunky hulls of these boats. Be sure to mix and chill the dough as instructed. The masts, cleats, and flags made of rolled fondant (or another modeling medium) should be shaped at least a day ahead of assembly to give them ample time to air-dry and firm up. Avoid White Chocolate Dough, especially for the masts; it is relatively heat sensitive and, therefore, less suitable for these slender pieces. If packaged in airtight containers at room temperature, this project will stay its best about 1 week.

1. Shape the masts (optional) and cleats. As noted in "Prep Talk," it's best to make these pieces at least a day in advance. Lollypop sticks can be used for masts, if preferred.

For masts (optional): Portion off about 1 ounce of the modeling medium and follow the instructions for Cords (p. 55) to make 11 ($1/8$ x 5-inch) cords for masts. Trim the ends to neaten and set aside on a parchment paper-lined cookie sheet to air-dry.

For cleats: Portion off another ounce or less of modeling medium. Form a cleat by rolling a small pinch of modeling medium into a tiny ($1/16$ to $1/8$ x $1/2$-inch) cord with tapered ends. Make 2 cleats per boat (about 22 in total) and set aside to air-dry, as instructed above.

The remaining modeling medium will be used for flags and boat wraps (optional) in subsequent steps, so wrap and contain it in the meantime to prevent it from drying out.

2. Prepare the Royal Icing as instructed on page 242. Reserve about $3/4$ cup for "glue," $1^1/2$ cups for outlining and flooding the hulls, $1/4$ cup for detailing the lifesavers, and $3/4$ cup for detailing the sails.

3. Shape the flags. Start work on this task after the masts have dried to the point that they can be rolled without misshaping. (Or start work immediately if using lollypop sticks for masts.) Portion off about 1 tablespoon of the $3/4$ cup icing reserved for "glue" and thin to top-coating consistency (p. 245). Save the rest for use in Steps 6 and 8. Portion off about 1 ounce of the leftover modeling medium.

Follow the instructions in Plain Ribbons (p. 56) to roll the modeling medium into thin ($1/16$-inch) sheets; then cut the sheet into small (about $1/2$ x $1^1/2$-inch) rectangles to make flags. Adorn with thin ribbons in contrasting colors, if desired. Simply dampen the backs of the ribbons with a bit of water; then set the ribbons atop the flags. (I prefer water to Royal Icing for gluing these tiny ribbons, as icing is more likely to show.) Lastly, glue the short end of each flag around the end of a mast with a dab of the loosened icing. (It's easiest to roll the masts onto the flags if the masts are still too soft to pick up.) Trim the flags to about 1 inch in length. Let the flags dry fully before moving. You should have 7 to 8 ounces modeling medium left over for use in Step 6.

4. Cut and bake the boat hulls. Start by cutting out a template to fit the boat hull outline on page 264. If you plan to make a lot of boats, consider making a custom cookie cutter; it will save cutting time in the long run. And, in this case, one will make for easier trimming of the boat hulls after baking, if desired. For more information about working with custom templates and cutters, see page 48.

On a lightly floured surface, roll the dough to a $3/8$-inch thickness. Using your template (or custom cutter) as a cutting guide, cut out about 11 hulls. Bake the cookies as directed until lightly browned on the bottom, or about 25 to 30 minutes. To neaten the cookie edges, trim the cookies while hot from the oven, as desired. Cool completely before icing.

5. Outline and flood the boat hulls. I like to outline and flood these cookies, as opposed to top-coating without any outlines, in order to get the icing as close to the cookie edges as possible. Tint the $1^1/2$ cups of icing reserved for outlining and flooding to a color of your choice; then thin to outlining consistency (p. 244). Fill a parchment pastry cone with the icing and cut a small ($1/16$-inch or more) hole in the tip. Outline each hull; then thin the leftover icing to flooding consistency (p. 245) and fill the interior of each outline using the flooding techniques described on page 31. Let the hulls dry completely before further decorating.

6. Wrap the boat hulls (optional). Thin about $1/4$ cup of the icing reserved for "glue" (Step 3) to top-coating consistency (p. 245) and set aside. Follow the instructions in Plain Ribbons (p. 56) to roll the leftover modeling medium into a thin ($1/16$-inch) sheet. Cut the sheet into 12-inch strips about $7/8$ inch wide at their center and tapering to the height of the iced hulls (about $3/8$ inch) at each end. You'll need 1 strip for each boat, though cut only a few strips at a time to keep them from drying out. *Note:* The strips can also be stitched or embossed, as pictured on page 178 and described in Ribbons (pp. 56 to 57).

Work on one boat at a time. Spread a thin layer of the loosened "glue" on the back of a strip and wrap the strip around the boat so that the widest part lands at the bow. Trim any excess modeling medium where the ends of the strip meet. Repeat to wrap all of the boats, as desired.

7. Make the tuile sails. Cut out a $5^1/8$ x $3^1/4$-inch-tall triangle in the center of a piece of acetate following the instructions for making custom stencils (p. 49). Prepare Traditional Tuiles as instructed. Portion off about $1/4$ cup batter (for lines on the sails) and tint to a color of your choice or leave as-is. Transfer this batter to a parchment pastry cone and cut a small ($1/16$-inch or more) hole in the tip. Leave the remaining batter (for the sail) as-is or tint to a color that contrasts the color mixed for the lines. Since the sails must be shaped very quickly once they come out of the oven, it's best to make only a few at a time.

Set the stencil on a prepared cookie sheet (remember, tuiles require silicone baking mats). (a) Spread a thin layer of the "sail" batter over the stencil opening using a medium offset spatula. The batter need not be any thicker than the thickness of the acetate. I use a medium spatula rather than a small one in order to evenly fill this relatively large stencil in the fewest possible swipes.

a.

(b) Pipe a line (or lines) of the other batter on top. Lift the template and repeat this process to fill the cookie sheet with a few more sails, if possible. Bake as directed until set and dull on top, but not browned, or about 3 to 4 minutes.

{ come sail away, continued }

Short and Sweet. *(a) Cut out shortbread boat hulls using a custom template (or custom cutter, pictured here). Bake and cool. Outline and flood with Royal Icing; then wrap any exposed sides with rolled fondant or another modeling medium, as desired. (b) Spread tuile batter through a custom stencil to make sails. Bake and shape while hot from the oven. (c) Use thick Royal Icing to glue the sails to masts made of rolled fondant, another modeling medium, or lollypop sticks; then glue a mast to each boat using Lifesavers candies as supports. Embellish with icing ropes and other decorations.*

(c) While the tuiles are still hot from the oven, give them shape by bending them around a lollypop stick.

Repeat Steps (a) to (c) to make at least 11 sails. *Note:* You will have enough batter to make many more sails, but it's difficult to mix the batter in any smaller quantity. Save the extra sails for snacking, or in case any crack or break during assembly.

If you don't plan to assemble the cookies immediately, package the sails in airtight containers as soon as they've cooled. Tuiles will quickly get soft under humid conditions.

8. Decorate and assemble the boats. Use leftover "glue" (Step 3) to attach 2 cleats on either side of each boat toward the stern. Tint the 1/4 cup icing reserved for detailing the Lifesavers candies to a color that contrasts the candy; then thin the icing to outlining consistency. Pipe crisscross lines on the Lifesavers to mimic ropes. Let the ropes dry and then glue one candy to the back of each boat to mimic (yes, you guessed it) a lifesaver. Lastly, glue another Lifesavers candy to the bow of each boat to serve as a support for the mast.

Add the masts and sails within a few hours of serving so the sails stay crispy. Work on one boat at a time. Trim a mast (or lollypop stick) to about $3^7/8$ inches, or just tall enough that the bottom of a sail can rest on the Lifesavers support when the mast is inserted in the center of the candy. Glue a sail to the mast and then glue the mast in the center of the candy. Prop the mast upright until the icing dries. Repeat to add masts and sails to all 11 boats.

As a finishing touch, use the $3/4$ cup icing reserved for sail details to pipe thin lines along the bottom of each sail and around the cleats to simulate ropes. (Thin the icing to outlining consistency for this task.) Add dots and other details to the sails, as desired, adjusting the consistency of the icing as needed for your task.

9. Display (optional). Serve the boats singly or in a vignette with other boats, brownie islands, Meringue (p. 253) clouds, and cookies in the nautical theme. For brownie islands, bake Basic or Blonde Brownies (p. 247) in round cake pans. Stack rounds to make taller islands.

along came a spider

WHILE YOU'VE PROBABLY SEEN CANDY-FILLED COOKIES masquerading as Christmas ornaments before, this cookie construction is even cooler when used for Halloween décor. Here, I've filled the interior of cutout gingerbread spider webs with bright green sugar syrup. When the syrup cools, it sets into shimmering plates of sugar glass with the translucence of real-life spider webs.

Makes about 1 dozen (6³⁄8-inch) webs with 1 to 2 (1³⁄16-inch) spiders per web

About 3 ounces (¹⁄16 recipe) Cutout Cookie
    Gingerbread (p. 236), for spiders

Small (1³⁄16-inch) plain round
    cookie cutter, for spiders

About 2¹⁄4 cups (¹⁄3 to ¹⁄2 recipe)
    Royal Icing (p. 242), divided

13 to 14 (1³⁄4-inch) wheels licorice lace
    (such as Haribo Wheels), for spider legs

Soft-gel food colorings (p. 14) of your choice

Parchment pastry cones (p. 13)

5 to 6 ounces chocolate jimmies
    (p. 26), for spider hair

Small candies (such as mini M&Ms or
    Skittles), for spider eyeballs

About 1 pound (¹⁄3 recipe) Construction
    Gingerbread (p. 238) or Cutout Cookie
    Gingerbread (p. 236), for webs

Large (about 6³⁄8-inch) and medium (about
    4³⁄8-inch) cobweb cookie cutters

3 to 4 cups isomalt crystals (p. 24), divided

Candy thermometer

Metal trussing needle (p. 15) or toothpicks

Thin twine or monofilament, for
    hanging webs and spiders

Stand-in: A Tangled Web We Weave. *Intricate, yes! But complicated? No! If you'd rather not have your kids around the hot sugar syrup used for the windows in the webs pictured on page 184, then make these speedy marbled webs instead. Simply top-coat web cookies in white and apply a center dot and concentric circles of black marbling icing on top. Then follow the instructions in "Marbling a Starburst Pattern" (p. 36) to create this spine-tingling effect!*

TYPES:

Cutout Cookie Gingerbread (p. 236); Construction

Gingerbread (p. 238) just for webs

{ along came a spider, continued }

PREP TALK:

While any of my rolled doughs can be used here, I prefer the darker color of gingerbread for its spookier effect! For the smaller spiders, I much prefer the delicacy of Cutout Cookie Gingerbread. For the relatively large and fragile webs, I have a slight preference for Construction Gingerbread because it's stronger and spreads less. (The windows cut in the webs therefore close less.) Be sure to mix and chill the doughs as instructed. If packaged in airtight containers at room temperature, this project will stay its best about 1 week. When not boxed, this project is best displayed in a cool, dry place, as the sugar windows can quickly get cloudy and sticky if exposed to humidity. You will need a candy thermometer for working with the isomalt (sugar) syrup in Step 5.

---

1. Cut and bake the spider bodies. It's best to make the spiders before the webs, since once filled with isomalt syrup, the windows of the webs are prone to clouding.

On a lightly floured surface, roll the (3 ounces) dough to a $1/8$- to $3/16$-inch thickness and cut out 1 to 2 dozen spider bodies (1 to 2 per web) using the $1\,3/16$-inch round cookie cutter. Bake as directed until lightly browned around the edges, or about 8 to 9 minutes. Cool completely before decorating in Step 3.

2. Prepare the Royal Icing as instructed on page 242. Reserve about $1/2$ cup for "glue," $1/2$ cup for the spiders' eyes, and another $1/2$ cup for the webs.

3. Dip the spider bodies and attach the legs and eyes. Start by prepping the spider legs. Unwind the licorice lace and cut it into 2- to $2\,1/4$-inch segments. You'll need 8 segments for each spider body. Set aside.

Tint the remaining $3/4$ cup icing to a color of your choice. (I'm partial to black.) Thin to thick dipping consistency (p. 245) and transfer to a small bowl, if needed, so the icing sits at least 1 inch deep. Tint the $1/2$ cup icing reserved for "glue" to a matching color. Transfer to a parchment pastry cone bag and cut a relatively large ($1/8$-inch or more) hole in the tip.

Work on one round cookie at a time.

(a) Using the Nose-Dive Dipping technique (p. 32), submerge the cookie in the icing to completely coat its top and sides. Shake off any excess icing and place the cookie on a parchment paper-lined cookie sheet.

a.

(b) While the icing is still wet, stick 8 licorice legs into the sides of each body (4 per side). The legs should stand up with the bends at the top. Pipe additional Royal Icing "glue" on each leg where it meets the body.

Short and Sweet. *(a) Dip round cookies (for spider bodies) in Royal Icing and, while the icing is still wet, add licorice legs and sprinkle with jimmies. Dry to the touch before adding candies and Royal Icing for eyes. (b) Fill web cookies with tinted isomalt syrup and let the isomalt set. (c) Pipe a spider web onto the isomalt using Royal Icing of outlining consistency. Attach spiders (and twine for hanging) with Royal Icing "glue."*

(c) Immediately sprinkle chocolate jimmies on top to make hair. Repeat with the remaining cookie rounds.

Let the spider bodies dry to the touch before adding the eyes, but do not move the spider bodies until they are completely dry. (Otherwise, the legs can fall down or off!)

(d) Glue 2 pieces of small candy to each cookie to create eyeballs. Tint the $1/2$ cup icing reserved for the eyes to a color of your choice and thin to the consistency for beadwork (p. 245). Fill a parchment pastry cone with the icing, cut a small ($1/16$-inch or more) hole in the tip,

d.

and pipe a small dot on the top of each eyeball to create pupils.

4. Cut and bake the spider webs. On a lightly floured surface, roll the (1 pound) dough to a $^{1}/_{8}$- to $^{3}/_{16}$-inch thickness. Since the webs are relatively large, it's best to cut them directly on prepared cookie sheets to avoid the misshaping that can occur in transferring from work surface to cookie sheet. Use the large (6$^{3}/_{8}$-inch) cobweb cutter to cut out about 1 dozen webs. As you go, cut out a smaller (4$^{3}/_{8}$-inch) web in the center of each cookie. Remove the dough from the center and be sure to reroll so that you end up with the right number (12) of large open webs.

Bake the cobweb cookies as directed until lightly browned around the edges, or about 11 to 13 minutes. Cool completely before filling in the next step.

5. Fill the spider webs with isomalt syrup. This step is best left to adults or big kids, since the isomalt syrup gets quite hot and must be carefully handled. Transfer the webs baked in Step 4 to cookie sheets lined with silicone baking mats. *Note:* Parchment paper-lined pans can also be used. However, the paper tends to buckle once the syrup is poured on it, introducing wrinkles and bubbles. Also, bubbles in the syrup take longer to dissipate on paper.

Because the syrup cools quickly and can become difficult to pour, it's best to make it in 3 or more batches and to fill a few cookies at a time. For 1 batch of isomalt syrup, combine 1 cup isomalt crystals and $^{1}/_{3}$ cup water in a saucepan to form a thick sludge. Place over medium-high heat and bring to a boil, stirring regularly until the isomalt crystals are dissolved. When the syrup reaches 250°F on a candy thermometer, add food coloring of your choice. (For the green webs pictured on page 184, I used about 2 drops green and 2 drops yellow.) Stir just to evenly distribute the coloring. Continue to cook the syrup until it reaches the hard crack stage (315°F); then remove from the heat and quickly pour into a liquid measuring cup with a pouring spout. Do not cook the syrup any longer, or it will begin to caramelize and turn brown.

Immediately pour the syrup into center of as many webs as you can. Carefully tilt the cookie sheets until the sugar fills the interior of each web. If the bubbles in the sugar don't dissipate on their own, pop them with a metal trussing needle or toothpick while the sugar is still warm. Fill the remaining web cookies with as many additional batches of isomalt syrup as needed.

Let the cookies cool completely on the cookie sheets before moving. Gently guide an offset spatula under each cookie to disengage the cooled sugar and transfer the cookies to airtight containers lined with parchment paper until ready to decorate. Avoid pulling the cookies off the cookie sheets, as this can put tiny stress fractures in the sugar, causing it to later crack as it fully cools. Also avoid handling the sugar to prevent fingerprints.

6. Pipe the spider webs. Tint the remaining $1/2$ cup icing to a color of your choice. (Again, I prefer black.) Thin to outlining consistency (p. 244).

Fill a parchment pastry cone with the icing and cut a small ($1/16$-inch or more) hole in the tip. Pipe a spider web (mimicking the one shown on page 184) onto the sugar window in each web cookie. Let the icing dry and then immediately package the cookies in airtight containers if you do not plan to assemble the webs right away.

7. Assemble the spider webs. Attach 1 to 2 spiders to the face of each web cookie with leftover Royal Icing "glue" (Step 3). You can also suspend the webs (from light fixtures, rafters, or anything overhead) by gluing a piece of thin twine or monofilament between the web and a spider cookie anchored at the top of the web. Let the icing dry completely, ideally overnight, before hanging or otherwise moving the cookies.

jack o' lanterns

SET YOUR HALLOWEEN TABLE AGLOW with these edible votive candle holders, or turn them into boxes by filling them with candy for your favorite trick-or-treaters.

Makes about 3 (3 x 4 to 5 x 4- to 5-inch-tall) jack o' lantern votive candle holders or boxes

About 13 ounces (¼ recipe) Construction Gingerbread (p. 238) or Cutout Cookie Gingerbread (p. 236)

Large (4 to 5 x 4- to 5-inch) pumpkin cookie cutter

Assorted small cookie cutters, for cutting pumpkin eyes, noses, and mouths (see Step 1)

Ruler or custom rectangular templates in 2 sizes (see Step 1)

About 3 cups (⅔ recipe) Royal Icing (p. 242), divided

Orange, black, brown, yellow, or other soft-gel food colorings (p. 14) of your choice

Parchment pastry cones (p. 13)

Pastry bag fitted with ¹¹⁄₁₆-inch basketweave tip (Ateco #895)

About 6 small (1- to 1½-inch) Embossed Leaves (p. 59, 2 per votive)

About 6 small (1½- to 2-inch) Vines (p. 60, 2 per votive)

1 cup isomalt crystals (p. 24)

Candy thermometer

Metal trussing needle (p. 15) or toothpicks

3 (1½-inch) tea candles (1 per votive, optional)

Stand-in: 2-D Tease. *It's more than okay to forego the 3-D votive holder construction and the shiny sugar windows behind these pumpkins' faces. 2-D pumpkins can be given extra dimension by standing them upright in cookie crumb dirt or in jelly beans or other Halloween candy, as pictured here. You can even stick a candle behind each one to cast eerie shadows.*

TYPES:

Construction Gingerbread (p. 238) or Cutout Cookie Gingerbread (p. 236)

{ jack o' lanterns, continued }

PREP TALK:

While any of my rolled doughs can be used here, I prefer the darker color of gingerbread for its spookier effect! And even though this is a small 3-D construction project that wouldn't ordinarily require the strength of Construction Gingerbread, I have a slight preference for it. Because it spreads less than Cutout Cookie Gingerbread, pumpkin faces rarely have to be recut after baking. Be sure to mix and chill the dough as instructed. If packaged in airtight containers at room temperature, this project will stay its best about 1 week. When not boxed, this project is best displayed in a cool, dry place, as the sugar faces can quickly get cloudy and sticky if exposed to humidity. You will need a candy thermometer for working with the isomalt (sugar) syrup in Step 5.

It's also best to make the leaves and vines from rolled fondant (or another modeling medium) at least a day before assembly to give them ample time to air-dry and firm up.

---

1. Cut and bake the votive pieces. Each votive will be comprised of 2 pumpkin cookies, 2 rectangular sides, and 1 rectangular bottom.

For the pumpkin cookies: On a lightly floured surface, roll the dough to a $1/8$-inch thickness. (It's best to roll extra thinly, as the dough will spread less, making it less necessary to recut faces after baking.) Cut out about 6 pumpkins (2 per votive) using a large (4 to 5 x 4- to 5-inch) relatively flat-bottomed pumpkin cutter. (The flatter the cookie cutter bottom, the better you can conceal the votive bottoms when assembling.) Use assorted small cookie cutters to cut out the eyes, noses, and mouths. *Note:* I used the cutters in a 9-piece jack o' lantern cookie cutter set manufactured by R & M International from fancyflours.com (p. 268).

For the rectangular pieces: Following the instructions for custom templates (p. 48), make rectangular templates in 2 sizes: about $2^1/4$ to $2^1/2$ x $2^1/2$ inches for the votive bottoms and 2 x $2^1/2$ inches for their sides. (*Note:* The width of the bottoms will vary with the size of the pumpkin cutter used. A narrower pumpkin cutter requires a narrower bottom, so that the bottom will not be visible in the final assembly. Be sure to test-fit the templates with your pumpkin cutters before you cut any dough.) Alternatively, you can use a ruler as a cutting guide. Or if you plan to make a lot of votives, consider making custom cookie cutters; they will save cutting time in the long run. For more information about working with custom templates and cutters, see page 48. Roll the remaining dough to the same ($1/8$-inch) thickness. Cut out 3 bottoms (1 per votive) and 6 sides (2 per votive).

Bake the pumpkins, sides, and bottoms as directed until lightly browned around the edges, or about 9 to 12 minutes, depending on cookie size. If the pumpkin faces have closed more than you'd like, or if the edges of the votive sides and bottoms have bulged, trim the cookies while still hot from the oven. Cool completely.

2. Prepare the Royal Icing as instructed on page 242. Reserve about $1/2$ cup for pumpkin contours, $1/2$ cup for outlining the faces, $1/2$ cup for stems, and another $1/2$ cup for "glue."

Short and Sweet. *(a) Outline, flood, and add details, such as embossed leaves and vines, to the pumpkin faces. (b) Pour tinted isomalt syrup onto a silicone mat and set the decorated pumpkins on top. (c) Use thick Royal Icing to assemble the pumpkins, along with rectangular sides and bottoms, into votives.*

3. Outline and flood the pumpkin cookies. I prefer to outline and flood the pumpkin cookies, as opposed to top-coating without any outlines, in order to get the icing as close to the cookie edges as possible. Tint the remaining 1 cup icing to a dark orange. Thin to outlining consistency (p. 244) and transfer to a parchment pastry cone. Cut a small ($1/16$-inch or more) hole in the tip and proceed to outline each pumpkin cookie following the outlining technique tips on page 29. Thin the leftover icing to flooding consistency (p. 245) and flood the interior each pumpkin cookie, taking care to keep the icing from flooding into the faces. (You can also outline around these openings to prevent overflow; however, I usually don't. I prefer the look of a single prominent black outline applied later.) Let the cookies dry to the touch.

4. Add details to the pumpkin cookies. Tint the $1/2$ cup icing reserved for contours to a light orange or another color of your choice. Thin to outlining consistency and pipe delicate lines at the top and bottom of each pumpkin, similar to those pictured on page 190, to suggest contours.

Tint the $1/2$ cup icing reserved for outlining the faces to a deep black or another color of your choice; then thin once again to outlining consistency. Pipe lines around the eyes, noses, and mouths to accentuate them.

Lastly, tint the $1/2$ cup icing reserved for stems to a dark brown or another color of your choice. Transfer the icing to a pastry bag fitted with a $11/16$-inch basketweave tip (Ateco #895). Hold the tip ridge side up and pipe a stem on each jack o' lantern. (*Note:* The icing should be thick enough to hold the ridged basketweave pattern. If the pattern disappears, the icing is too loose and needs to be thickened further with powdered sugar.) While the stems are still wet, insert Embossed Leaves (p. 59) and Vines (p. 60) into them.

Let the cookies dry completely before adding isomalt to the faces.

{ jack o' lanterns, continued }

5. Back the pumpkin faces with isomalt. This step is best left to adults or big kids, since the isomalt syrup gets quite hot and must be carefully handled. (Alternatively, the pumpkin faces can be left unbacked.) Line 2 cookie sheets with silicone baking mats. *Note:* Parchment paper-lined pans can also be used. However, the paper tends to buckle once the syrup is poured on it, introducing wrinkles and bubbles. Also, bubbles in the syrup take longer to dissipate on paper.

Combine the isomalt with $1/3$ cup water in a saucepan to form a thick sludge. Place over medium-high heat and bring to a boil, stirring regularly until the isomalt crystals are dissolved. When the syrup reaches 250°F on a candy thermometer, add food coloring of your choice. (For the bright yellow pictured on page 190, I used about 2 to 3 drops yellow.) Stir just to evenly distribute the coloring. Continue to cook the syrup until it reaches the hard crack stage (315°F); then remove from the heat. Do not cook the syrup any longer, or it will begin to caramelize and turn brown.

Immediately pour the syrup into 6 small pools spanning the 2 cookie sheets. Space the pools far enough apart to fit the pumpkin cookies in between. Because the face openings are relatively small, it's much easier to pour the isomalt into pools, and set the pumpkin cookies on top, than it is to pour the isomalt directly into the openings. It's also best to use as little syrup as possible in each pool, no more than needed to fill each pumpkin face. If the syrup spreads and coats too much of the cookie backs, it can interfere with votive assembly in Step 6. Let the syrup cool slightly, just until any bubbles in it subside; then set a decorated pumpkin cookie on top of each pool. Press the cookie gently into the syrup until the syrup fills the empty face openings. Pop any large bubbles in the sugar with a metal trussing needle or toothpick.

Let the cookies cool completely on the cookie sheets before moving. Gently guide an offset spatula under each cookie to disengage the cooled sugar; then transfer the cookies to airtight containers lined with parchment paper until ready to assemble the votives. Avoid pulling the cookies off the cookie sheets, as this can put tiny stress fractures in the sugar, causing it to later crack as it fully cools. Also avoid handling the sugar to prevent fingerprints.

6. Assemble the votives. Tint the $1/2$ cup icing reserved for "glue" to a brown that matches the gingerbread. Work on one votive at a time. Set a cookie bottom on your work surface and glue 2 (2 x $2^{1}/_{2}$-inch) votive sides to the opposing ($2^{1}/_{2}$-inch) edges of the bottom. Prop with paper towels or other lightweight objects, if needed, to keep the sides standing straight up. To form the remaining sides of the votive, glue a pumpkin cookie to each of the open ends, again propping the pieces as needed. Let the votive dry completely before moving. Repeat to make the rest of the votives.

7. Display (optional). If desired, set tea candles inside the votives and light when you're ready to set the mood. (*Note:* Never leave lit candles unattended, especially around kids.) If you'd rather fill the boxes with candies, be sure to support them underneath with small plates.

what a hoot

WITH WITCH CRAFT VARIATION

THIS HALLOWEEN HOOT FIRST APPEARED IN MY BOOK *COOKIE SWAP* as an example of a compound cookie (a cookie on a cookie). Back by popular demand, he is now joined by edible tree branches, a cookie bat, and step-by-step instructions that allow even the newest of decorators to replicate him with ease. And if that's not enough, apply your craft to my larger variation with a wicked witch (p. 199).

Makes about 10 (4³⁄₄-inch) compound moon-owl-bat cookies

About 6¹⁄₂ cups (1¹⁄₃ to 1¹⁄₂ recipes) Royal Icing (p. 242), divided

Brown, black, yellow, orange, or other soft-gel food colorings (p. 14) of your choice

Pastry bag fitted with ¹⁄₄-inch round tip (Ateco #10 or #11), for tree branches

About 1 lb 11 ounces (¹⁄₂ to ²⁄₃ recipe) Cutout Cookie Gingerbread (p. 236) or (1 to 1¹⁄₃ recipes) Signature Sugar Cookie Dough (p. 234)

Large (about 4³⁄₄-inch) plain round cookie cutter, for moons

Small (1³⁄₈ x 3¹⁄₄-inch) owl cookie cutter

Small (1¹⁄₂ x 4¹⁄₂-inch) bat cookie cutter

Small (⁷⁄₈-inch) plain round cookie cutter, for supports for owls and bats

Small craft paintbrush (handle about ¹⁄₄-inch diameter)

Parchment pastry cones (p. 13)

Pastry bag fitted with ¹⁄₄-inch leaf tip (Ateco #352), for wing feathers

Small offset spatula (p. 14)

TYPES:

Cutout Cookie Gingerbread (p. 236) or Signature Sugar Cookie Dough (p. 234)

PREP TALK:

Either dough, above, can be used for this project, though I prefer gingerbread or a spiced sugar cookie variation (p. 235) to launch me into this project's Halloween spirit. Be sure to mix and chill the dough as instructed. If packaged in airtight containers at room temperature, this project will stay its best about 1 week. Also, it's best to make the Royal Icing tree branches at least a day before assembly to give them ample time to air-dry.

{ what a hoot, continued }

1. Prepare the Royal Icing as instructed on page 242. Reserve about $5\frac{1}{2}$ cups of the icing: $1\frac{3}{4}$ cups for top-coating the moons, $\frac{1}{2}$ cup for beadwork on the moons, $\frac{3}{4}$ cup for top-coating the owls, $\frac{1}{4}$ cup for top-coating the bats, 1 cup for owl feathers, $\frac{1}{2}$ cup for detailing the owls and bats, $\frac{1}{4}$ cup for reinforcing the owls' necks, and $\frac{1}{2}$ cup for "glue."

2. Make the tree branches. Divide the remaining 1 cup icing in half. Tint one half to a light brown and the other to a dark gray using black food coloring. Adjust the icings, as needed, to make sure they are thick enough to hold their shape when piped through a pastry bag.

Line a cookie sheet with parchment paper. Load the icings side by side in a pastry bag fitted with a $\frac{1}{4}$-inch round tip (Ateco #10 or #11). By loading both icings in the bag at the same time, you'll end up with two-tone branches! Pipe at least 20 (3- to 5-inch) lines on the prepared cookie sheet. For craggy branches, the more irregular the lines, the better. Dry the branches completely, ideally overnight, before assembling with the moons in Step 8. *Note:* Avoid pulling the branches off the paper, as they are fragile and can easily break. Instead, slide a thin-bladed paring knife under each to separate it from the paper.

3. Cut and bake the moons, owls, and bats. On a lightly floured surface, roll the dough to a $\frac{1}{8}$- to $\frac{3}{16}$-inch thickness. Using a $4\frac{3}{4}$-inch round cookie cutter, cut out about 10 moons. If you don't have a wide spatula, cut these cookies directly on prepared cookie sheets to minimize the misshaping that can occur in transferring from work surface to cookie sheet. Cut out the same number of owls and bats (1 of each per moon) and about 40 small ($\frac{7}{8}$-inch) rounds (4 per moon) for cookie supports.

Bake the cookies as directed until lightly browned around the edges, or about 11 to 13 minutes for the moons, 10 to 11 minutes for the owls and bats, and 7 to 10 minutes for the round supports. Cool completely before decorating.

4. Top-coat and detail the moons. Tint the $1\frac{3}{4}$ cups icing reserved for top-coating the moons to a bright yellow; then thin to top-coating consistency (p. 245). Using the handle-end of a craft paintbrush, apply a smooth coat of icing to each moon top. For top-coating technique details, see page 28. Let the icing dry to the touch.

Tint the $\frac{1}{2}$ cup icing reserved for beadwork to a bright orange or another color of your choice; then adjust to the appropriate consistency (p. 245). Fill a parchment pastry bag with the icing and cut a small ($\frac{1}{16}$-inch or more) hole in the tip. Pipe dots around each moon following the instructions for beadwork on page 34. Save the leftover icing for detailing the owls and bats in Step 7.

Let the moons dry thoroughly before assembling in Step 8.

5. Top-coat the owls and bats. Divide the $\frac{3}{4}$ cup icing reserved for top-coating the owls into 2 portions, one about twice the size of the other. Tint the larger portion to a dark brown and leave the other portion white; then thin both portions to top-coating consistency (p. 245). Using the handle-end of a craft paintbrush, apply the white icing in a "V"-shaped area on each owl's chest. Next, apply a smooth coat of the brown icing to each head and body. To minimize bleeding of colors, keep the brown icing from touching the white.

Tint the $\frac{1}{4}$ cup icing reserved for top-coating the bats to a deep black; then thin to top-coating consistency. Apply a smooth coat of icing to each bat.

Let the icings dry to the touch before further decorating.

6. Add feathers to the owls. Tint $\frac{3}{4}$ cup of the icing reserved for owl feathers to match the brown icing used in Step 5. Adjust the consistency, as needed, so it is very thick. Leave the remaining $^1/_4$ cup white and thin to out-lining consistency (p. 244). Transfer the white icing to a parchment pastry cone and cut a small ($^1/_{16}$-inch or more) hole in the tip.

(a) Use the Trailing Beaded Border technique (p. 46) to apply white crests to the tops of the owls' heads and feathery texture to the chests. Let the icing dry to the touch. Save the leftover white icing for use on the bats in Step 7.

b.

a.

Transfer the brown icing to a pastry bag fitted with a $^1/_4$-inch leaf tip (Ateco #352).

(b) Work on one owl at a time. Hold the bag at a 45-degree angle to the cookie with the pointed end of the tip facing up. Starting at the bottom tip of a wing, pipe a feather by applying pressure at the start and then releasing pressure as you pull the bag away from the cookie. Pipe another couple of feathers in a row directly above the first feather, such that the rows of feathers overlap. Continue to add rows of feathers in this fashion until the wing is com-pletely filled. Repeat with the other wing and then with the other owls.

7. Add finishing details to the owls and bats. Divide the $^1/_2$ cup icing for detailing the owls and bats in half. Tint one half yellow and the other black. Adjust both the yellow and black icings to beadwork consistency.

(c) Add a pair of eyeballs (dots) to each owl and bat using the yellow icing and the beadwork technique. Let the eye-balls dry to the touch; then pipe black dots (for pupils) onto the eyeballs, as desired. Use the leftover white out-lining icing from Step 6 to add ears on the bats and spiny details to their wings. Lastly, thicken the leftover orange icing from Step 4 to outlining consistency and add feet and beaks.

c.

8. Assemble the compound moon-owl-bat cookies. Thin the $1/4$ cup icing reserved for reinforcing the owls' necks to top-coating consistency. (If desired, tint it to match the gingerbread to keep slipups from showing.) Using a small offset spatula, spread a thin layer on the back of each owl, especially around the neck where there may be little icing on top of the cookie. (The added icing will keep the necks from sagging or cracking once the owls are mounted on the supports.) Let the icing dry to the touch.

Tint the $1/2$ cup icing reserved for "glue" to a yellow that matches the moons. Work on one moon at a time. Glue 2 to 3 ($7/8$-inch) round support cookies (one on top of the other) close to the bottom of the moon and 1 support cookie near the top. Glue a bat to the top support and a Royal Icing branch on either side of the bottom support. Glue an owl on top of the bottom support and prop as needed until it has dried in place. Repeat to make about 10 compound cookies.

VARIATION
{ Witch Craft }

For a scarier spin, change up the 3-D moon-owl-and-bat vignette (p. 196) by cutting larger (6- to $6 1/4$-inch) round moon cookies and mounting 1 or 2 decorated bat cookies, 1 decorated witch cookie, and a couple of Royal Icing branches on each moon. For the compound witch cookie pictured here, I used a $4 1/2$ x $6 1/2$-inch witch cutter and 6 ($7/8$-inch) rounds for supports. *Note:* Closer to 2 pounds dough is needed to make 6 compound witch cookies of this size; plus, the Royal Icing in Step 1 (p. 197) needs to be increased accordingly.

Pictured from back: *O Christmas Tree, Sleigh Cool, and Snow Honeys (front and back).*

YULETIDE YUMMIES

Okay, I know, I know. Just a few pages ago I said we should make a celebration of cookies year-round. I still stand by those words, but that doesn't mean we shouldn't go all out at Christmastime! Deck your table with any one of these yuletide projects to quickly get in the holiday spirit. Or bundle several together for an unforgettable and supremely tasty winter centerpiece.

snow honeys

CHARM YOUR CHRISTMAS GUESTS WITH THESE DELIGHTFUL HIS-AND-HERS SNOWMEN and women fashioned from Goofproof Macarons (p. 249). I've accessorized these honeys with rolled fondant scarves, top hats, and other decorations. And in the spirit of more is merrier, I've made smaller snow children to complete the happy snow family!

Makes about 10 (2 x 4½-inch) 3-macaron snowmen or about 1¾ dozen (1¾ x 2¾-inch) 2-macaron snow children

2 to 3 ounces dark brown rolled fondant (p. 53) or other modeling medium, for hats, arms, and broomsticks (latter, optional)

12-piece plain round cookie cutter set (Ateco #5457, p. 14)

About 1 ounce (each) red and green rolled fondant or other modeling medium, for hat bands and scarves

Less than ½ ounce orange rolled fondant or other modeling medium, for carrot noses

1 large Shredded Wheat biscuit, for broom heads (optional)

1 recipe Goofproof Macarons (p. 249)

Pastry bag fitted with ½-inch round tip (Ateco #806)

About 1 cup (⅕ to ¼ recipe) Italian Buttercream (p. 257) or (⅔ to 1 recipe) White Chocolate Ganache (p. 259)

About 10 (6-inch) cardboard lollypop sticks (p. 268, optional)

About 1¼ to 1½ cups (¼ to ⅓ recipe) Royal Icing (p. 242), divided; quantity will vary

Stand-in: Snow Balls. *No time to decorate? Simply fill the macarons with Italian Buttercream or Ganache (made with white chocolate), and you've got cookies that pass for little snowballs, especially when presented atop drifts of powdered sugar or an icicle-clear glass plate, as shown here.*

TYPE:

Goofproof Macarons (p. 249)

{ snow honeys, continued }

Parchment pastry cones (p. 13)

Assorted small ($^1/_2$- to $^7/_8$-inch) readymade royal icing embellishments (p. 26), such as wreaths, holly, and/or candles (1 per snowman, optional)

Brown (optional) and other soft-gel food colorings (p. 14) of your choice

Powdered sugar, for display (optional)

PREP TALK:

The egg whites for Goofproof Macarons (the snow balls) must be dehydrated for 20 to 24 hours before baking. Once baked, the macarons may be filled with Italian Buttercream or White Chocolate Ganache up to a few days prior to final assembly. (I like to use light colored fillings to keep the snowmen white through and through.) Since both fillings are perishable, be sure to refrigerate the filled macarons until you're ready to serve. However, for best flavor and texture, bring them to room temperature before serving.

It's also best to shape the hats, arms, carrot noses, and broomsticks, whether made of rolled fondant or another modeling medium, at least a day before assembly to give them ample time to air-dry and firm up. Avoid White Chocolate Dough for the broomsticks and arms; it is relatively heat sensitive and, therefore, less suitable for these slender pieces.

1. Shape the hats, arms, carrot noses, and broomsticks (optional). As noted in "Prep Talk," it's best to make these pieces at least a day ahead. They'll be easier to place on the finished snowmen if firm. Broomsticks may need more time to air-dry, as they must be quite rigid to support the broom heads on top.

To make hats: Follow the instructions on page 54 to roll the brown modeling medium into a thin ($^1/_{16}$-inch) sheet. Cut out about 10 round brims with a $^7/_8$-inch round cookie cutter. Reroll the leftover dough to a $^3/_8$- to $^1/_2$-inch thickness and cut out about 10 ($^1/_2$-inch) round hat tops to fit the brims. Stick the hat tops to the brims with a dab

of water. Finish by wrapping a thin ($^1/_8$-inch-wide) red or green ribbon made of modeling medium around the base of each hat, where it meets the brim. See Ribbons (p. 56) for ribbon making instructions.

To make arms: Follow the instructions for Cords (p. 55) to roll the leftover brown modeling medium into small ($^1/_{16}$ to $^1/_8$ x $1^3/_4$- to 2-inch) cords (2 per snowman) that taper to a point on one end. Attach even smaller twigs to the tapered end of each twig with a dab of water, as desired.

To make carrot noses: Roll the orange modeling medium into small ($^1/_{16}$ x $^3/_4$-inch) cords (1 per snowman) that taper to a point on one end. Trim the nontapered ends to straighten.

Short and Sweet. *(a) Fill three sizes of Goofproof Macarons with Italian Buttercream or White Chocolate Ganache. (b) Decorate the macarons with Royal Icing buttons and faces, carrot noses made of rolled fondant (or another modeling medium), and other readymade royal icing embellishments; then glue the body parts together with thick Royal Icing. (c) Once the icing "glue" is dry, add arms and scarves made of modeling media.*

To make broomsticks (optional): Roll the remaining brown modeling medium into $1/8$ x $3 3/4$- to 4-inch cords. Trim the ends to straighten. Cut a biscuit of Shredded Wheat cereal into small ($3/4$ x $1 1/4$-inch) rectangles (1 per broomstick, for broom heads). Leave one side of the original biscuit intact when cutting, so the broom heads don't fall apart. Let the broomsticks dry thoroughly before applying the broom heads in Step 7.

2. Bake the macarons. Prepare 2 cookie sheets by tracing about 20 ($1 7/8$-inch), 20 ($1 1/2$-inch), and 20 ($7/8$-inch) circles on pieces of parchment paper sized to fit the cookie sheets. Use plain round cookie cutters from the cutter set as your tracing guides. Leave no less than $3/4$ inch between circles and draw like sizes on the same cookie sheet(s). Turn over the papers and secure them to the cookie sheets with a dab of shortening or butter in each corner. *Note:* Turning over the paper keeps the tracing marks from being transferred onto the cookies during baking.

Prepare Goofproof Macarons as instructed. Transfer the batter to a pastry bag fitted with a $1/2$-inch round tip (Ateco #806) and pipe it into the outlines just traced, leaving a little room to spare to allow for spreading. Air-dry the cookies as directed on page 251 and then bake until set but not at all brown. To keep these cookies as white as possible, bake in a slow (275°F) oven from the start, usually about 20 minutes for the $7/8$-inch and $1 1/2$-inch rounds and closer to 25 minutes for the $1 7/8$-inch rounds. But watch the cookies closely, as they can quickly get too dark to pass as snowmen. Cool completely before filling.

3. Fill the macarons. Prepare either Italian Buttercream or White Chocolate Ganache (chilled to piping consistency) and transfer to a pastry bag fitted with a $1/2$-inch round tip (Ateco #806). Turn half of the cookies (in each of the 3 sizes) upside down and pipe a small mound of filling on the back of each cookie. Top each with a macaron of the same size to make about 30 sandwiches, 10 of each size. Refrigerate the macarons in airtight containers until you're ready to decorate in Step 5. They'll be easier to handle if the filling is set up. *Note:* If you'd like to make lollypops of the snowmen, you can also sandwich the macarons around lollypop sticks (3 sandwiches per stick, 1 in each size) as in Cream of the Crop (p. 107). In this case, skip the assembly instructions in Step 6.

4. Prepare the Royal Icing as instructed on page 242. Reserve about $3/4$ cup for snowmen details and $1/4$ cup (optional) for "glue." You can omit the latter if you did not make broomsticks in Step 1.

5. Decorate the snowmen's heads and bodies. Transfer the remaining $1/2$ cup icing to a parchment pastry cone and cut a small ($1/16$-inch or more) hole in the tip. Use the icing as "glue" to fix the hats and noses from Step 1 onto the $7/8$-inch macaron sandwiches, or heads. You can also use readymade royal icing embellishments, such as wreaths and holly, instead of hats or to embellish the hats.

Divide the $3/4$ cup icing reserved for details in half; then tint each portion to a color of your choice. (I usually use black for coal faces and red for buttons.) Thin both portions to beadwork consistency (p. 245) and transfer to separate parchment pastry cones. Cut a small ($1/16$-inch or more) hole in each tip. Apply dots of one color to the $7/8$-inch sandwiches (for faces) and dots of the other color to the $11/2$-inch sandwiches (for buttons). Let the icing dry to the touch before assembling in Step 6.

6. Assemble the snowmen. To make a 3-macaron snowman, arrange a $17/8$-inch sandwich, a $11/2$-inch sandwich, and a $7/8$-inch sandwich in a straight line, from big to small, so that they touch edge to edge; then glue them together at the contact points using the "glue" left over from Step 5. You can also make smaller 2-macaron snow children

by gluing together $11/2$-inch and $7/8$-inch sandwiches in the same fashion. Repeat to make about 10 (3-macaron) snowmen. Let the "glue" dry completely before adding scarves in the next step.

7. Add decorative embellishments. *To add scarves:* Follow the instructions for Plain Ribbons (p. 56) to cut small 10 ($3/8$ to $1/2$ x 7- to 8-inch) ribbons from the leftover red and green modeling media. Cut 10 thinner ($1/8$-inch) ribbons of the same length. Keep the ribbons covered with plastic so they don't dry out while you complete this step. Work on one snowman at a time.

(a) Dampen the back of a thin ribbon with water and fix it to the top of a wider one of contrasting color. Keep water off the top of the ribbons, as it will dry and leave behind unwanted shiny spots! Trim the scarf ends to neaten.

a.

(b) Flip over the double-decker ribbon while still pliable and set an assembled snowman on top. Wrap the ribbon around the snowman's neck and fix it together in the center with a dab of water or leftover Royal Icing.

b.

Repeat Steps (a) and (b) to add scarves to all of the snow-men, as desired.

Stick arms from Step 1 into the icing between the $1^1/_2$-inch sandwich in each snowman.

To finish the broomsticks (optional): Tint the $^1/_4$ cup icing reserved for "glue" in Step 4 to a brown that matches the broomsticks. Use this icing to fix a broom head, reserved in Step 1, to the end of each broomstick. Dry completely before moving.

8. Display (optional). For an extra wintry presentation, perch the snowmen upright in mounds of powdered sugar with broomsticks nearby, as pictured on page 202. Handle the snowmen carefully, ideally with the support of a spatula.

sleigh cool

TIRED OF THE TYPICAL GINGERBREAD HOUSE? Then skip it this year and turn your holiday showpiece into this way cool gingerbread sleigh instead. Drawn by a retinue of cookie reindeer and stuffed with (yes, you guessed it) cookie gifts, penguins, and a Christmas tree, it's even cooler.

Makes about 2 (3⅛ x 9 x 5⅞-inch-tall) sleighs, plus reindeer and assorted cookies to fill sleighs

Custom sleigh template (p. 267)

Ruler or custom rectangular template, for sleigh supports (see Step 1)

About 2 pounds 10 ounces (¾ to 1 recipe) Cutout Cookie Gingerbread (p. 236; *Note:* About 1¼ pounds dough is used for the 2 sleighs alone.)

Large (5½ x 6- to 6½-inch) reindeer cookie cutter

6-cutter plain square cookie cutter set (Ateco #5253, p. 14), for gifts

Assorted (1½- to 5-inch) Christmas cookie cutters, such as trees and penguins, for filling sleighs

1¼-inch plain round cookie cutter, for reindeer pedestals (optional)

About 6¼ cups (1¼ to 1⅓ recipes) Royal Icing (p. 242), divided; quantity will vary

Brown and other soft-gel food colorings (p. 14) of your choice

Parchment pastry cones (p. 13)

Assorted (3 to 6 mm) dragées or sugar beads (p. 26)

Assorted small (½- to 1¼-inch) readymade royal icing and sugar embellishments (p. 26), such as poinsettias and cardinals, for decorating sleighs and reindeer

Stand-in: Props to Powdered Sugar. *Powdered sugar is of course essential to Royal Icing, but did you know that it can also be a timesaver in cookie displays? Here it props a simple 2-D sleigh, allowing the 3-D assembly in Step 5 (p. 212) to be skipped! As for the sleigh cargo? It's standing in a glass of powdered sugar hidden behind the sleigh.*

TYPES:

Cutout Cookie Gingerbread (p. 236); Construction Gingerbread (p. 238) just for sleighs; Signature Sugar Cookie Dough (p. 234) just for small pieces

{ sleigh cool, continued }

Powdered sugar, for display

5 to 6 ounces rolled fondant (p. 53) or
    other modeling medium, color(s)
    of your choice, for reins

PREP TALK:

I prefer the delicacy of Cutout Cookie Gingerbread and Signature Sugar Cookie Dough for the smaller pieces (reindeer, gifts, and trees) of this project. However, for the larger 3-D sleigh, I prefer either Cutout Cookie Gingerbread or Construction Gingerbread. Both doughs spread less than sugar cookie dough, making it less necessary to trim the sleigh pieces after baking; plus, the latter lends extra stability. When all's said and done, I usually use Cutout Cookie Gingerbread for everything to avoid making different doughs. Whatever you do, be sure to mix and chill the doughs as instructed. If packaged in airtight containers at room temperature, this project will stay its best about 1 week.

---

1. Cut and bake the sleigh, reindeer, and other cookies. Start by making a sleigh template using the outline on page 267, and a 2 x 3-inch rectangular template for the sleigh supports. For the latter, you can also use a ruler as a cutting guide. If you plan to make a lot of sleighs, consider making custom cookie cutters; they will save cutting time in the long run. For more information about working with custom templates and cutters, see page 48.

On a lightly floured surface, roll the dough to a $1/8$- to $3/16$-inch thickness. Since the sleigh pieces are relatively large, it's best to cut them directly on prepared cookie sheets to avoid the misshaping that can occur in transferring from work surface to cookie sheet. Using your sleigh template (or custom cutter) as a cutting guide, cut out 4 sleigh pieces (2 per assembled sleigh).

Reroll the leftover dough to the same thickness. Using your rectangular template (or ruler or custom cutter) as a cutting guide, cut out 8 (2 x 3-inch) rectangles (4 per

sleigh) for sleigh supports. Also cut out about 10 reindeer (5 per sleigh) and assorted squares (for gifts) and other Christmas cookies to fill the sleighs. (I usually allow 2 pairs of reindeer, a single reindeer to pose as Rudolph, and 4 to 5 other cookies per sleigh.) As desired, cut out 2 ($1^1/4$-inch) plain rounds per reindeer (10 per sleigh) to serve as pedestals for freestanding reindeer.

Group like-size cookies on the same cookie sheet(s). Bake the cookies as directed until lightly browned around the edges, or about 10 to 11 minutes for the sleighs and 8 to 10 minutes for smaller pieces. Baking time will vary considerably with cookie size. While the cookies are still hot from the oven, trim the sleigh supports and rudders if they've misshapen. Cool completely before outlining and flooding in Step 3.

2. Prepare the Royal Icing as instructed on page 242. Reserve about $2^1/2$ cups for detailing the reindeer, sleighs, and other cookies, and $3/4$ cup for "glue." *Note:* The quantity

Short and Sweet. *(a) Cut out sleigh and rectangular support cookies using custom templates (or custom cutters). (Not pictured: also cut out reindeer and assorted Christmas cookies to fill each sleigh.) (b) Outline and flood the sleigh cookies; dry and then detail with Royal Icing, dragées, sugar beads, and/or readymade royal icing embellishments. (c) Make sleigh bottoms from half of the supports; then assemble 3-D sleighs by using thick Royal Icing to glue matching sleigh cookies and the remaining supports to the bottoms. Prop until dry.*

of icing will vary with the number of colors and consistencies mixed. It's best to allow no less than $1/4$ to $1/2$ cup icing per color or consistency for easiest mixing and handling.

3. Outline and flood the sleigh, reindeer, and other cookies. I typically like to outline and flood these cookies, as opposed to top-coating without any outlines, in order to get the icing as close to the cookie edges as possible. Divide the remaining 3 cups icing into as many portions as you want flooding colors, taking care to scale the portions to the size of the cookies they'll decorate. For instance, I usually allot about $1 1/4$ cups icing for the sleighs and, again, no less than $1/4$ to $1/2$ cup icing per color. Tint each portion to a color of your choice. (Don't forget red and green for Christmas!)

Thin each portion to outlining consistency (p. 244) and transfer to separate parchment pastry cones. Cut a small ($1/16$-inch or more) hole in each tip and proceed to outline each cookie following the instructions for outlining on page 29. Thin the leftover icings to flooding consistency (p. 245) and then flood the interior of each outlined cookie with the same color used to outline it. You can also use the same outlining and flooding techniques to apply multiple colors to a single cookie, as shown on the cookies on page 208. Simply use the outlining colors to delineate the areas of the cookie that should contain different colors; then flood each area with the corresponding color. Let the icing dry to the touch before detailing in Step 4. *Note:* I chose to decorate the front-facing sides of each sleigh cookie pictured on page 208, however if you'd prefer to decorate the front and back views of the sleigh instead, then flip over one sleigh cookie in each pair and decorate its underside instead.

4. Detail the sleigh, reindeer, and other cookies. These cookies can be styled in countless ways, which is always the fun of cookie decorating, isn't it?! However, as a general rule, I like to decorate the sleigh and reindeer cookies in identical matched pairs, since they'll be assembled in duos in Step 5. I've allotted $2 1/2$ cups icing for this task, but, again, the quantity will vary widely with the factors noted in Step 2.

Remember to adjust the icing to the proper consistency for your chosen decorating task. For example, I used icing of outlining consistency (p. 244) for the delicate white scrollwork on the upper edge of the sleigh carriage and also along the rudder; whereas I used thick icing "glue" to attach the dragées, sugar beads, and readymade royal icing poinsettias around the carriage door.

5. Assemble the reindeer (optional) and sleighs. Tint about $1/2$ cup of the icing reserved for "glue" to a brown that matches the gingerbread. (The "glue" will be less likely to show this way.) For freestanding reindeer, tint the remaining $1/4$ cup "glue" to match the icing on the round pedestals. Transfer the icings to separate parchment pastry cones and cut a relatively large ($1/8$-inch or more) hole in each tip.

For freestanding reindeer (optional): Use the $1/4$ cup "glue" to stand each reindeer on 2 round pedestals (1 pedestal per foot).

For each sleigh: Use the $1/2$ cup brown "glue" to secure 2 (2 x 3-inch) supports on top of one another. Stand up 1 sleigh cookie and attach it to the longer side of the double-decker support; then glue 2 more supports onto each of the shorter sides. Lastly, glue a second sleigh cookie to the remaining long side to form a closed chamber. If needed, shave the support cookies with a paring knife to ensure the best fit.

Prop both the reindeer and sleighs until the icing is dry. Repeat to make another sleigh and reindeer retinue.

6. Add reins and display. Arrange a sleigh, 2 reindeer pairs, and Rudolph on a bed of powdered sugar snow. (If the reindeer are not freestanding, prop them with the sugar.) Connect the reindeer to one another with thin ribbons of rolled fondant or another modeling medium, as pictured on page 208. See Plain Ribbons (p. 56) for ribbon making instructions. For the finishing touch, tuck decorated gift packages and other Christmas cookies inside the sleigh. Repeat to make another display, or enjoy the remaining cookies immediately!

boughs of holly

A PLATTER OF CHRISTMAS COOKIES IS DE RIGUEUR DURING THE HOLIDAY SEASON, but you can bet few have seen a cookie collection as festive as this. Here, cookie holly leaves and macaron berries are gathered into an edible wreath that can deck your halls either lying down as a centerpiece or hanging up as shown on page 214.

Makes about 3 (11 to 12 x 13- to 15-inch) wreaths

10-inch round custom template (or cake pan or bowl)

About 1 pound 8 ounces ($^1/_2$ recipe) Construction Gingerbread (p. 238), for support rings

Large ($4^3/_4$- to 5-inch) plain round cookie cutter

About 2 pounds ($^2/_3$ recipe) Cutout Cookie Gingerbread (p. 236) or ($1^1/_3$ recipes) Signature Sugar Cookie Dough (p. 234), for holly leaves and bows

Assorted ($1^1/_4$ x 2-inch to $2^1/_8$ x $3^3/_4$-inch) holly cookie cutters

Custom templates (p. 263), for bow ribbons

2 x $3^1/_8$-inch teardrop cookie cutter, for bow loops

About 8 cups ($1^2/_3$ to $1^3/_4$ recipes) Royal Icing (p. 242), divided

Green, red (optional), and other soft-gel food colorings (p. 14) of your choice

Small craft paintbrush (handle about $^1/_4$-inch diameter)

2 to 3 (8 x 11-inch) sheets printed wafer paper (p. 26), pattern(s) of your choice, for decorating bows (optional)

Small sponge brush, for decorating bows (optional)

Stand-in: Kiss and Tell. *Short on time? Make small mistletoe kissing balls instead. Use Royal Icing "glue" to attach tiny ($^3/_8$- to $1^1/_4$-inch) teardrop cookies (for leaves) and white sugar beads (for berries) to top-coated 4- to $4^1/_2$-inch cookie disks. Mount pairs of decorated cookie disks back to back with a piece of ribbon in between. Once the icing is dry, hang a ball or two over the nearest threshold. Oh, and don't forget to demand a kiss in exchange for any decorating tips!*

TYPES:

Construction Gingerbread (p. 238) for supports;

Cutout Cookie Gingerbread (p. 236) or Signature Sugar Cookie Dough (p. 234) for holly leaves and bows;

Goofproof Macarons (p. 249, optional) for berries

{ boughs of holly, continued }

A few tablespoons light corn syrup, for decorating bows (optional)

Parchment pastry cones (p. 13)

1/2 recipe Goofproof Macarons (p. 249), for berries (optional; *Note:* Or substitute 1/2-inch red gumballs.)

Pastry bag fitted with 1/4-inch round tip (Ateco #10 or #11), for berries (optional)

1/4 cup Ganache (p. 259), Italian Buttercream (p. 257), or Royal Icing, for filling berries (optional)

3 large (3/4-inch) gumballs, for decorating bows

Large (6 to 8 mm) dragées or sugar beads (p. 26)

PREP TALK:

Since it's the least fragile of my rolled cookie doughs, Construction Gingerbread is best used for the rings that support each wreath. However, I prefer the delicacy of either Cutout Cookie Gingerbread or Signature Sugar Cookie Dough for the holly leaves and bows. Be sure to mix and chill the doughs as instructed.

The egg whites for Goofproof Macarons (optional berries) must be dehydrated for 20 to 24 hours before baking. Once baked, the macarons may be filled with Ganache or Italian Buttercream up to a few days prior to serving. Since both fillings are perishable, be sure to refrigerate the filled macarons until you're ready to eat. To avoid refrigeration, the macarons can be filled with Royal Icing, or gumballs can be used instead. Wreaths topped as such will be their best up to 1 week if stored in airtight containers.

---

1. Cut and bake the support rings. Following the instructions for custom templates (p. 48), make a 10-inch circle template. Alternatively, you can use a cake pan or bowl as a cutting guide. If you plan to make a lot of wreaths, consider making a custom cookie cutter; it will save cutting time in the long run. For more information about working with custom templates and cutters, see page 48.

On a lightly floured surface, roll the dough to a 1/8- to 3/16-inch thickness. Since these supports are very large, it's best to cut them directly on prepared cookie sheets to avoid the misshaping that can occur in transferring from work surface to cookie sheet. Cut out a 10-inch circle using your template (or pan or bowl) as a cutting guide. Cut a 4 3/4- to 5-inch round out of the center of the 10-inch

circle to leave behind a ring about 2 1/2 to 2 5/8 inches wide. Reroll the leftover dough (including that cut from the center) and repeat to make 3 support rings (1 per cookie sheet). Bake as directed until lightly browned around the edges, or about 15 to 20 or more minutes, depending on the thickness of the dough.

2. Cut and bake the holly leaves and bows. Set aside about 6 ounces of the 2 pounds dough for bows. On a lightly floured surface, roll the remaining dough to a 1/8- to 3/16-inch thickness. Cut out holly leaves in assorted sizes. (Variety will make for more interesting wreaths.) I usually use about 20 medium (1 3/4 x 2 1/4-inch) to large (2 1/8 x 3 3/4-inch) leaves and 10 to 12 small (1 1/4 x 2-inch) leaves on each of the 3 wreaths. Bake as directed until lightly

Short and Sweet. *(a) Top-coat a large ring cookie (the wreath support); also, top-coat and outline assorted sizes of holly cookies. (b) Use thick Royal Icing to glue the holly leaves onto the ring, along with a cookie bow (cut from custom templates and wafer-papered, as desired). Prop the bow until its pieces dry in place. (c) Glue berries made with Goofproof Macarons and large dragées or sugar beads onto the wreath. Finish the center of the bow with a large gumball.*

browned around the edges, or about 7 to 9 minutes for the small leaves and 10 to 12 minutes for the larger leaves.

Make 2 different templates for the bow ribbons using the 2 outlines (long and short) on page 263 and the instructions for making templates on page 48. Again, if you plan to make a lot of wreaths, consider making custom cookie cutters (p. 49). Roll the reserved dough (6 ounces) to the same thickness as above and cut out 6 bow ribbons (3 in each length) using the templates as cutting guides; then cut out 6 (2 x $3^1/_8$-inch) teardrops (2 per wreath) for bow loops. Bake as directed until lightly browned around the edges, or about 10 to 12 minutes. Watch these pieces carefully, as the tips of the ribbons tend to brown very quickly. Cool all cookies completely before decorating.

3. Prepare the Royal Icing as instructed on page 242. Reserve about $1^1/_2$ cups for outlining the holly leaves and bows and $1/_2$ cup for "glue."

4. Top-coat the holly leaves, supports, and bows. Portion off about 1 cup of the remaining 6 cups icing. Tint this portion, as desired, and thin to top-coating consistency (p. 245). (This icing will be used for the bows. I usually leave it white if wafer-papering the bows in Step 5.) Divide the remaining 5 cups icing in half. Tint one half to a dark holly green and the other to a light green. Thin both portions to top-coating consistency.

Using the handle-end of a craft paintbrush, apply a smooth coat of green icing to the holly cookies. (I usually top-coat half of the holly cookies with the dark green and the other half with the light green). Likewise, top-coat the 3 wreath supports with green icing, and the bow loops and ribbons with the reserved white (or other) icing. For top-coating technique details, see page 28.

If wafer-papering the bows in Step 5, let them dry completely, ideally overnight. Otherwise, let them dry to the touch before proceeding to Step 6.

5. Apply wafer paper to bows (optional). Cut out wafer paper to fit the top coats on the bow loops and ribbons. Work on one cookie at a time. Use a small sponge brush to spread a thin layer of corn syrup on the cookie top coat; then gently press a matching piece of wafer paper on top. Repeat to paper all 12 pieces that make up the 3 bows. Dry about 1 hour before applying borders in the next step. For more wafer-papering details, see page 38.

6. Outline the holly leaves and bows. Divide the $1^1/2$ cups icing reserved for outlining into thirds; tint two of the portions to match the colors mixed in Step 4 (i.e., dark green and light green). Tint the third portion to contrast the top coats (or wafer paper) on the bows. Thin the icings to outlining consistency (p. 244) and transfer to separate parchment pastry cones. Cut a relatively large ($1/8$-inch or more) hole in each tip. Outline the dark green holly leaves with the light green icing and the light green holly leaves with the dark green icing; then outline the bow pieces with the icing reserved for that purpose.

7. Make and fill the macaron berries (optional). If you'd rather use gumballs for berries, proceed to Step 8. Otherwise, prepare $1/2$ recipe Goofproof Macarons as instructed, except tint the batter by adding about 12 drops red food coloring at the end of Step 3 (p. 250). Using a pastry bag fitted with a $1/4$-inch round tip (Ateco #10

or #11), pipe about 120 ($1/2$-inch) rounds onto prepared cookie sheets. Air-dry the rounds as instructed on page 251; then bake about 10 minutes. Cool before filling. *Note: $1/2$ recipe will make many more macarons than needed, but it's difficult to mix the batter in any smaller quantity. Save any extra macarons for snacking!*

Using a pastry bag fitted with a $1/4$-inch round tip (Ateco #10 or #11), pipe a small mound of Ganache (chilled to piping consistency), Italian Buttercream, or Royal Icing onto the flat side of half of the macarons. Top each icing mound with another macaron to make about 60 sandwiches (aka berries), or 20 per wreath. Again, you will have leftover icing. Use it to fill the macaron surplus, above.

8. Assemble the wreaths. Tint the $1/2$ cup icing reserved for "glue" to a green that coordinates with the leaves. (Green "glue" will be less likely to show against green cookies!)

Work on one wreath at a time. Cluster 2 bow loops and 2 bow ribbons (of different lengths) at the bottom of a wreath support so that the narrowest ends of each piece meet in the center. Fix the pieces in place with the "glue," and prop, if needed, while the "glue" dries. Conceal the point at which the pieces meet with a $3/4$-inch gumball. Attach the holly leaves around the bow and wreath support, alternating colors of leaves as you go. Glue macaron or gumball berries (again, about 20 per wreath) and dragées or sugar beads on top of the wreath in small clusters. Repeat to make 2 more wreaths. Let the icing dry completely before moving the wreaths.

COMPLEXITY 2

snow globes

WITH NAME DROPPER VARIATION

A FLURRY OF SNOWFLAKE CONFETTI, SANDING SUGAR, AND NONPAREILS ADDS SPARKLE to these fun yuletide favors. You can make your own Royal Icing figures for the central vignettes or, to avoid the holiday rush, use readymade decorations as pictured left.

Makes 6 ($2^{1}/_{2}$ x $4^{1}/_{8}$ x $4^{1}/_{2}$-inch-tall) snow globes

About 1 pound 5 ounces ($^{1}/_{2}$ recipe) Cutout Cookie Gingerbread (p. 236) or (1 recipe) Signature Sugar Cookie Dough (p. 234)

12-piece fluted round cookie cutter set (Ateco #5407, p. 14)

12-piece plain round cookie cutter set (Ateco #5457, p. 14)

About 3 cups ($^{2}/_{3}$ recipe) Royal Icing (p. 242), divided; quantity will vary

Soft-gel food colorings (p. 14) of your choice

Small craft paintbrush (handle about $^{1}/_{4}$-inch diameter)

Parchment pastry cones (p. 13)

A few tablespoons sanding sugar, nonpareils, and/or edible glitter (p. 26)

Assorted small ($^{1}/_{2}$- to $1^{1}/_{4}$-inch) readymade royal icing embellishments (p. 26), such as santas, snowmen, penguins, and Christmas trees, for central vignettes

Snowflake sugar confetti (p. 26)

Assorted (2 to 3 mm) dragées or sugar beads (p. 26)

Pastry bag fitted with tip of your choice, for borders

TYPES:

Cutout Cookie Gingerbread (p. 236) or Signature Sugar Cookie Dough (p. 234)

PREP TALK:

Either dough, above, works well for this small-scale 3-D construction project. Just be sure to mix and chill the dough as instructed. If packaged in airtight containers at room temperature, this project will stay its best about 1 week.

{ snow globes, continued }

1. Cut and bake the snow globe pieces. Each snow globe will be comprised of 4 cookies: 1 (3^1/$_2$-inch) plain round cookie for the central vignette, 2 (4^1/$_8$-inch) fluted rounds (the first cut into a ring to frame the central vignette; the other left solid to reinforce the back of the vignette), and 1 (2^1/$_2$-inch) fluted round for the base.

On a lightly floured surface, roll the dough to a ^{1}/$_8$- to ^{3}/$_{16}$-inch thickness. Start by cutting out the 4^1/$_8$-inch fluted rounds and rings. It's best to cut the latter directly on prepared cookie sheets to minimize the misshaping that can occur in transferring from work surface to cookie sheet. Cut out 12 rounds with the 4^1/$_8$-inch fluted cutter; then cut out a window in the center of half of the rounds using a 2^7/$_8$-inch plain round cutter. Reroll the remaining dough to the same thickness and cut out 6 (3^1/$_2$-inch) plain rounds and 6 (2^1/$_2$-inch) fluted rounds. Group like-size cookies on the same cookie sheet.

Bake as directed until lightly browned around the edges, or about 9 to 11 minutes for the 4^1/$_8$-inch rings (or frames) and 2^1/$_2$-inch rounds, and 11 to 13 minutes for the 3^1/$_2$-inch and 4^1/$_8$-inch rounds. Cool completely before decorating.

2. Prepare the Royal Icing as instructed on page 242. Reserve about ^{1}/$_2$ cup for beadwork, ^{1}/$_2$ cup for "glue," ^{1}/$_4$ cup for flocking (aka sanding), and ^{1}/$_2$ cup for inner borders on the rings. *Note:* The quantity of icing will vary with the number of colors and consistencies mixed. It's best to allow no less than ^{1}/$_4$ to ^{1}/$_2$ cup icing per color or consistency for easiest mixing and handling.

3. Top-coat the bases, central vignettes, and rings. Divide the remaining 1^1/$_4$ cups icing into as many portions as you want top-coating colors. For this quantity of icing, I limit the colors to three: pale blue for sky and white for snow on the central vignettes (3^1/$_2$-inch rounds), and another color, such as red or green, for the bases and the 4^1/$_8$-inch rings. (*Note:* It isn't necessary to top-coat the solid 4^1/$_8$-inch rounds; they will be used as props to keep the vignettes from leaning and will not be seen in the final construction.) Thin each portion to top-coating consistency (p. 245).

Using the handle-end of a craft paintbrush, apply a smooth coat of icing to each cookie top. For top-coating technique details, see page 28. As noted earlier, I usually ice the bottom halves of the 3^1/$_2$-inch rounds in white and the top halves in blue, for snow and sky. For greater control over the placement of these icings, outline each area first and then flood inside, as pictured in "Short and Sweet." Let the icing dry until very firm.

4. Add dots to the outer rings and bases. Tint the ^{1}/$_2$ cup icing reserved for beadwork to a color that complements the top-coating colors; then thin to the proper consistency (p. 245). Transfer the icing to a parchment pastry cone and cut a small (^{1}/$_{16}$-inch or more) hole in the tip. Pipe small dots around the outside edge of each 2^1/$_2$-inch base and each 4^1/$_8$-inch ring following the instructions for beadwork on page 34. (Alternatively, choose a different border from among those listed in "7 Essential Piping Techniques," p. 46.) Let the icing dry to the touch.

5. Frame and create central vignettes. Use the ^{1}/$_2$ cup icing reserved for "glue" to tack a ring onto each 3^1/$_2$-inch round, taking care to center the rings on top.

Create a holiday-themed vignette inside each ring by flocking (aka sanding) areas with sanding sugar, nonpareils, and/or edible glitter and then gluing readymade royal icing embellishments, snowflake confetti, and/or dragées or sugar beads on top. *Note:* I usually flock the bottom half of each round with white nonpareils and edible glitter to mimic snow. To flock, thin the ^{1}/$_4$ cup icing reserved for this purpose to top-coating consistency and spread a thin layer on the area to be flocked. Sprinkle nonpareils or

Short and Sweet. *(a) Top-coat (or outline and flood) the cookies for the central vignettes, bases, and rings. Add Royal Icing dots or other borders to the edges of the bases and rings. (b) Glue a ring around each central vignette cookie with thick Royal Icing. Use an assortment of readymade royal icing embellishments, sugar confetti, and other decorations to create a wintry picture within each ring. Reinforce the back of each vignette with another round cookie. (c) Pipe a border on the inner edge of each ring. Use thick Royal Icing to stand up each vignette on a cookie base. Prop until dry.*

sanding sugar over the wet icing and shake off the excess into a bowl. For more flocking technique details, see page 42. Lastly, glue a solid $4^1/_8$-inch round to the back of each $3^1/_2$-inch round so that the $4^1/_8$-inch ring and the $4^1/_8$-inch round line up.

6. Add borders to the inner rings. Tint the $^1/_2$ cup icing reserved for inner ring borders to a color of your choice and choose a border style from among those listed on page 46. Adjust the icing to the appropriate consistency for your border and transfer to a parchment pastry cone or pastry bag fitted with the right tip. Proceed to pipe a border around the inner edge of each ring. *Note:* I piped a Trailing Star Border (p. 47) with thick icing and a pastry bag fitted with a $^1/_4$-inch star tip (Ateco #18 or #27).

7. Assemble the snow globes. Work on one snow globe at a time. Glue a framed cookie vignette upright to the center of a cookie base using as little icing "glue" as possible to keep it from showing. Prop the vignette, as needed, until the "glue" is dry. Repeat to assemble 6 snow globes in total. Do not move until completely dry.

VARIATION
{ Name Dropper }

Snow globes can go from frivolous favor to polished place card simply by swapping the readymade royal icing figures for mini roses and names printed on wafer paper. Here, I've used an elegant script font called Eutemia I, flowers from fancyflours.com, and Royal Icing leaves piped with a $^1/_4$-inch leaf tip (Ateco #352).

o christmas tree

WHILE YOU MAY HAVE SEEN MY COOKIE CHRISTMAS TREES IN *COOKIE SWAP,* I've taken these trees to new heights by adding gingerbread trunks. The trunks not only make the trees taller, but also leave more room for decorating the branches with royal icing poinsettias, dragées, sugar birds, cookie stars. . . the sky's the limit!

Makes about 5 (5¼ x 11-inch-tall) Christmas trees

About 2 pounds 11 ounces (2 recipes) Signature Sugar Cookie Dough (p. 234), for branches and treetop stars

Green, yellow, brown, or other soft-gel food colorings (p. 14) of your choice

6-piece star cookie cutter set (Ateco #7805, p. 14), for upper branches

2 large (5¼-inch and 4½-inch) star cookie cutters, for lower branches

Small (1⅛-inch) star cookie cutter, for treetops and treetop stars

About 1 pound 4 ounces (⅓ to ½ recipe) Cutout Cookie Gingerbread (p. 236), for trunks

12-piece plain round cookie cutter set (Ateco #5457, p. 14)

1 standard pastry tip (i.e., Ateco #10), for cutting ¹¹/₁₆-inch rounds

About 7 cups (1½ recipes) Royal Icing (p. 242), divided

Small offset spatula (p. 14)

Parchment pastry cones (p. 13)

Pastry bag fitted with ¼-inch leaf tip (Ateco #352)

Stand-in: See the Forest for the Trees. *You'll be able to make a veritable forest of trees quite quickly if you stick to smaller trees (foreground and right) crafted with fewer pairs of branches and a single cookie trunk between the pairs. For an additional timesaver, skip the icing on the cookie edges and let the green-tinted Signature Sugar Cookie Dough stand on its own (foreground).*

TYPES:

Signature Sugar Cookie Dough (p. 234) for branches;

Cutout Cookie Gingerbread (p. 236) for trunks

{ o christmas tree, continued }

Pastry bag fitted with $^{11}/_{16}$-inch
    basketweave tip (Ateco #895)

Large (6 to 8mm) dragées or
    sugar beads (p. 26)

Assorted small ($^1/_2$- to $1^1/_4$-inch) readymade
    royal icing or sugar embellishments
    (p. 26), such as poinsettias and
    cardinals, for decorating trees

Assorted ($^1/_2$- to $^3/_4$-inch) gumballs,
    for treetops (optional)

PREP TALK:

Either dough in "Types" is suitable for the relatively small pieces that comprise this large 3-D construction project. However, I like to use Signature Sugar Cookie Dough for the star cookies (branches) because it can be tinted green. For the round cookies (trunks), I prefer Cutout Cookie Gingerbread, again for reasons of color. Be sure to mix and chill the doughs as instructed. If packaged in airtight containers at room temperature, this project will stay its best about 1 week.

---

1. Cut and bake the branches (or star cookies). Prepare the Signature Sugar Cookie Dough as instructed. Portion off about 1 ounce and set it aside for use in Step 2. Tint the remaining dough by beating in green food coloring in Step 4 (p. 235). I typically add about 20 drops food coloring to each batch of dough to get the dark hues shown on page 222.

On a lightly floured surface, roll the dough to a $^1/_8$- to $^3/_{16}$-inch thickness. For each of 5 trees, cut out 2 stars in each of the following 9 sizes using the full range of cutters in the star cutter set, as well as the large and small star cutters indicated on page 223: $5^1/_4$ inches (measured tip to tip), $4^1/_2$ inches, $3^1/_2$ inches, $3^3/_{16}$ inches, $2^{13}/_{16}$ inches, $2^1/_2$ inches, 2 inches, $1^3/_4$ inches, and $1^1/_8$ inches. (*Note:* I use the $1^1/_8$-inch star cutter from the Ateco #4848 aspic cutter set.) You should end up with 18 star cookies per tree, or $7^1/_2$ dozen stars in total.

Bake the cookies as directed until barely browned around the edges, or about 6 to 7 minutes for the smallest ($1^1/_8$-inch) stars and closer to 10 to 12 minutes for the larger ($5^1/_4$-inch and $4^1/_2$-inch) stars. Watch the cookies closely; I like to bake them slightly less than usual to avoid turning

their lovely green hue to brown. Cool completely before reinforcing the backs in Step 5.

2. Cut and bake the treetop stars. Tint the 1 ounce dough reserved in Step 1 by working in about 5 drops yellow (or other) food coloring. Roll the dough as instructed in Step 1 and cut out about 10 stars (2 per tree) using the small ($1^1/_8$-inch) star cookie cutter. Bake as directed in Step 1.

3. Cut and bake the trunks (or round cookies). On a lightly floured surface, roll the Cutout Cookie Gingerbread to a $^1/_8$- to $^3/_{16}$-inch thickness. For each of 5 trees, cut out the following number of round cookies using cutters in the plain round cutter set, as well as the wide end of a standard pastry tip for the $^{11}/_{16}$-inch rounds: 8 ($1^7/_8$-inch), 4 ($1^1/_2$-inch), 4 ($1^1/_4$-inch), 4 ($^7/_8$-inch), and 4 ($^{11}/_{16}$-inch) rounds. Bake the cookies as directed until lightly browned around the edges, or about 7 to 12 minutes, depending on cookie size. Cool completely before assembling in Steps 8 and 9.

4. Prepare the Royal Icing as instructed on page 242. Reserve about $^1/_2$ cup for "glue" for the treetop stars and tree branches, $2^3/_4$ cups for pine needles, $1^1/_2$ cups for

Short and Sweet. *(a) Bake star cookies in graduated sizes for each tree. Reinforce the backs of the stars with Royal Icing. (b) Use thick Royal Icing to glue like-size stars together in pairs. Pipe pine needles on the cookie edges with a small leaf tip. Glue large gingerbread rounds together to form tree trunks and add brown Royal Icing bark with a basketweave tip. (c) Glue alternating layers of star pairs and gingerbread rounds on top of the tree trunks. Move from the biggest star pair at the bottom to the smallest at the top. Trim finished trees with dragées, sugar beads, and/or readymade royal icing decorations.*

bark, and another $1^1/2$ cups for "glue" for stacking trees and adding decorations. You may not use all of this icing, but it's helpful to fill your pastry cones and bags relatively full to provide ample hand clearance when assembling and decorating the trees.

5. Reinforce the branches. Because the tree branches (star cookies) won't be fully top-coated, it's best to reinforce their backs with a thin layer of Royal Icing to keep them from sagging or cracking under humid conditions and at the pressure points where the branches meet the trunks. To reinforce, simply tint the remaining $^3/4$ cup icing to a green that matches the branches (you'll be less likely to see any mistakes this way) and thin to top-coating consistency (p. 245). Using a small offset spatula, spread a thin layer of icing on the back of each star cookie. Let the icing dry to the touch.

6. Stack the treetop stars and branches in pairs. Start by making 5 treetop cookie stars by gluing the yellow stars made in Step 2 back to back using a small portion of the $^1/2$ cup icing reserved for this purpose.

Tint the remaining "glue" for the tree branches to a green that matches those cookies. Transfer the icing to a parchment pastry cone and cut a relatively large ($^1/8$-inch or more) hole in the tip. Glue like-size pairs of stars together so that the cookies are offset to one another. For each tree, you should have a pair of each of the 9 stars cut in Step 1.

7. Add pine needles to the branches. Tint the $2^3/4$ cups icing reserved for pine needles to a dark pine green (or other shade). Adjust the icing, as needed. It should be thick enough to hold its shape when piped through a pastry bag fitted with a $^1/4$-inch leaf tip (Ateco #352). Pipe leaves (aka needles) around the edges of the star pairs assembled in Step 6. Continue to add leaves in the inner parts of the stars, if desired, but be sure to leave room in their centers to later attach the cookie trunks. Let the icing dry completely before assembling the branches with the trunks in Step 9.

8. Assemble the trunks and add bark. Tint the 1^1/$_2$ cups icing reserved for bark to a dark brown. Adjust the icing, as needed; it should remain "glue"-like. To make a trunk, glue 8 (1^7/$_8$-inch) plain round cookies together in a stack. Repeat to make 4 more trunks. (*Note:* To vary the heights of the trees, make shorter 4- and 6-cookie trunks, as desired.) Let the icing set.

Transfer the leftover brown icing to a pastry bag fitted with a ^{11}/$_{16}$-inch basketweave tip (Ateco #895). Before adding the icing bark, set each trunk on a small piece of parchment paper-lined cardboard. The cardboard makes it easy to rotate the trunk while icing; plus, the trunk will more readily slide off lined (vs. unlined) cardboard once it is dry. Work on one trunk at a time. Hold the pastry tip ridge side up and pipe bands of icing from the top of the trunk to the bottom, and extending onto the parchment paper to mimic roots. Continue all the way around the trunk until its sides are completely covered. Before the icing dries, level any icing on the top of the trunk with your finger or a paring knife. This way, your tree branches are more likely to sit level on the trunk in the final assembly. Repeat to add bark to the 4 remaining trunks.

9. Assemble the branches with the trunks. Tint the 1^1/$_2$ cups "glue" reserved for stacking the trees to a green that matches the tree branches. Transfer the icing to a parchment pastry cone and cut a relatively large (1/8-inch or more) hole in the tip.

You can make any tree configuration from the star pairs and disks already prepped, but the configuration described here is for the biggest (11-inch-tall) trees pictured on page 222. Feel free to begin tree assembly while the trunks are still drying. However, if the trees seem too wobbly at any point, allow more drying time between layers. In a nutshell, order the star pairs from largest at the bottom to smallest at the top and separate each star pair with 2 appropriately sized gingerbread rounds, using the "glue" to hold the cookies to each other. More specifically, for each tree, glue a pair of 5^1/$_4$-inch stars to the top of a tree trunk; then add trunk pieces and pairs of stars in the following quantities and order: 2 (1^1/$_2$-inch) rounds, 1 (4^1/$_2$-inch) star pair, 2 (1^1/$_2$-inch) rounds, 1 (3^1/$_2$-inch) star pair, 2 (1^1/$_4$-inch) rounds, 1 (3^3/$_{16}$-inch) star pair, 2 (1^1/$_4$-inch) rounds, 1 (2^{13}/$_{16}$-inch) star pair, 2 (^{7}/$_8$-inch) rounds, 1 (2^1/$_2$-inch) star pair, 2 (^{7}/$_8$-inch) rounds, 1 (2-inch) star pair, 2 (^{11}/$_{16}$-inch) rounds, 1 (1^3/$_4$-inch) star pair, 2 (^{11}/$_{16}$-inch) rounds, and 1 (1^1/$_8$-inch) star pair. Repeat to make 4 more big trees.

10. Decorate the trees. As is usually the case with decorating cookies, the styling options here are limitless. Use the leftover "glue" from Step 9 to adorn the tree branches with dragées, sugar beads, and/or readymade royal icing or sugar do-dads. Whatever you do, don't forget to finish each treetop with one of the yellow stars assembled in Step 6 or a gumball, if preferred. *Note:* To stand a star on end, it's easiest to prop it from the back with a 6mm to 8mm dragée or sugar bead.

Dry the trees completely before moving off the cardboards. If the trees don't readily slide off, run a thin-bladed paring knife under the icing to separate it from the parchment paper. To avoid breakage, it's best to slide (rather than lift) the trees into position and to always handle them from their trunks.

counting the days

WHAT COULD BE MORE FUN THAN COUNTING DOWN THE HOLIDAYS WITH COOKIES? While this garland may look purely decorative, it also functions practically as an advent calendar with an ornament cookie for each of the 25 days of Christmas. To reveal the surprises stamped on the cookies, family and friends must pluck out and eat the central cookie numbers. (Oh, darn!)

Makes about 1 (25-ornament) garland with 2½- to 5-inch cookies; yield will vary considerably with cookie size

---

About 2 pounds 14 ounces (1 recipe) Cutout Cookie Gingerbread (p. 236) or (2 recipes) Signature Sugar Cookie Dough (p. 234)

Assorted cookie cutter sets (i.e., Ateco #5407, #7805, #5253, #5234, p. 14), or other 2½- to 5-inch cookie cutters of your choice

Assorted (1½- to 2¼-inch) plain round or other cookie cutters, for cutting windows

About 8¼ cups (1⅔ to 1¾ recipes) Royal Icing (p. 242), divided; quantity will vary

Black and other soft-gel food colorings (p. 14) of your choice

Parchment pastry cones (p. 13)

Small craft paintbrush (handle about ¼-inch diameter)

A few (8 x 11-inch) sheets plain wafer paper (p. 26), for printing numbers and messages (optional)

Food-safe marking pens (p. 26, optional)

1⅛- to 1½-inch round or other craft paper punch (optional)

Small sponge brush (optional)

A few tablespoons light corn syrup (optional)

Stand-in: Ornament-al Treat. *Don't want to string out this project? Then skip the garlands and central cookie numbers, and make a few stylish Christmas ornaments, like this one, instead.*

TYPES:

Cutout Cookie Gingerbread (p. 236) or Signature

Sugar Cookie Dough (p. 234)

{ counting the days, continued }

Rubber stamps of your choice, sized to fit 1$\frac{1}{2}$- to 2$\frac{1}{4}$-inch cookie cutters, above

Un-inked felt or foam ink pad (p. 24)

Pastry bag fitted with tip of your choice, for borders

8 to 12$\frac{1}{2}$ yards ribbon, for ornament ties

A few yards garland, for stringing ornaments

PREP TALK:

Either dough in "Types" works well for this project. Just be sure to mix and chill the dough as instructed. If packaged in airtight containers at room temperature, this project will stay its best about 1 week.

---

1. Cut and bake the ornament pieces. Each of the 25 ornaments on the garland will be comprised of 1 cookie frame, 1 backing cookie mounted behind the frame (with a surprise design on it), and 1 window cutout that fits the frame. The frames can be cut in any shape, though I often keep them simple by using the largest cutters in various cookie cutter sets. Assorted Christmas cookies cutters, such as stars, trees, and snowmen, also work well. To ensure a yield close to that indicated on page 227, size the frames and backing cookies to about 2$\frac{1}{2}$ to 5 inches and cut an even mix of cookies in this range.

On a lightly floured surface, roll the dough to a $\frac{1}{8}$- to $\frac{3}{16}$-inch thickness. Cut out 25 large cookies (in sizes indicated above) and transfer to prepared cookie sheets. Use smaller (1$\frac{1}{2}$- to 2$\frac{1}{4}$-inch) plain round or other cutters to cut a window in each cookie. Remove the window cutouts to leave behind large frames. (*Note:* It's best to cut out the windows directly on the cookie sheets; otherwise the frames can misshape in transferring from work surface to cookie sheet.) Place the cutouts on another prepared cookie sheet. Cut out another 25 backing cookies to match the frames; however, do not cut any windows in them.

Bake the cookies as directed until lightly browned around the edges, or about 9 to 11 minutes for the window cutouts and smaller frames and 12 to 13 minutes for bigger

frames and backing cookies. While the cookies are still hot from the oven, trim the window cutouts, as well as the windows cut in the frames, with the cutters originally used to cut them. Once trimmed, the cutouts should fit comfortably in the frames. Cool completely before decorating in Step 3.

2. Prepare the Royal Icing as instructed on page 242. Reserve about 2 cups for top-coating the backing cookies, 3 cups for borders (or other details) on the frames and window cutouts, and $\frac{1}{2}$ cup for "glue." *Note:* The quantity of icing will vary with the number of colors and consistencies mixed. It's best to allow no less than $\frac{1}{4}$ to $\frac{1}{2}$ cup icing per color or consistency for easiest mixing and handling.

3. Outline and flood the frames and window cutouts. I prefer to outline and flood the frames and window cutouts, as opposed to top-coating without any outlines, in order to get the icing as close to the cookie edges as possible.

Divide the remaining 2$\frac{3}{4}$ cups icing into as many portions as you want colors. I usually limit the colors to white and a couple of others, typically red and green. Tint the icing as desired and thin each portion to outlining consistency (p. 244). Transfer each portion to a separate parchment pastry cone and cut a small ($\frac{1}{16}$-inch or more) hole in

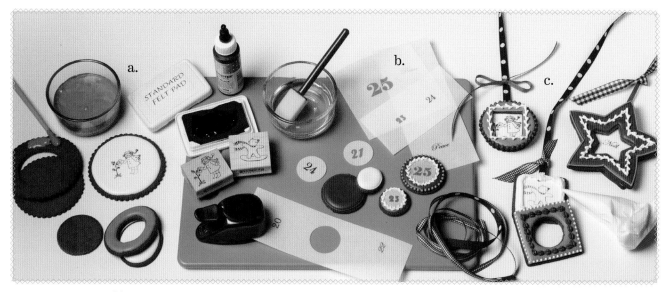

Short and Sweet. *(a) Outline and flood large cookie frames and their window cutouts with Royal Icing; also top-coat matching backing cookies. (b) Rubber-stamp a holiday pattern on each backing cookie. Print numbers on wafer paper, cut out, and affix to the window cutouts. (Alternatively, write the numbers with icing or food-safe markers.) Add icing details to the frames and numbered window cutouts. (c) Use thick Royal Icing to mount ribbons between matching frames and backing cookies and to glue the cookies together. Dry completely. Insert a numbered window cutout in each frame and tie the finished cookies on a garland in numerical order.*

each tip. Outline all of the frames and window cutouts in colors of your choice following the outlining instructions on page 29. Thin the leftover icing to flooding consistency (p. 245) and flood the interior of each outlined cookie with the same color of icing used to outline it. Let the window cutouts dry completely before wafer-papering in Step 5.

4. Top-coat the matching backing cookies. Tint the 2 cups icing reserved for this purpose to a pale color or leave it white. (You'll be rubber-stamping Christmas patterns on these cookies in Step 6, and the patterns will show better on light icings.) Thin the icing to top-coating consistency (p. 245). Using the handle-end of a craft paintbrush, apply a smooth coat of icing to the each cookie top. Dry completely before rubber-stamping in Step 6.

5. Wafer-paper the window cutouts (optional). The window cutouts will be the equivalent of the numbered doors on an advent calendar, so they need some numbers right about now! Print numbers (from 1 to 25) in showy fonts on plain wafer paper. Just make sure the numbers fit the top coats on the window cutouts with some room to spare. *Note:* You can use a dedicated printer with edible ink (p. 24) as I have here. If you don't have one or don't want to make the investment, you can write numbers with food-safe markers on the paper or directly on the cookie top coats, or pipe them with Royal Icing, again directly on the top coats.

To apply the wafer paper to an entire window cutout, trace around a number using the cutter originally used to cut that window; then cut along the tracing marks. (Alternatively, cut out the numbers to any size and shape using craft paper punches.) Use a small sponge brush to spread a thin layer of corn syrup on a cookie top coat (if covering it entirely with paper) or onto the back of the paper (if partially covering the cookie). Gently press the paper onto the cookie. Smooth out any air bubbles and re-press the paper edges, which have a tendency to lift. For more wafer-papering details, see page 38. Repeat to paper all 25 window cutouts. Let the paper dry at least 1 hour before detailing in Step 7.

6. Rubber-stamp the backing cookies. Arrange matching frames and backing cookies in pairs. Choose a rubber stamp (or stamps) sized to fit the windows in your cookies. Work on one cookie pair at a time. Ink a felt or foam ink pad with black food coloring, blot any excess coloring with paper towels, and then ink your stamp. Stamp each backing cookie so the pattern is centered in the window in the matching frame. Repeat to stamp all of the backing cookies. For more rubber-stamping technique details, see page 40.

7. Add borders and other details to the frames and window cutouts. Tint the 3 cups icing reserved for this purpose to a color (or colors) of your choice and choose a border style (or styles) from among those listed in "7 Essential Piping Techniques" (p. 46). Adjust each icing color to the appropriate consistency for your task and transfer to separate parchment pastry cone(s) or pastry bag(s) fitted with the right tip(s). Proceed to add details as desired. *Note:* I piped a Trailing Star Border (p. 47) around many of the ornaments (pictured p. 228) with thick icing and a pastry bag fitted with a $1/4$-inch star tip (Ateco #18 or #27). I also used icing of outlining consistency (p. 244) for Zig Zag Borders (p. 47) as pictured on the big red star

(p. 228, bottom left). Tiny icing dots and lines can also be added to the stamped patterns on the backing cookies, just so long as they don't interfere with the fit of the numbered windows.

8. Assemble the ornaments and cookie garland. Work on one ornament at a time. Place a backing cookie face up on your work surface and use the $1/2$ cup icing reserved for "glue" to attach a piece of ribbon to the top of the cookie. (Allow about 1 to $1^1/2$ feet ribbon per ornament so there is plenty of length for tying the ornaments to the garland.) Glue a matching frame on top. Assemble the remaining 24 cookies. When the icing is dry, fit numbered cutouts in each window and tie the cookies in numerical order on a long piece of paper or evergreen garland. Then promptly hang on your mantel for all to admire—and eat!

HOW THE COOKIE CRUMBLES
Recipes

I love a beautiful cookie. But I'm also the first to insist that decorators pay attention to taste, texture, ingredients, and the many other variables that dictate how a cookie ultimately crumbles—that is, whether it dances or falls flat on our tongues. Just as my mom fought the infiltration of store-bought cookies into my childhood house (p. 7), I urge you now to resist the use of them in my projects. You'll be happier with the tastier results. Plus, the extra time with friends and family, mixing batter, licking bowls, and stealing the first warm cookie bites, is always time well spent.

Still not sure if you'll bake or buy? Well, I'm hoping the recipes in this chapter will be your tipping point. Some of them are of long-standing Usher tradition, handed down by my mom and passed on once before in *Cookie Swap*, whereas others, especially the rolled cookie variations, are new taste sensations developed just for this book. For your convenience, I've organized the recipes into two sections. In the first, "Cookie Cutter Approaches" (p. 233), you'll find those recipes that I use most frequently in my projects, namely rolled cookie doughs that require cookie cutters and the Royal Icing used to decorate them. Also included in this section are the recommended Royal Icing consistency adjustments for each of my "15 Bottom-to-Top Decorating Techniques." In "Extras," starting on page 247, you'll find other recipes, such as Traditional Tuiles and Goofproof Macarons, that I call on less frequently, yet use to wonderful effect to add extra flavor and dimension to cookie projects. But first, take a look at "Before You Bake,"—yes, ideally before you bake! It contains useful tips for ensuring consistently delicious and gorgeous results.

Before You Bake

1. Read the recipe. Don't start measuring, or doing anything for that matter, until you've read the recipe from start to finish. Some ingredients require advance preparation, such as the softening of butter in Italian Buttercream (p. 257) or the dehydrating of egg whites in Goofproof Macarons (p. 249). Reading in advance will also help you identify any ingredients or tools you might be lacking. There's nothing worse than coming up shorthanded in the middle of an unstoppable step.

2. Follow orders. It may go without saying, but follow the recipe in the order in which the steps are laid out. I've done my best to sequence tasks to minimize downtime between them and overall time in the kitchen.

3. Measure mindfully. So the recipes come out just as intended, measure all dry ingredients (especially flour) by the spoon-and-scrape method, unless otherwise specified. By this, I mean: spoon the ingredient into the measuring cup, gently tap the surface to make sure any large air pockets are filled, and then level the top with an offset spatula. Never plunge the cup into the bin, again, especially with flour. Plunging compresses the flour, which will leave you with more flour by weight than desired—and, in turn, a heavier, drier end product. For superior accuracy and control, you can always weigh dry ingredients using the conversions on page 272.

4. Always add flavorings to taste. I purposely start my icing and rolled cookie recipes, with the exception of gingerbread, with a minimum of flavorings so you can add any extract or oil and scale it to personal taste. If experimentation isn't your strong suit, then check out the recipe variations for my favorite flavor combinations or "Flavor Behavior" (p. 239) for general flavoring guidance.

5. Get ready to roll. If you're making rolled cookies, don't forget to chill the dough well before rolling and to read "Handling Rolled Cookie Dough" (p. 15) for additional tips. Remember, if you work with dough that is too warm and soft or add too much flour to prevent sticking, you're more likely to end up with misshapen and/or tough cookies.

6. Avoid crowds. To ensure even baking and browning of cookies, place them on the back of cookie sheets (if the sheets have sides) and don't crowd them in the oven. Follow the suggested cookie spacing provided in each recipe and bake one cookie sheet at a time in the center of the oven whenever you've got the time. Otherwise, actively manage the oven by rotating cookie sheets from front to back, and from lower to higher racks, and vice versa.

7. Keep an eye out. I test all of my recipes in two different ovens and many times over in order to tune the preparation times as accurately as possible. Even so, no two mixers, ovens or bakers(!) are alike, and suggested mixing and baking times should never be the sole measure of doneness. Start checking for doneness before the time suggested in the recipe has elapsed and pay attention to the visual cues that I provide alongside. If the recipe looks or behaves as it's described, then pull it from the oven or move onto the next step.

signature sugar cookie dough

WITH VARIATIONS

WHAT CAN I SAY? I'M NOSTALGIC AT HEART, which is why you'll find this cookie in so many projects throughout the book. You see, the Anise Seed Variation (p. 235) was my mom's invention—and the very same cookie that my sibs and I decorated so happily each and every Christmas. Look closely at the photo of me circa 1971 (p. 4), and you'll see me coddling one of these prized possessions! As one of my most delicate cookies, it's best used for 2-D projects and small or non-weight-bearing 3-D constructions.

Makes about 1 pound 6 ounces dough or 3 to 3½ dozen (2½-inch) round cookies

2 cups all-purpose flour

1½ teaspoons baking powder

¼ teaspoon salt

Additional spices (per Variations, p. 235)

6 tablespoons (¾ stick) unsalted butter, softened

⅓ cup (⅓ stick) shortening

¾ cup granulated sugar

1 large egg

1 tablespoon whole milk

½ teaspoon pure vanilla extract (or to taste, or per Variations)

PREP TALK:

For easiest handling, the dough should be chilled about 3 hours before rolling and cutting. The dough can be frozen for 1 month or more with minimal loss of flavor if wrapped tightly in plastic and then foil. For best eating, store baked cookies in airtight containers at room temperature and enjoy within 1 to 1½ weeks.

1. Combine the flour, baking powder, salt, and any additional spices (per Variations, p. 235) in a small bowl. Set aside for use in Step 4.

2. Using an electric mixer fitted with a paddle attachment, beat the butter and shortening on medium speed until creamy. Gradually add the sugar and beat until light and fluffy, about 1 minute. Do not overbeat, or your cookies will dome upon baking, making them more difficult to decorate later.

3. Whisk together the egg, milk, and vanilla extract in another bowl. Add additional flavoring(s) to taste, or see Variations. Slowly blend into the butter mixture on low to medium speed and mix until smooth. Scrape down the sides of the bowl, as needed, to ensure even mixing.

4. Turn the mixer to low speed and gradually add the reserved dry ingredients, mixing until just incorporated. Flatten the dough into a disk, wrap tightly in plastic, and refrigerate about 3 hours, or until firm enough to roll without sticking.

5. Position a rack in the center of the oven and preheat the oven to 375°F. Line 2 cookie sheets with parchment paper (or silicone baking mats) and set aside.

6. On a lightly floured surface, roll the dough to a $1/8$- to $3/16$-inch thickness. (*Note:* It's best to roll these cookies no thicker than $3/16$ inch in order to keep them their flattest for decorating.) Cut out assorted shapes with your favorite cookie cutters or the cutters or templates specified in the project you've chosen. Carefully transfer the cookies to the prepared cookie sheets with an offset spatula, leaving no less than $3/4$ inch between each cutout.

7. Baking time will vary considerably with cookie size and thickness. Bake until the cookies are lightly browned around their edges, about 8 to 10 minutes for $2 1/2$-inch round cookies or as specified in your project. Let particularly long or delicately shaped cookies cool 1 to 2 minutes on the cookie sheets before transferring to wire racks. Otherwise, immediately transfer to racks and cool completely before frosting and/or assembling with Royal Icing (p. 242) or storing.

VARIATIONS

{ Anise, courtesy of my mom }

Add $1/2$ teaspoon anise extract along with the vanilla extract. Sprinkle each cookie sheet with $1 1/2$ teaspoons whole anise seed before placing and baking the cookies. The seeds will bake into the bottom of the cookies and impart a tasty crunch.

{ Cinnamon }

Add $1 1/2$ teaspoons ground cinnamon to the dry ingredients. Increase the vanilla extract to $3/4$ teaspoon. *Note:* The ground cinnamon will tint the dough pale brown.

{ Lemon-Cardamom }

Add $1 1/4$ teaspoons ground cardamom to the dry ingredients. Add $1 1/2$ teaspoons lemon extract and 2 teaspoons finely grated lemon zest along with the vanilla extract.

{ Orange-Clove }

Add $3/4$ teaspoon ground cloves to the dry ingredients. Increase the vanilla extract to 1 teaspoon and add $1 1/2$ teaspoons finely grated orange zest with the liquid ingredients.

cutout cookie gingerbread

WITH CORIANDER SEED VARIATION

HIGH ON SPICE YET RELATIVELY DELICATE IN TEXTURE, this dough is perfect for 2-D cookies and small-scale 3-D construction projects. It also spreads less than Signature Sugar Cookie Dough, making it more suitable for tight-fitting angular constructions, insofar as it requires less trimming. For projects with very large weight-bearing pieces, such as Full Plate (p. 101) or Open Your Heart Box (p. 165), the safer bet is sturdier Construction Gingerbread.

Makes about 3 pounds dough or $6^1/_2$ to 7 dozen ($2^1/_2$-inch) round cookies

5 cups all-purpose flour

$2^1/_2$ teaspoons ground ginger

$1^1/_4$ teaspoons ground cinnamon

1 teaspoon ground cloves

$1^1/_2$ teaspoons baking soda

$^1/_2$ teaspoon salt

1 cup (1 stick) shortening

1 cup granulated sugar

1 large egg

1 cup mild molasses

2 tablespoons distilled white vinegar

PREP TALK:

For easiest handling, the dough should be chilled about 3 hours before rolling and cutting. The dough can be frozen for 1 month or more with minimal loss of flavor if wrapped tightly in plastic and then foil. For best eating, store baked cookies in airtight containers at room temperature and enjoy within 1 to $1^1/_2$ weeks.

1. Combine the flour, spices, baking soda, and salt in a large bowl. Set aside for use in Step 4.

2. Using an electric mixer fitted with a paddle attachment, beat the shortening and sugar until well combined. Add the egg and beat on medium-high speed until light and fluffy, about 1 minute. Scrape down the sides of the bowl, as needed, to ensure even mixing.

3. Turn the mixer to medium speed and add the molasses and vinegar. Mix well. Scrape down the sides of the bowl, as needed.

4. Turn the mixer to low speed and gradually add the reserved dry ingredients. Mix until just incorporated; however, make sure there are no dry spots.

5. Flatten the dough into a disk (or 2 disks for easier handling). Wrap tightly in plastic and refrigerate about 3 hours, or until firm enough to roll without sticking.

6. Position a rack in the center of the oven and preheat the oven to 375°F. Line 2 or more cookie sheets with parchment paper (or silicone baking mats) and set aside.

7. On a lightly floured surface, roll the dough to a $1/8$- to $3/16$-inch thickness. (*Note:* It's best to roll these cookies no thicker than $3/16$ inch in order to keep them their flattest for decorating.) Cut out assorted shapes with your favorite cookie cutters or the cutters or templates specified in the project you've chosen. Carefully transfer the cookies to the prepared cookie sheets with an offset spatula, leaving no less than $3/4$ inch between each cutout.

8. Baking time will vary considerably with cookie size and thickness. Bake until the cookies are firm to the touch and lightly browned around the edges, about 8 to 10 minutes for $2 1/2$-inch round cookies or as instructed in your project. Let particularly long or delicately shaped cookies cool 1 to 2 minutes on the cookie sheets before transferring to wire racks. Otherwise, immediately transfer the cookies. Cool completely before frosting and/or assembling with Royal Icing (p. 242) or storing.

VARIATION

{ Coriander Seed }

Since I've forever been infatuated with my mom's Anise Seed Variation of Signature Sugar Cookie Dough, a similar whole seed spin on this gingerbread seemed like the next most logical twist!

Sprinkle each cookie sheet with $1 1/2$ teaspoons crushed or coarsely ground coriander seeds before placing and baking the cookies in Steps 7 and 8, left.

There's More to Storing Rolled and Iced Cookies

- Some may disagree, but I find that cookie taste and texture almost always suffers if cookies are baked and then frozen. Not to mention, cut and/or baked cookies take up tons of freezer space. To manage my time and space in the kitchen, I prefer to only mix the dough in advance. I then wrap it tightly into compact disks and freeze it. When I'm ready to start a project, I portion off just the amount I need and bake as close to eating time as possible.

- Humidity is the root of much trouble in baking. To keep baked cookies their crispest, store them as soon as they've cooled in airtight containers. *Note:* This same rule applies to Meringues, Goofproof Macarons, and Traditional Tuiles, and even more so. As high in hygroscopic (moisture-attracting) sugar, these cookie types are especially vulnerable to humidity.

- Avoid commingling cookie types in the same container, as flavors will also mingle and quickly become indistinguishable.

- Cookies frosted with Royal Icing should also be stored at room temperature in airtight containers. Refrigeration or freezing can cause icing colors to bleed or spot and the cookies to soften.

- However, never contain, or even loosely cover, frosted cookies until the icing is completely dry. Icing dries more slowly this way, leading to trouble with colors bleeding and spotting. I usually allow top coats to air-dry overnight, uncovered.

construction gingerbread

PROTEIN-RICH BREAD FLOUR STANDS IN FOR ALL-PURPOSE FLOUR, making this gingerbread exceptionally strong. It's less prone to spreading during baking, and to breaking or softening with humidity once baked, than any of my other rolled cookie doughs. However, there's a trade-off: bread flour also makes the dough less tender and more difficult to roll. At the end of the day, I only use it for projects that benefit from its strength, such as ones intended for extended display or involving small precision cuts, tight or angular constructions, and/or unusually large weight-bearing pieces.

Makes about 3 pounds dough or $6^{1}/_{2}$ to 7 dozen ($2^{1}/_{2}$-inch) round cookies

5 cups bread flour

2 tablespoons ground cinnamon

1 tablespoon ground cloves

1 tablespoon ground ginger

$1^{1}/_{4}$ teaspoons baking soda

$^{1}/_{4}$ teaspoon salt

1 cup plus 2 tablespoons granulated sugar

$^{3}/_{4}$ cup light corn syrup

$^{1}/_{2}$ cup (1 stick) plus 7 tablespoons margarine, cut into tablespoon-size pieces

$^{1}/_{4}$ cup plus 2 tablespoons whole milk

PREP TALK:

Though not essential, a candy thermometer is helpful in Step 2. Chill the dough several hours or until it can easily be rolled without sticking. If you find it too difficult to roll straight from the fridge, let it soften, wrapped, at room temperature about $^{1}/_{2}$ hour. The dough can be frozen for 1 month or more with minimal loss of flavor if wrapped tightly in plastic and then foil. Once baked, cookies will stay crisp and construction-ready for several months in airtight containers, stored at room temperature. Flavor will dissipate over time, so if you intend to eat your construction project, bake the cookies no more than 1 to $1^{1}/_{2}$ weeks ahead.

1. Combine the bread flour, spices, baking soda, and salt in a large bowl. Set aside for use in Step 3.

2. Combine the sugar, corn syrup, margarine, and milk in a large ($6^{1}/_{2}$-quart) nonreactive (stainless steel or coated) saucepan. Place the pan over medium to medium-high heat. Cook, stirring frequently, until the butter is completely melted and the mixture is the consistency of thick syrup. (The syrup should look cloudy, with minimal oil separation from the margarine, and feel slightly warm to the touch. When ready, it will register 115°F to 125°F on a candy thermometer.)

3. Remove the pan from the heat and add half of the reserved dry ingredients. Mix until lump-free. Add the remaining dry ingredients and mix until the flour is just incorporated. The dough will be sticky and somewhat shiny at this point, but do not add more flour. (Excess flour and handling will only toughen the dough.) Cover the surface of the dough with plastic wrap and cool to room temperature. If left uncovered, the dough will crust and dry out.

4. Flatten the dough into a disk (or 2 disks for easier handling). Wrap tightly in plastic and refrigerate several hours, or until firm enough to roll without sticking.

5. Position a rack in the center of the oven and preheat the oven to 375°F. Line 2 or more cookie sheets with parchment paper (or silicone baking mats) and set aside.

6. For large weight-bearing construction projects (of the scale of Open Your Heart Box, p. 165), I like to roll the dough about $3/16$ inch thick so the resulting cutouts are extra sturdy. For smaller projects, the dough can be rolled thinner, but generally no less than $1/8$ inch thick. You'll need little to no flour for dusting your work surface—this dough is not at all sticky and it doesn't need to be any sturdier than it already is.

Cut out assorted shapes using your favorite cookie cutters or the cutters or templates specified in the project you've chosen. Using an offset spatula, carefully transfer your cookies to the prepared cookie sheets, leaving no less than $3/4$ inch between each piece. If your pieces are very big or difficult to handle with a spatula, as they can be with some of my larger construction projects, cut them directly on the cookie sheet.

7. Baking time will vary considerably with cookie size and thickness. Bake until the cookies are firm to the touch and lightly browned around the edges, about 10 to 12 minutes for $2^1/2$-inch round cookies or as instructed in your project. For large-scale support pieces, it is especially important to bake the cookies all the way through. Even though this dough doesn't spread much, any cookies intended for tight-fitting angular constructions may need some trimming while hot from the oven.

8. Let the cookies cool 1 to 2 minutes on the cookie sheets before transferring to wire racks. Cool completely before frosting and/or assembling with Royal Icing (p. 242) or storing.

Flavor Behavior

- Always use 100 percent natural extracts and oils whenever possible. The simple reason being: they taste better!

- Though extracts and oils of the same flavor may be interchanged, oils are more potent and will lose less flavor during baking. When substituting oil for extract, I generally start with about one quarter of the specified quantity of extract and gradually add more oil to taste.

- Similarly, some flavorings within the same family (i.e., extract or oil) are stronger than others, meaning that you'll need far less of those flavorings to get an equivalent flavor intensity. For instance, lemon and vanilla extract are relatively mild compared to almond and peppermint extract.

Further, some recipes, especially those high in fat, tend to carry flavor better. All this to say: never assume that different flavors of extract (or oil) can be substituted one for one, or in the same quantity across recipes. When in doubt about the amount of flavoring, start with very little and gradually add more to taste.

- If I've learned one thing after all my years of recipe development and testing, it's that flavor is very subjective. I tend to be a high flavor kind of gal; if you prefer subtlety, then treat the recommended amounts of flavoring in my recipe variations as guideposts rather than gospel.

shortbread, straight up

WITH VARIATIONS

SHORTBREAD IS THE ONE ROLLED COOKIE THAT I PREFER TO ROLL THICKER than $^1/_8$ to $^3/_{16}$ inch thick. Why? Well, for starters, its buttery texture is better accentuated and appreciated this way. Second, it remains quite tender at thicknesses of $^1/_4$ inch or more, which is not the case for gingerbread. And, lastly, it holds its shape quite well when cut thick. The flip side: it's the most fragile of my doughs, making it far less suitable for big 2-D or 3-D constructions. As such, I typically reserve it for small cookie projects that benefit from thicker cookie layers, such as Come Sail Away (p. 179) and Take the Cake (p. 113).

Makes about 1 pound 6 ounces dough or 2 dozen ($2^1/_2$-inch-diameter; $^1/_4$-inch-thick) round cookies

2 cups all-purpose flour

$^1/_2$ cup blanched slivered almonds
(or per Variations, p. 241)

$^1/_2$ teaspoon salt

1 cup (2 sticks) unsalted butter, softened

$^1/_4$ cup granulated sugar

$^1/_4$ cup sifted superfine sugar

1 teaspoon pure vanilla extract (or
to taste, or per Variations)

About 2 tablespoons granulated sugar,
for sprinkling on top (optional)

PREP TALK:

For easiest handling, chill the dough 1 to 2 hours before rolling and cutting. If chilled longer, the dough will get quite firm and may be difficult to roll straight from the fridge. In this case, let it sit, wrapped, at room temperature for 15 minutes or more, until it becomes workable. The dough can also be frozen for 1 month or more with minimal loss of flavor if wrapped tightly in plastic and then foil. For best eating, store baked cookies in airtight containers at room temperature and enjoy within 1 to $1^1/_2$ weeks.

1. Combine the flour, almonds (and/or other nuts and spices per Variations, p. 241), and salt in a food processor fitted with a metal blade. Process until the nuts are finely ground but not pasty.

2. Place the softened butter and sugars in the bowl of an electric mixer fitted with a paddle attachment. Mix on low speed to bring the ingredients together; then beat on medium to medium-high speed until light and fluffy, about 1 minute. Turn the mixer to low speed and add the vanilla extract. Add additional flavoring(s) to taste, or see Variations. Gradually blend in the flour-nut mixture, mixing until just incorporated. Scrape down the sides of the bowl, as needed, to ensure even mixing.

3. Flatten the dough into a disk and wrap tightly in plastic. Refrigerate 1 to 2 hours or until firm enough to roll without sticking.

4. Position a rack in the center of the oven and preheat the oven to 300°F. Line 2 or more cookie sheets with parchment paper (or silicone baking mats) and set aside.

5. On a lightly floured surface, roll the dough to a $1/4$-inch thickness or to the thickness specified in the project you've chosen. Cut out assorted shapes with your favorite cookie cutters or the cutters or templates specified in your project. Using an offset spatula, carefully transfer the cookies to the prepared cookie sheets, spacing them no less than $3/4$ inch apart.

6. If you want to eat these cookies straight up, without any icing, then sprinkle the remaining 2 tablespoons sugar evenly over the cookie tops. (This dough isn't nearly as sweet as Signature Sugar Cookie Dough.) Baking time will vary considerably with cookie size and thickness. Bake until the cookies are lightly browned on the bottom and firm to the touch, about 25 to 30 minutes for $2^{1}/_2$-inch round cookies or as specified in your project. (By the time these cookies brown on their edges or on top, they are usually overdone, in my opinion.) Immediately transfer the cookies to wire racks to cool using an offset spatula to prevent breakage. Cool completely before frosting and/or assembling with Royal Icing (p. 242) or storing.

VARIATIONS

{ Crystallized Ginger }

Add $3/4$ cup coarsely chopped crystallized ginger and 1 teaspoon ground ginger to the flour along with the almonds and salt.

{ Pecan-Brown Sugar }

Substitute 1 cup pecan halves for the almonds and $1/2$ cup firmly packed light brown sugar for the granulated and superfine sugars.

{ Pistachio-Rosewater }

Substitute $1/2$ cup shelled salted pistachios (with the skins rubbed off) for the almonds and 1 teaspoon rosewater for the vanilla extract.

{ Walnut-Cardamom }

Substitute $3/4$ cup walnut halves for the almonds and add $1/2$ cup diced candied orange peel and 1 teaspoon ground cardamom to the flour along with the walnuts and salt.

royal icing

AKA "GLUE" WITH CONSISTENCY ADJUSTMENTS

I'VE SAID IT BEFORE AND I'LL SAY IT AGAIN: Royal Icing is—by far—my favorite cookie decorating medium! Even if I intend to use a relatively loose Royal Icing, I always start by mixing the icing to a very thick consistency using the egg white to powdered sugar ratio below. When mixed thick, the icing ends up with fewer air bubbles and holds coloring better with less mottling. Also, the thicker the icing, the faster it dries, which makes this thick formulation ideal for securing decorations to cookie tops and sticking together compound cookies (p. 45) or larger 3-D structures. In short, it acts like "glue," and that's how I refer to it throughout the book. Most other decorating techniques require looser icing, which is easily achieved by thinning thick icing with water. See "Consistency Adjustments" (p. 244) for details.

Makes about 2 pounds 4 ounces or 4½ to 5-plus cups; yield
will vary with egg size, egg temperature, and beating time

2 pounds powdered sugar

½ teaspoon cream of tartar

5 large egg whites, cold (about 11 to
12 tablespoons pasteurized whites,
or see "Substitutions," p. 243)

Flavoring(s) of your choice, to taste
(*Note:* Don't skimp on the flavoring,
or the icing can taste chalky.)

Soft-gel food coloring (p. 14) of
your choice (optional)

PREP TALK:

If tinted, the icing is best used the day it's mixed. Otherwise, the icing can be made 1 to 2 days ahead and stored in the fridge. When ready to use, bring the icing to room temperature, stir vigorously to restore its original consistency (especially if any separation has occurred), and tint as desired. Once applied to cookies, the icing should remain at room temperature so it sets into a crunchy candy-like coating.

Important: Unless you're using the icing, always cover the surface flush with plastic wrap to prevent a crust from quickly forming.

1. Combine the powdered sugar and cream of tartar in the bowl of an electric mixer. Mix in the egg whites by hand to moisten the sugar.

2. Fit the electric mixer with a whip attachment. To avoid a flurry of powdered sugar, beat the mixture on low speed just until the egg whites are evenly incorporated. Scrape down the sides of the bowl; then turn the mixer to its highest speed and continue to beat about 2 to 3 minutes. (The icing will lighten and thicken as you beat it. However, avoid beating too long; you'll introduce excess air bubbles, which are tough to remove and interfere with smooth top-coating.) When done, the icing should be bright white, glossy, and very thick—and at what I call "glue" consistency. At this consistency, the icing will cling to a spoon (held upside down) indefinitely without falling off. See "Visual Cue #1," right.

3. Beat in flavoring(s) and/or coloring, as desired. Mix well before using or store, covered flush with plastic wrap, as instructed in "Prep Talk."

Visual Cue #1: *Royal Icing of "glue" consistency clings to a spoon indefinitely!*

Substitutions: Raw Egg Whites

Some bakers steer clear of Royal Icing and Italian Buttercream (p. 257) because of the risks of salmonella and other bacterial poisoning associated with raw egg whites. But there's no reason to let fear get in the way of superior decorating! These risks can be substantially reduced by substituting about 2 to 3 tablespoons pasteurized egg whites for each large white in my recipes. Pasteurized whites can be found in the refrigerated section of most grocery stores.

Alternatively, meringue powder (a mixture of dehydrated whites and often sugar, vegetable gum, and preservatives) can be combined with water. About 2 teaspoons meringue powder plus 2 tablespoons water is equivalent to 1 large egg white. However, there are some downsides to meringue powder: (1) it's often harder to find than pasteurized whites; (2) you must take extra care to completely dissolve it with warm water, or the resulting icing will be gritty; and (3) because of its additives, it results in much sweeter, often stiffer icings than those made with raw eggs or pasteurized whites.

Consistency Adjustments, by Decorating Technique

In cookie decorating, icing consistency is king! Your success or failure, or pleasure or frustration, with each of my "15 Bottom-to-Top Decorating Techniques" (p. 27) is likely to be determined by one thing: whether your icing is the right consistency. To set you on the path to success, I've compiled here the recommended consistency adjustments for each of my major decorating techniques and ordered them from thickest to thinnest consistency.

Note: These consistency adjustments are *approximate guidelines for 1 cup of untinted, unflavored Royal Icing* made with raw egg whites and freshly mixed to thick "glue" consistency. The addition of food coloring or flavoring, beating time, humidity, prior refrigeration, and variations in egg size can all affect the final consistency of your icing. Royal Icing made with pasteurized whites or hydrated meringue powder (per "Substitutions," p. 243) generally starts out a bit thicker and may require more loosening to achieve the ideal consistency for each technique.

If after making these adjustments, you think your icing is too thin or too thick for your application, don't worry. The icing consistency can be adjusted at any stage of the decorating process simply by adding powdered sugar to thicken, or water to thin. Just be sure to sift powdered sugar before adding, as sugar clumps can be hard to break up and will block small holes in pastry bags and cones. Water should always be stirred in, vs. beaten in with an electric mixer, to avoid introducing excess air bubbles.

For outlining: Add about $1/2$ to $3/4$ teaspoons water per 1 cup icing "glue." For crisp, well-defined outlines, start with $1/2$ teaspoon water. If the icing is too thick to easily pipe through the desired hole in your parchment pastry cone (or tip in your pastry bag), gradually add more water. See "Visual Cue #2," right, for more details.

For stenciling: Generally, $1/2$ to $11/2$ teaspoons water per 1 cup icing "glue" works best, though the exact quantity will vary with the size and complexity of your stencil and the other variables noted earlier. The icing must be thin enough to spread easily into the stencil openings without leaving peaks or tracks when the spatula is lifted. At the same time, it must be sufficiently thick

Visual Cue #2: *Royal Icing of outlining consistency is thick and stretchy and drops off a spoon in relatively large blobs. When piped, it holds a thin line with minimal to no spreading.*

to keep from creeping under the stencil into areas where it's not wanted. For stencils with delicate, closely spaced openings (such as the one pictured right in "Beginner vs. Advanced Stencil," p. 37), it's best to start on the thicker end of this spectrum to avoid icing creep and blurring of the pattern. Stencils with more space ($1/8$ inch or more) between openings (pictured left, p. 37) are less sensitive to icing creep and, therefore, icing consistency. Lastly, large stencils (greater than about 2 inches across) typically require icing on the thinner end of this spectrum so that they can be smoothly covered without leaving tracks.

For marbling: Generally, marbling begins with the application of top-coating icing (p. 245) to a cookie; then contrasting icings of marbling consistency are immediately piped on top. For the marbling icings, I like to use icing that is slightly thicker than the one used for top-coating, i.e., mixed in the ratio of about $3/4$ to $11/3$ teaspoons water per 1 cup icing "glue." A thinner consistency will marble smoothly, but as you add more water, you're more likely to experience bleeding of colors as the icing dries.

Conversely, thicker marbling icings will marble less smoothly; that is, the trussing needle or toothpick (used to marble the colors) may actually break the marbling icing rather than leave behind long, graceful tracks.

For top-coating: Ideal top-coating consistency usually varies from about $1^1/_2$ to $2^1/_2$ teaspoons water per 1 cup icing "glue," depending on cookie size. To avoid icing runoff on cookies under 2 inches, start on the lower end of this spectrum. Gradually increase to $2^1/_2$ teaspoons water, as needed, to improve spreadability on larger cookies. You can also use what I've dubbed "the 15-second rule" to quickly gauge whether icing is at top-coating consistency for an average (2- to 3-inch) cookie. See "Visual Cue #3," below, for details.

Visual Cue #3: *Royal Icing of top-coating consistency flows slowly off a spoon. Tracks largely disappear into the bulk of the icing in about 15 seconds.*

For beadwork: About 2 to 3 teaspoons per 1 cup icing "glue" works best, though expect some variability with the factors noted on page 244. At the proper consistency, a smooth, well rounded dot should form when the icing is piped through a small ($^1/_{16}$-inch or more) hole in a parchment pastry cone. If the icing forms a peak, it is too thick. Conversely, if it spreads a great deal, it is too loose.

For flooding: Ideal flooding consistency varies widely with cookie size and also icing color. I generally add anywhere from 2 to 3 or more teaspoons water per 1 cup icing "glue." However, the goal should be to keep the icing as thick as possible, yet still flowing freely enough to prevent tracks. Why? Again, the thinner the icing, the greater the likelihood of colors bleeding, especially if the flooding color is much darker (or lighter) than the adjacent outlining color. As a rule of thumb, 2 teaspoons should be plenty for cookies under 2 inches; only very large cookies, in excess of 5 to 6 inches, will require 3 or more teaspoons to ensure smooth spreading. See "Visual Cue #4," below.

Visual Cue #4: *Royal Icing of flooding consistency flows quickly off a spoon. Tracks largely disappear into the bulk of the icing in 10 seconds or less.*

For dipping: Again, ideal dipping consistency varies with cookie size and also the type of dipping, i.e., either Nose-Dive Dipping (p. 32) or Roundabout Dipping (p. 34). I generally add anywhere from 2 to 4 teaspoons of water per 1 cup icing "glue"—lesser amounts for Roundabout Dipping or Nose-Dive Dipping of small (2-inch or less) cookies, and larger amounts for Nose-Dive Dipping of larger cookies, such as the egg whites in Breakfast in Bed (p. 95).

A (Big) Hint on Tint

- For best results, tint Royal Icing at "glue" consistency before thinning it with water. I've found that if icings are tinted when very thick, they are less likely to dry with spotting or mottling, even if later loosened. (Don't ask me to explain the food science here! You'll just have to take my word for it!)

- As noted earlier (p. 14), I recommend only one food coloring for cookie decorating: soft-gel coloring, a relatively thick, concentrated dye that comes in a container fitted with a dropper. A little goes a long way; it is less likely to alter your icing consistency than is liquid coloring; and the dropper takes the guesswork out of getting the right color. And, again, my preferred brand is Chefmaster; it doesn't have the strong taste of some other brands.

- Count the drops of coloring as you add them to the icing. This way, if you run out of icing later, you can more easily match the original color.

- Tinted icing will dry darker than it appears wet, and some colors (such as red) are notorious for drying much darker than others. To get a truer sense of the end color, I recommend painting a test splotch on a piece of white cardboard and allowing the splotch to dry before applying any icing to your cookies. If the icing dries too dark for your tastes, you can lighten it by adding untinted Royal Icing. *Note:* When working with a lot of colors, I always paint a full test palette, let it dry, and then check to make sure the dried colors work in harmony together.

- Avoid mixing lots of colors together, as the final color is more likely to migrate and mottle upon drying. Fortunately, this is easy to do, since soft-gel coloring comes in almost every shade of the rainbow. I usually limit my color mixing to adding a small amount of brown or black to tone down brighter colors, or yellow to brighten darker, duller colors.

- If the particular decorating technique you're using permits, it's best to allow a tinted icing, especially a very dark one, to dry until it is dull and firm to the touch before applying another color, especially a much lighter one, next to it. This precaution reduces the risk of the darker color bleeding into the lighter one. *Note:* For techniques that require direct application of pressure, such as stenciling (p. 37), the top-coating icing, regardless of color, must dry even longer—generally overnight or until completely solid—before applying more icing on top.

- Of course, some techniques, such as marbling (p. 35) and wet-on-wet layering (p. 31), call for different icing colors to touch when wet. In these cases, I always push the icing to the thickest possible consistency for the technique at hand. Thicker icings dry faster and will minimize the chances of bleeding.

basic brownies
WITH BLONDE BROWNIES VARIATION

QUICK AND EASY, THESE BROWNIES ARE UNDENIABLE KID-PLEASERS. (I should know; when my mom didn't get around to making them for me, I often whipped them up for after-school snacks.) Bake them thick, as I have here, for turning into chunky cookie rocks and landscapes, or as instructed in the project you've chosen.

Makes 16 ($1^3/_4$ x $1^3/_4$-inch-thick) squares

6 ounces premium (see "Definitions," p. 258) unsweetened chocolate, chopped

1 cup (2 sticks) plus 2 tablespoons unsalted butter, cut into tablespoon-size pieces

$2^1/_2$ cups granulated sugar

5 large eggs, lightly beaten

$1^1/_2$ teaspoons pure vanilla extract and/or other flavoring(s) of your choice, to taste

$1^3/_4$ cups all-purpose flour

$1/_8$ teaspoon salt

PREP TALK:

Store at room temperature for 1 to $1^1/_2$ weeks. The brownies will stay moist longer if kept in a block in the pan, wrapped tightly in foil, and only cut when ready to serve. The brownies may also be frozen for 1 month or more if wrapped tightly in plastic and then foil. Again, keep them in one big block in the freezer until you're ready to thaw, cut, and serve.

1. Prep the baking pan(s) described in the project you've chosen. If you aren't making a particular project and just want to enjoy these brownies in simple squares, then line an 8 x 8 x 2-inch baking pan with foil, leaving a 1-inch overhang around the top edge of the pan. Smooth out any big wrinkles in the foil and then lightly coat the foil with nonstick cooking spray. *Note:* In an 8 x 8 x 2-inch pan, the brownies will rise to very near the top, a perfect thickness for cutting into chunky brownie rocks for cookie landscapes. If you prefer a thinner brownie, prep a 9 x 9 x 2-inch pan instead.

2. Position a rack in the center of the oven and preheat the oven to 350°F.

3. Combine the chopped chocolate and butter in a large bowl (at least 4-quart capacity) that fits a double boiler. Place the bowl over barely simmering water over low heat. Stir as needed until the chocolate and butter are melted. Remove from the heat, cool slightly, and whisk in the sugar, followed by the beaten eggs, vanilla extract, and any additional flavoring(s). (I often like to pump up the flavor with coffee, mint, or orange extract.) Stir in the flour and salt, mixing until smooth.

4. Turn the batter into the pan(s) specified in your project and bake according to those instructions.

Or if you're making simple squares, turn the batter into the prepared 8 x 8 x 2-inch baking pan. Bake until a cake tester inserted in the brownie center comes out with damp crumbs on it, or about 45 to 50 minutes. If you prefer fudgy brownies to cakey ones, bake closer to 45 minutes. The brownies will dome and crack on top before they bake completely through to the center, especially if baked in a 8 x 8 x 2-inch pan, so be sure to test doneness with a cake tester. (*Note:* The brownies will bake faster and somewhat more evenly in a 9 x 9 x 2-inch pan.) Set on a wire rack and cool completely in the pan. Any doming of the brownie top will settle upon cooling.

5. For simple squares only. Remove the brownies from the pan in one block by gently pulling up on the foil overhang, or by easing the block out with an offset spatula. Place directly on a cutting board. Remove all foil and trim any uneven edges before cutting into $1^3/4$-inch squares. For the neatest cuts, use a sharp knife, wiped clean with a warm, damp cloth between slices.

VARIATION
{ Blonde Brownies }

If you're not fond of chocolate but love the chewy texture of brownies, these cookies are a fine substitute for Basic Brownies, though they are considerably sweeter.

$2^1/2$ cups all-purpose flour

2 teaspoons baking powder

$3/8$ teaspoon salt

$1^1/4$ cups ($2^1/2$ sticks) unsalted butter, cut into tablespoon-size pieces

$2^1/4$ cups firmly packed light brown sugar

3 large eggs, room temperature

$1^1/2$ teaspoons pure vanilla extract, or to taste

3 tablespoons dark rum (*Note:* I love how the rum diminishes this brownie's sweetness. Only omit it if you must.)

2 cups pecan halves, toasted and coarsely chopped (optional; *Note:* For certain projects where no lumpiness is preferred, such as Beetlemania, the nuts are best left out.)

1. Prep baking pan(s) and preheat the oven as described for Basic Brownies (p. 247).

2. Combine the flour, baking powder, and salt in a small bowl.

3. Melt the butter in a medium (at least 3-quart) saucepan over medium to medium-high heat. Remove the pan from the heat, cool the butter slightly, and whisk in the sugar, eggs, vanilla extract, rum, and nuts, as desired. Stir in the flour mixture, mixing just until the batter is lump-free.

4. Turn the batter into the pan(s) and bake, cool, and cut as indicated for Basic Brownies.

goofproof macarons

NOT TO BE CONFUSED WITH THE CHUBBY COCONUT MACAROON COMMON IN THE UNITED STATES, macarons are sleek, sophisticated French sandwich cookies, notorious for requiring the utmost baking finesse. But have no fear! I've created a recipe that's infallible, whether you weigh the ingredients (as many bakers profess you must) or simply measure everything in cups. (I've given instructions to do both, so take your pick.) Just heed the egg white prep and cookie drying instructions and the visual cues provided at key steps, and every macaron should end up picture-perfect with characteristic smooth top and crinkly foot.

Makes 3 to 3½ dozen (1⅞- to 2⅛-inch) rounds or 1½ to 1¾ dozen sandwiches

½ cup (about 4 ounces) egg whites (from about 4 large eggs), dehydrated for 20 to 24 hours

2⅓ cups plus 1 tablespoon (about 8½ ounces) powdered sugar

1⅓ cups plus 2 tablespoons (about 5 ounces) blanched almond flour (*Note:* Also called almond meal, this flour is available in many organic and health food stores. Even if made with blanched almonds, almond flour can contain lots of ground skins. Choose the least speckled bag you can find, as skins leave dark spots on the cookies.)

Pinch salt

Pinch cream of tartar

2 tablespoons (about 1 ounce) granulated sugar

Flavoring(s) of your choice, to taste (optional; *Note:* These cookies are very almond-y as-is, so I often only add flavoring to the filling.)

Soft-gel food coloring (p. 14) of your choice (optional)

About 1 cup (less than ½ recipe) Ganache (p. 259) or (⅕ to ¼ recipe) Italian Buttercream (p. 257), for filling

PREP TALK:

Remember to dehydrate the egg whites, as described in Step 1, about 20 to 24 hours before mixing the batter and to air-dry piped batter about 45 to 60 minutes before baking. Once baked, unfilled macarons should be immediately stored in airtight containers at room temperature. (Because of their high sugar content, macarons can quickly get tacky under humid conditions.) However, once filled with Ganache or Italian Buttercream, both of which are perishable, macarons must be refrigerated. Unfilled cookies remain their best up to 1½ weeks if stored as directed above. Filled macarons are best eaten within a few days. For optimal flavor and texture, bring the macarons to room temperature before serving.

{ goofproof macarons, continued }

1. Prep the egg whites. Place the egg whites in a bowl and cover with a clean cloth towel. Let rest in a cool area (but not the refrigerator) about 20 to 24 hours. This step essentially dehydrates the egg whites and accelerates the drying process in Step 4, which, in turn, leads to less cracking or other misshaping of cookies during baking. Don't skip or rush this step.

2. Prep the cookie sheets following the instructions in the project you've chosen. Or if you're making the macarons just to eat and have no particular project in mind, trace about 3 dozen (1⁷/₈- to 2-inch) circles on parchment paper for piping guides. You'll need 2 pieces of parchment paper sized to fit your cookie sheets, provided you space the circles no less than ³/₄ inch apart. Flip over the papers so the tracing marks are on the underside and use a piece to line each cookie sheet. (If you don't flip over the papers, the tracing marks will transfer onto the cookies during baking.) Secure the parchment paper to the cookie sheets with a dab of butter or shortening applied to each corner.

3. Mix the macaron batter. Sift the powdered sugar and almond flour into a medium bowl. Discard any coarse grains of meal or dark almond skins remaining in the sifter. (Or add them to the mixture, but recognize that the surface of your macarons will end up more lumpy and freckled than pictured on page 252.) Add the salt and gently whisk to evenly distribute the ingredients.

Place the dehydrated egg whites and cream of tartar in a clean bowl of an electric mixer fitted with a whip attachment. (*Note:* The bowl, whip attachment, and all mixing utensils should be completely free of fat, or the egg whites will not stiffen.) Beat on medium-high speed until frothy. Turn the mixer to high speed and gradually add the granulated sugar. Stop briefly, if needed, to scrape any sugar off the sides of the bowl; add any flavoring(s) and then continue beating until the whites are billowy and stiff, but not dry, usually another 15 to 45 seconds. (See "Visual Cue #1," below.) Do not overbeat, as you'll find it more difficult to incorporate the dry ingredients without overfolding.

Note: Now is the time to tint the macarons, if desired. If you fold in coloring after incorporating the dry ingredients, below, you risk overfolding the batter, which can result in heavy, lopsided macarons. Add no more than 20 to 25 drops coloring. If you add more or use liquid coloring (heavens no!), you defeat the purpose of dehydrating the egg whites in Step 1. Too much moisture will prolong drying time in Step 4 and/or result in macarons with cracks or overextended feet. Beat to just incorporate the coloring.

Visual Cue #1: *Macarons start with meringue that is billowy and stiff, but not dry.*

Remove the bowl from the mixer and transfer the meringue to a large bowl. Sift the reserved almond flour mixture over the top of the meringue in thirds, folding with a large rubber spatula between each addition. It may seem as if there is more almond flour mixture than you can possibly incorporate, but, trust me, you can! It is normal for

Visual Cue #2: *The macaron batter will be quite thick immediately after the dry ingredients are added. Keep folding, but watch the texture of the batter closely!*

Visual Cue #3: *A properly folded macaron batter is one that has just turned shiny. Also, tracks from lifting the spatula should largely disappear after about 20 to 30 seconds; that is, the batter should flow like magma.*

the meringue to deflate quite a bit after the dry ingredients are added and for the batter to be very thick at first. (See "Visual Cue #2," left.) Continue to fold until the batter just turns shiny and loosens slightly. At the ideal consistency, the batter should "flow like magma," as other bakers before me have said, meaning that tracks created by lifting up the spatula should largely disappear into the bulk of the batter, except for a faint outline, after 20 to 30 seconds. (See "Visual Cue #3," below left.) Again, avoid overfolding.

4. Pipe and air-dry the macarons. Turn the batter into a pastry bag fitted with a $1/2$-inch round coupler (or tip specified in your project). Pipe the batter onto the prepared cookie sheets so it fills the tracing marks made in Step 2 with a little room to spare. (For $1^7/_8$-inch tracings, I usually leave about $1/_{16}$ to $1/_8$ inch all the way around.) Rap the cookie sheets on a tabletop to release trapped air bubbles in the cookies; then flatten any peaks in the batter with a barely damp fingertip. If you've mixed the batter to the optimal consistency, it should spread on its own into smooth, flat rounds with few to no peaks to flatten. (See "Visual Cue #4," below.)

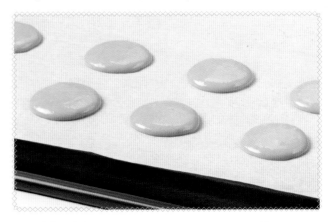

Visual Cue #4: *Piped macarons should be very flat, without any peaks or air bubbles.*

{ goofproof macarons, continued }

Air-dry until a skin has formed on the cookie tops, generally about 45 to 60 minutes. Drying time will vary with humidity, air temperature, and the length of time the egg whites were dehydrated in Step 1. When ready, the macarons will have lost their stickiness and sheen.

5. Position a rack in the center of the oven and preheat the oven to 300°F.

6. Bake about 18 to 20 minutes for $1^7/_8$-inch rounds, or as instructed in your project. (To minimize browning, bake for 10 minutes at 300°F; then drop the oven temperature to 275°F and continue to bake for the remaining time. For some projects, I recommend baking at a lower temperature from the start in order to avoid browning altogether.) When done, the cookies should feel dry and firm and begin to lift off the parchment paper when gently nudged. They should also have risen to $1^1/_2$ to 2 times their initial height and have smooth, crack-free tops and crinkly feet. (See "Visual Cue #5," below.)

Slide the cookies, still on the parchment paper, onto a wire rack and let cool a few minutes until they can easily be removed from the paper. If the cookies stick even after cooling, set them back in the oven on a very low temperature (about 125°F) to dry further. Alternatively, release them with a thin-bladed paring knife. Avoid abruptly pulling them because they can break.

Cool completely before filling with Ganache or Italian Buttercream, or storing.

7. Fill the macarons. Prepare either Ganache (chilled to piping consistency) or Italian Buttercream and transfer to a pastry bag fitted with a $^1/_2$-inch round tip (Ateco #806). Turn half of the macarons upside down so their flat sides face up. Pipe enough filling on each cookie to just cover it; then top with another macaron, placed flat side down, to make a sandwich. Again, once filled, the macarons should be refrigerated as described in "Prep Talk" until you're ready to eat.

Visual Cue #5: *Picture-perfect macarons have smooth tops and crinkly, but not overextended, feet.*

meringues

I ENJOY THE INTERPLAY OF VARIOUS COOKIE TYPES AND TEXTURES, SO I OFTEN USE MERINGUES as building blocks for compound cookies (p. 45), such as the frosting topper on Move Over, Cupcake! (p. 124) and the soft swirl ice cream on Soft Spot (p. 112). Both sweet and light (no fat), they are also a wonderful any-time-of-day standalone snack.

Makes about 3 dozen (2-inch) rosettes

4 large egg whites, room temperature

$1/4$ teaspoon cream of tartar

1 cup sifted superfine sugar

$1^1/2$ teaspoons cornstarch

Flavoring(s) of your choice, to taste

Soft-gel food coloring (p. 14) of
    your choice (optional)

PREP TALK:

Because sugar quickly attracts moisture, and meringue contains a lot of sugar, package these treats in airtight containers as soon as they've cooled and keep them packaged until ready to serve. For best eating, store at room temperature and enjoy within 1 to $1^1/2$ weeks.

1. Prep the cookie sheet(s) as described in the project you've chosen. If you aren't making a particular project and simply want to enjoy these treats on their own, trace about 3 dozen (2-inch) circles on parchment paper for piping guides. You'll need 2 pieces of parchment paper sized to fit your cookie sheets, provided you space the circles no less than $3/4$ inch apart. Flip over the papers so the tracing marks are on the underside and use a piece to line each cookie sheet. (If you don't flip over the papers, the tracing marks will transfer onto the meringues during baking.) Secure the parchment paper to the cookie sheets with a dab of butter or shortening applied to each corner. Alternatively, you can skip the tracing guides and make free-form meringues in Step 4.

2. Position a rack in the center of the oven and preheat the oven to 225°F. If you have two ovens, preheat both. Meringue needs to be baked immediately or it softens and deflates. The cookies will also dry more evenly with one cookie sheet per oven. If you don't have two ovens, then mix and bake $1/2$ recipe at a time.

3. Place the egg whites and cream of tartar in a clean bowl of an electric mixer fitted with a whip attachment. *Note:* Be sure the whites are at room temperature, as cold meringue is more likely to crack in heat of the oven. The bowl, whip attachment, and all mixing utensils should also be completely free of fat, or the egg whites will not stiffen.

Beat on medium speed until the whites are frothy. Very gradually add the superfine sugar in a continuous stream. Quickly scrape down the sides of the bowl and then turn the mixer to its highest speed. Continue beating until the whites are very stiff and glossy and the sugar is completely dissolved, about 7 to 10 minutes. The meringue may look stiff at less than 5 minutes, but generally the longer you beat, the more sharply defined your meringues will be once they're piped. (A caveat: for $1/2$ recipe, beat closer to 5 to 7 minutes; otherwise the meringue can get too stiff and won't form graceful peaks.) Sprinkle the cornstarch evenly over the top and beat until just incorporated. Beat in flavoring(s) of your choice and soft-gel food coloring, if desired. *Note:* Limit the food coloring to no more than 20 drops to avoid loosening the meringue too much. And because different colors tint to different intensities, it's best to add the coloring a drop at a time, especially to achieve a pale shade.

4. *For rosettes:* Transfer the meringue to a pastry bag fitted with a large ($7/16$- to $9/16$-inch) star tip (Ateco #825, #826, or #827). Work quickly before the meringue deflates.

(a) Hold the bag perpendicular to a prepared cookie sheet and center it over one of the circles traced in Step 1. Apply gentle pressure while drawing the bag in a circle to fill the traced outline.

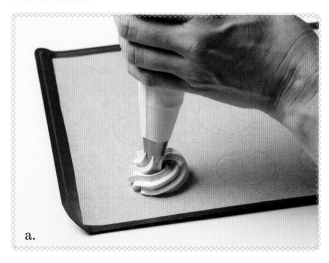

a.

(b) Draw the bag into the center of the circle, stop applying pressure, and lift up abruptly to create a central peak. Repeat to fill all of the traced outlines.

b.

For free-form meringues: Simply dollop the meringue with a tablespoon onto the prepared cookie sheets.

5. Bake about $1 1/2$ to 2 hours, or until the meringues are bone-dry to the touch and only minimally discolored, if at all. If the meringue begins to discolor or crack at any point during baking, drop the oven temperature to 200°F and continue to bake until dry. (Humidity can greatly affect baking time.) Immediately transfer to wire racks and let cool before storing as described in "Prep Talk."

traditional tuiles
WITH COCOA VARIATION

FRAGILE AND FLEXIBLE? AN OXYMORON AS IT RELATES TO MOST THINGS, BUT NOT THESE TUILES. Thin as paper, these cookies dance swiftly over the palate before they dissolve into satisfying sweetness on the tongue. Plus, if you catch them straight from the oven, you can bend them any which way. Once the cookies cool, they'll hold their shape just as long as you keep them properly stored. *Note:* Tuile "dough" is actually a loose batter, most often spread through a stencil to create a defined shape.

Makes 3½ to 4 dozen (2⅞- to 3-inch) tuiles; yield will vary with egg size, beating time, and stencil size

¹/₂ cup all-purpose flour

¹/₈ teaspoon salt

¹/₂ cup superfine sugar

2 egg whites, room temperature

2¹/₂ tablespoons unsalted butter, melted and cooled slightly

1¹/₂ tablespoons heavy cream

Flavoring(s) of your choice, to taste (or per Variation, p. 256; *Note:* Because these cookies are so thin, they require more flavoring than you might expect to pack any punch. I typically use as much as 1 to 2 or more teaspoons extract, depending on the flavoring.)

Soft-gel food coloring (p. 14) of your choice (optional)

PREP TALK:

Silicone baking mats are a must for this recipe. Mats distribute heat extremely evenly, which is important when baking these paper-thin cookies. Plus, the cookies will lift off them easily without any sticking. Parchment paper can buckle in the heat of the oven, causing the cookies to misshape. The cookies will also get doughy if baked on greased and floured pans. Nonstick pans can work, though you'll need to slide a thin-bladed paring knife under the cookies to release them, which can often result in rips or misshaping.

Before you mix the batter, be sure you've made the stencil for shaping the cookies, as indicated in your project. These cookies are especially vulnerable to humidity, so for the crispest results, bake on a dry, sunny day and package the cookies in airtight containers as soon as they've cooled. For best eating, store at room temperature and enjoy within 1 to 1¹/₂ weeks.

{ traditional tuiles, continued }

1. Position a rack in the center of the oven and preheat the oven to 400°F. Line 2 or more cookie sheets with silicone baking mats.

2. Combine the flour and salt in a small bowl. Set aside for use in Step 4.

3. Place the sugar and whites in the bowl of an electric mixer fitted with a whip attachment. Beat on high speed until thick and milky white, about 1 to 2 minutes. (The egg whites will not get fluffy or hold peaks.) Gradually add the cooled, melted butter and heavy cream. Beat until the ingredients are well combined and the batter has thickened slightly.

4. Turn the mixer to low speed and slowly add the dry ingredients, beating just until smooth. Scrape down the sides of the bowl and stir in flavoring(s) and soft-gel food coloring, as desired. *Note:* To avoid loosening the batter too much, limit the food coloring to 5 to 10 drops, which is often all that's needed to create a deep color.

5. Lay the stencil for your project on a prepared cookie sheet. Use a small offset spatula to spread the batter in a thin layer over the openings of the stencil. The batter need be no thicker than the thickness of the stencil, which is about $2/100$ inch! (For tips on cutting and working with custom stencils, see page 49.) Carefully lift the stencil and repeat to make no more than 3 or 4 tuiles per cookie sheet, if you plan to shape the tuiles after baking. Shaping must happen very quickly while the tuiles are still hot, so it's best to bake only a few cookies at a time.

6. Bake as directed in your particular project, or adhere to the following general rules if you're baking these cookies to enjoy on their own. With most of the projects in this book, my goal is to avoid discoloration of the tuiles, so I bake just until the cookie tops are set and the edges are minimally browned, if at all. However, if you'd like more browning, that's fine, too. Either way, baking time is quite short (3 to 5 minutes), even for larger stencils, because these cookies are so thin. Watch the cookies carefully, as they'll go from done to burned in the blink of an eye.

7. Shape the cookies while hot from the oven as described in your project (or leave them unshaped); then store as instructed in "Prep Talk."

VARIATION
{ Cocoa }

Add 2 teaspoons unsweetened Dutch-process cocoa powder to the egg whites and sugar at the start of Step 3, left. (If you add it with the dry ingredients in Step 4, it won't distribute as evenly and your cookies will end up with visible specks.) Use 1 teaspoon orange extract for the flavoring, or substitute another flavoring of your choice.

italian buttercream

WITH CHOCOLATE VARIATION

UNLIKE AMERICAN BUTTERCREAM, which is usually comprised of butter or shortening and powdered sugar, Italian Buttercream starts with meringue, which makes it notably light and fluffy. I like to use it as a filling in macarons and other sandwich-style cookies. But bear in mind: it is perishable, and because it's made with 100 percent butter and no shortening, it will harden when refrigerated. Apply it to cookies as close to serving time as possible; if it sits too long next to certain cookies, especially tuiles, the cookies will soften.

Note: If a project calls for a fraction of this recipe, it's best to make a full batch and portion off what you need, as this recipe is difficult to mix in any smaller quantity.

Makes about 1 pound 8 ounces or 4 to 4³⁄₄ cups; yield will vary
with egg size, egg and butter temperature, and whipping time

4 large egg whites, room temperature
(about 9 tablespoons pasteurized egg
whites, or see "Substitutions," p. 243)

¹⁄₄ teaspoon cream of tartar

²⁄₃ cup granulated sugar

¹⁄₃ cup plus 1 tablespoon light corn syrup

1²⁄₃ cups (3 sticks plus 2²⁄₃ tablespoons)
unsalted butter, softened

1 teaspoon pure vanilla extract
(*Note:* Increase to 1 tablespoon if
you do not add other flavorings.)

Additional flavoring(s) of your choice, to taste

Soft-gel food coloring (p. 14) of
your choice (optional)

PREP TALK:

If you don't plan to use Italian Buttercream immediately, store it in an airtight container in the refrigerator up to 1 week, or in the freezer for 1 month or more. Once refrigerated or frozen, the icing should be softened at room temperature and then rebeaten until glossy, both for best eating and easiest handling.

{ italian buttercream, continued }

1. Combine the egg whites and cream of tartar in a clean bowl of an electric mixer fitted with a whip attachment. (*Note:* The bowl, whip attachment, and all mixing utensils should be completely free of fat, or the egg whites will not stiffen.) Beat on medium speed to stiff, but not dry, peaks.

2. Meanwhile, combine the sugar and corn syrup in a large nonstick skillet and stir to evenly moisten the sugar. Place the mixture over medium-high heat and bring to a boil, stirring as needed to make sure the sugar completely dissolves. Continue to boil approximately 30 seconds, until thick, syrupy, and bubbly through to the center.

3. Turn the mixer to medium-high speed and gradually add the hot sugar syrup in a slow, steady stream, with the mixer running. (If you turn down the mixer speed, shut off the mixer, or add the syrup too fast, you run the risk of curdling the egg whites with the hot syrup. And curdling means gritty buttercream.) Once the syrup is completely incorporated, stop the mixer and quickly scrape down the sides of the bowl, taking care not to scrape any hard crystallized sugar into the meringue. Resume beating at high speed until the meringue is lukewarm to cool to the touch, at least 5 minutes.

4. Add the butter a few tablespoons at time, beating well after each addition. The meringue will deflate and the icing may look grainy at first, but it will get quite thick and glossy as more butter is incorporated.

5. Add the vanilla extract and additional flavoring(s) or soft-gel food coloring, as desired, and mix well.

VARIATION
{ Chocolate }

Makes about 1 pound 12 ounces or $4^1/_2$ to $5^1/_4$ cups

Proceed as directed for Italian Buttercream (p. 257), but increase the vanilla extract to $1^1/_2$ teaspoons and add 6 ounces melted premium semisweet chocolate in Step 5. Be sure to cool the chocolate to lukewarm prior to adding it; otherwise, you may melt the buttercream.

Definitions

Premium chocolate is, by my definition, a chocolate made with pure cocoa butter and no hydrogenated or saturated fat substitutes, such as palm or coconut oil. Premium chocolates can be pricey, but their texture and flavor are superior to those of cheaper brands and chocolate types. Most grocery stores stock premium brands. Look for Valrhona, Scharffen Berger, Callebaut, Green & Black's, Lindt, or Ghirardelli.

Coating chocolate is inexpensive, due to its use of cocoa butter substitutes, and comes in a wide range of flashy colors. It's also a helpful shortcut in decorative chocolate work, such as No Finer Liners (p. 127), because it doesn't need to be tempered the way premium chocolate does. Tempering is an often finicky process of melting, working, and cooling premium chocolate so that it retains a glossy appearance and snap once it sets back up. The downside of coating chocolate is that it's simply very sweet, without having the complexity that one usually associates with "chocolate." And despite what its name suggests, it coats less smoothly than most premium chocolates.

ganache

WITH WHITE CHOCOLATE VARIATION

WHILE THIS SATINY CHOCOLATE-AND-CREAM BLEND can be poured warm as a glaze (which, BTW, I love over ice cream), I always chill it to piping consistency for use with the cookies in this book. At this consistency, it makes a wonderfully rich filling for tuile cones, macarons, and other sandwich-style cookies. Like Italian Buttercream, Ganache is perishable and will set up when refrigerated. I also apply it to cookies as I do buttercream—as close to serving time as possible. Otherwise, it can soften cookies if in contact for too long.

Makes about 1 pound 6 ounces or 2 ¼ to 2 ½ cups

12 ounces premium (see "Definitions," p. 258) semisweet chocolate, finely chopped or ground in a food processor

1 1/2 cups heavy cream

1 tablespoon light corn syrup

PREP TALK:

Allow at least 20 to 25 minutes for Ganache to chill to piping consistency (Step 4) before using in this book's projects. If you don't plan to use it immediately, store it tightly covered in the refrigerator up to 1 week, or in the freezer for 1 month or more. Once refrigerated or frozen, Ganache should be softened at room temperature until it reaches piping consistency (or gently heated in a double boiler until fluid, if you intend to pour it).

1. Place the chopped (or ground) chocolate in a large bowl so it forms a shallow layer.

2. Pour the cream into a medium (3-quart) nonreactive (stainless steel or coated) saucepan. Avoid aluminum and other noncoated metal pans, as they can impart a tinny flavor to the cream. Place the pan over medium to medium-high heat and scald the cream. (That is, heat the cream to just below the boiling point. The cream will put off steam, and a skin will form, but no bubbles should break on its surface.)

3. Immediately strain the hot cream through a fine-mesh sieve directly onto the chocolate. (Don't skip the straining; the sieve will remove the skin that formed during scalding

and ensure that your ganache ends up as smooth as can be.) Stir just to make sure that all of the chocolate comes in contact with the hot cream. Let the mixture sit 1 to 2 minutes without stirring; then gently whisk until the chocolate is entirely melted and the chocolate and cream come together into a satiny glaze. (If the chocolate does not melt completely, set the bowl over simmering water in a double boiler and stir regularly until smooth. Do not overheat, or the ganache may break.) Stir in the corn syrup to enhance the sheen.

4. To use the ganache as a glaze, pour it while lukewarm. Alternatively, for piping consistency (as used in this book), pour it into a shallow pan to a $^1/_2$- to $^3/_4$-inch depth. Cover the pan and refrigerate until the ganache is firm enough to pipe through a pastry bag easily without being a drippy mess, typically at least 20 to 25 minutes. Stir occasionally during chilling to maintain a uniform consistency. (Hard overchilled pieces of ganache should be broken up, as they can easily clog pastry tips when piping.) Chilling time will vary with ganache temperature, refrigerator temperature, and depth of the ganache. Watch the ganache closely, as it can quickly overchill and become difficult to pipe.

VARIATION
{ White Chocolate }

Makes about 1 pound or 1$^1/_2$ to 1$^3/_4$ cups

Substitute white chocolate for the semisweet chocolate in Step 1 (p. 259). Reduce the cream to $^3/_4$ cup and proceed as directed in Steps 1 to 4. All other factors (depth of ganache, ganache temperature, etc.) being the same, White Chocolate Variation will take longer than regular Ganache to set to piping consistency due to its higher cocoa butter content.

chocolate dough
WITH WHITE CHOCOLATE VARIATION

IF YOU'RE SEEKING A MORE FLAVORFUL MODELING MEDIUM THAN ROLLED FONDANT, then you're in the right place. Both the semisweet and white chocolate versions of this Tootsie Roll–like clay are extremely tasty, especially when made with premium chocolate (p. 258). But ... as palate-pleasing as these doughs are, they aren't without their own drawbacks. See "Know Your Modeling Media" (p. 53) for a complete comparison of modeling media.

Makes about 10 ounces dough

7 ounces premium (see "Definitions," p. 258) semisweet chocolate

$^1/_3$ cup light corn syrup

PREP TALK:

After the dough is mixed, it needs to sit, wrapped and contained, in a cool (60°F to 65°F) but unrefrigerated place to solidify to a pliable working consistency. Setting time can range from overnight to a few days depending on ambient conditions. (The hotter it is, the longer the dough will take to set.) When not in use, the dough should be wrapped tightly in plastic and then sealed in an airtight container; otherwise, it can quickly dry out.

1. Break the chocolate into small pieces and place in a double boiler over barely simmering water on low heat. Stir occasionally until the chocolate is completely melted.

2. Remove the chocolate from the heat and add the corn syrup. Stir until the mixture just turns into a thick paste, generally no longer than 30 seconds. Do not overstir or the mixture may break.

3. Cover the dough loosely with plastic wrap and cool until you can handle it comfortably. It will solidify slightly while cooling, but will still be very soft. Flatten it into a disk and pat any excess cocoa butter (greasy fluid) off the surface. (Otherwise, the cocoa butter will recrystallize upon cooling and make the dough gritty.) Seal tightly in plastic wrap, taking care to keep the plastic wrap as flat as possible. If the dough sets up around any wrinkles, the plastic will be difficult to remove later. Store in an airtight container, as instructed in "Prep Talk," until solidified to proper working consistency.

4. Before working with the dough, knead it until homogenous. If it has any grittiness, you can often work it out through additional kneading or by running the dough through the smallest setting on a pasta machine.

VARIATION
{ White Chocolate }

Makes about 9 ounces dough

Substitute premium white chocolate for the semisweet chocolate in Step 1, left. Reduce the corn syrup to $^1/_4$ cup and proceed as directed through Step 2.

Note: Cocoa butter naturally tends to separate more from White Chocolate Dough than from its darker counterpart, so it's best to take an extra precaution to remove the excess cocoa butter. Otherwise, you'll end up with a big grit problem. Let the dough cool until you can handle it comfortably; then knead it over a bowl for a few minutes to work out the cocoa butter. The dough will become slightly more elastic as you knead. Flatten the dough into a disk and pat it dry on both sides. Wrap in plastic and store as directed for Chocolate Dough.

Because White Chocolate Dough has a higher cocoa butter content than Chocolate Dough, it will generally take a little longer to set to proper working consistency. It's also more vulnerable to softening in the heat (including the heat of your hands), so avoid overhandling it.

A CUT ABOVE
Templates

Here, you'll find the outlines for all of the novel (meaning nonrectangular) custom templates used in the projects in this book. For the sake of conserving paper, the outlines are much smaller than those actually used. To replicate the project dimensions exactly, simply blow up each outline to the size indicated near the arrow (or arrows) in the sketch; then make a template from the enlargement as described in "Custom Templates and Stencils" (p. 48).

Breakfast in Bed (p. 95), Egg Whites

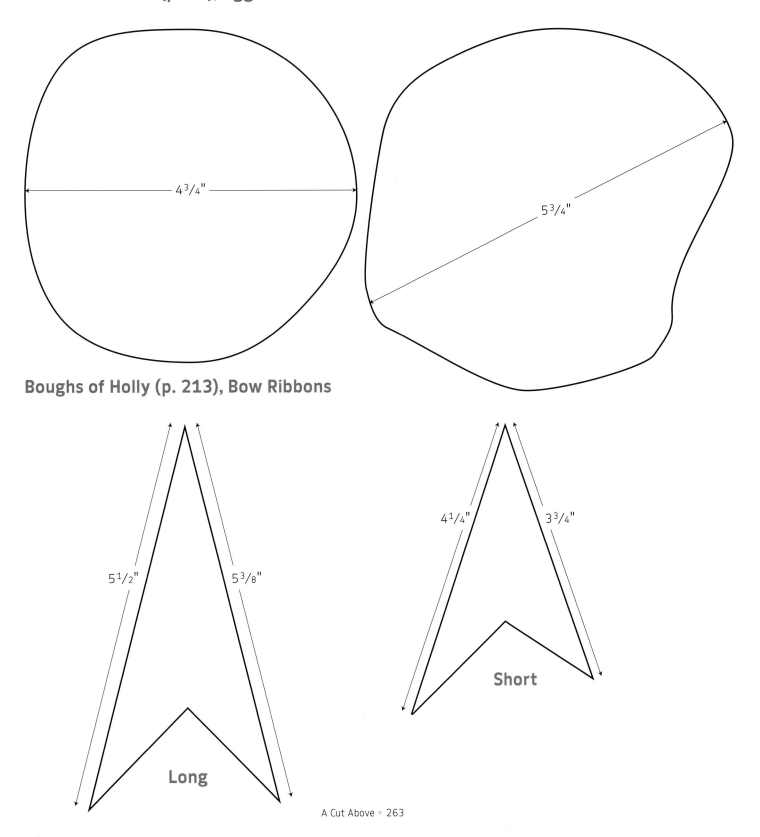

4³/₄"

5³/₄"

Boughs of Holly (p. 213), Bow Ribbons

5¹/₂"   5³/₈"

Long

4¹/₄"   3³/₄"

Short

**Come Sail Away (p. 179),
Boat Hull**

**Fit for a Queen (p. 77),
Headband**

**Lounge Lizards (p. 139),
Body**

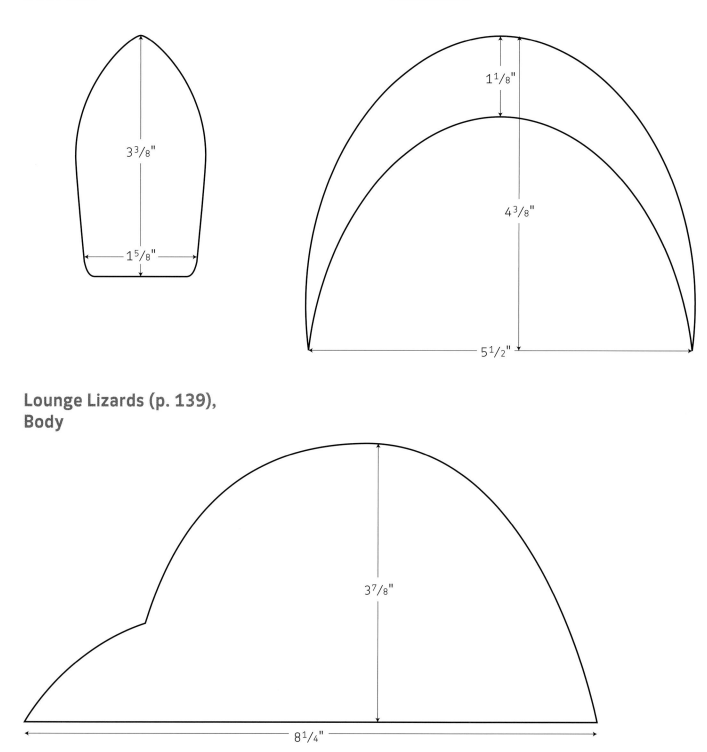

$3^3/_8"$

$1^5/_8"$

$1^1/_8"$

$4^3/_8"$

$5^1/_2"$

$3^7/_8"$

$8^1/_4"$

Lounge Lizards (p. 139), Front Feet

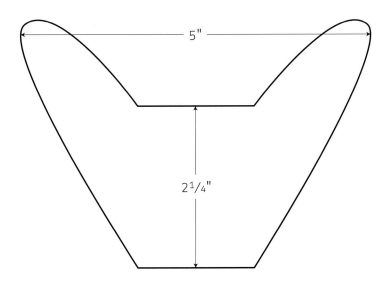

5"

2 1/4"

Lounge Lizards (p. 139), Back Haunch

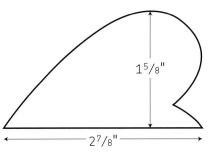

1 5/8"

2 7/8"

Lounge Lizards (p. 139), Front Haunch

1 1/4"

2 1/4"

Lounge Lizards (p. 139), Back Feet

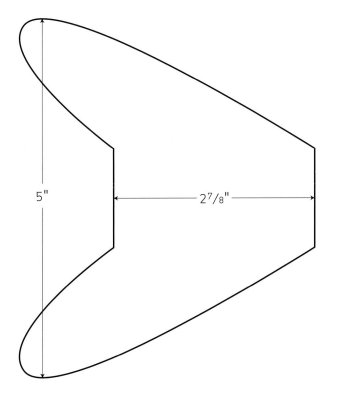

5"

2 7/8"

Lounge Lizards (p. 139), Tail

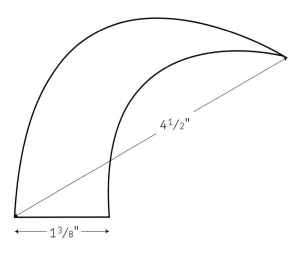

4 1/2"

1 3/8"

Mam-moth (p. 135), Wing

Proud as a Peacock (p. 155), Body

Proud as a Peacock (p. 155), Fan

Proud as a Peacock (p. 155), Wing

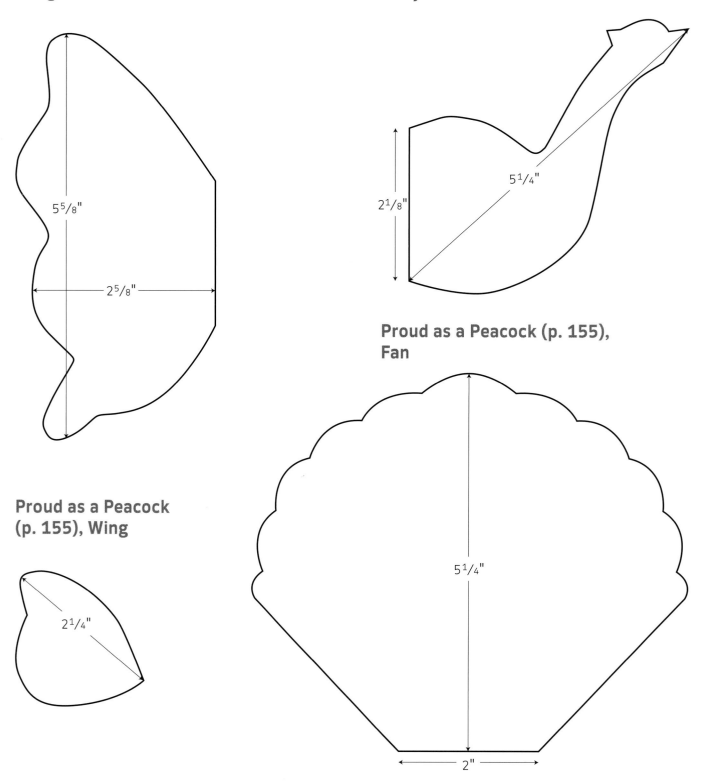

5⅝"

2⅝"

2⅛"

5¼"

2¼"

5¼"

2"

Sleigh Cool (p. 209), Sleigh

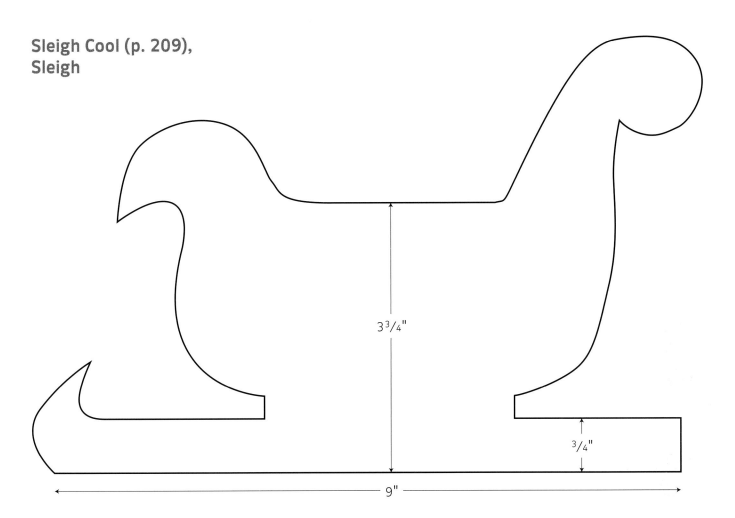

3³/4"

³/4"

9"

Snake Charmer (p. 149), Head

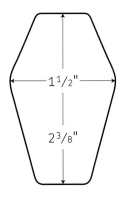

1¹/2"

2³/8"

Snake Charmer (p. 149), Tail

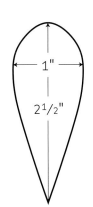

1"

2¹/2"

Snake Charmer (p. 149), Cactus

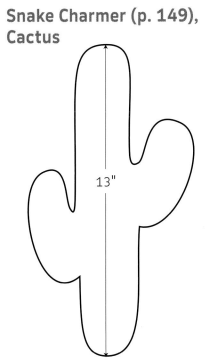

13"

resources

FAQ

In an effort to make this book as practical as I hoped it would be inspirational, I turned to my Facebook fans for input about midway through the project. I asked one simple question: what's your biggest cookie decorating conundrum? While the number of responses was initially overwhelming, I quickly discovered common themes and concerns, even common decorating mishaps. After a little boiling down, the many emails reduced to a few questions, which you'll find answered in the sidebars throughout the book. For a handy printout with all the FAQ in one place, visit www.juliausher.com.

TOOLS AND DECORATIONS

Many of the specialty decorating tools and treasures used in this book can be found locally in kitchenwares shops or craft stores, such as Michaels and Hobby Lobby. If these sources don't bear fruit, then check out my favorite online suppliers, listed below. Though some of the companies are full spectrum providers (those with lots of "X"s) and others are more specialized, all came through with quality products and reliable service every time I ordered.

Where to go:	Cookie cutters	Cookie cutter making kits	Crystallized roses and other edible flowers	Dragées and/or sugar beads	Edible ink cartridges for printers	Fondant, rolled	Food-safe markers	Gumballs	Isomalt	Leaf and flower plunger cutters	Leaf veiners	Licorice lace and other dime-store candies	Lollypop sticks	Luster, pearl, petal, and other dusts	Meringue powder	Modeling tools (i.e., ball and bone tools)	Readymade royal icing and/or sugar embellishments	Silicone baking pans and/or cupcake liners	Silicone molds	Soft-gel food coloring	Stencils	Sugar gems	Textured rolling pins and/or impression mats	Tiny sugar decorations, i.e., nonpareils, sanding sugar, jimmies, and confetti	Wafer paper, plain and/or printed	Wire stamens
Bakers Nook, LLC shopbakersnook.com 734-429-1320	X			X		X	X		X	X			X	X	X	X	X	X (liners only)		X	X		X (mats only)	X		X
Candy Warehouse candywarehouse.com 310-343-4099								X				X												X		
coppergifts.com 620-421-0654 866-898-3965	X	X				X							X	X	X		X	X (liners only)		X	X			X		
Crystalized Flower Co. crystallizedflowerco.com 440-478-5302			X																							
Designer Stencils designerstencils.com 302-475-7300 800-822-7836													X								X					
Fancy Flours fancyflours.com 406-587-0118	X	X	X	X					X				X	X			X	X (liners only)	X	X	X	X	X (mats only in cutter sets)	X	X	
First Impressions Molds firstimpressionsmolds.com 561-784-7186											X								X				X (mats only)			
Global Sugar Art globalsugarart.com 518-561-3039 800-420-6088	X			X		X	X		X	X	X			X	X	X			X	X	X	X	X			X

Where to go:

Company	Cookie cutters	Cookie cutter making kits	Crystallized roses and other edible flowers	Dragées and/or sugar beads	Edible ink cartridges for printers	Fondant, rolled	Food-safe markers	Gumballs	Isomalt	Leaf and flower plunger cutters	Leaf veiners	Licorice lace and other dime-store candies	Lollypop sticks	Luster, pearl, petal, and other dusts	Meringue powder	Modeling tools (i.e., ball and bone tools)	Readymade royal icing and/or sugar embellishments	Silicone baking pans and/or cupcake liners	Silicone molds	Soft-gel food coloring	Stencils	Sugar gems	Textured rolling pins and/or impression mats	Tiny sugar decorations, i.e., nonparells, sanding sugar, jimmies, and confetti	Wafer paper, plain and/or printed	Wire stamens
gumballs.com 800-307-7900								X				X														
H. O. Foose Tinsmithing Co. foosecookiecutters.com 610-944-1960	X	X		X																	X			X		
Kerekes Bakery & Restaurant Equipment, Inc. bakedeco.com 718-232-7044 800-525-5556	X					X				X				X	X	X (bone tool only)		X (pans only)	X	X	X		X (mats only)	X		X
Kitchen Collectables kitchengifts.com 402-597-0980 888-593-2436	X																									
Kitchen Krafts kitchenkrafts.com 563-535-8000 800-298-5389	X	X	X			X	X			X	X	X		X	X	X		X	X	X	X	X	X	X	X (plain only)	X
Kopykake kopykake.com 310-373-8906 800-999-5253					X																				X (plain only)	
Off the Beaten Path cookiecutter.com 816-415-8827 866-756-6543	X	X		X (sugar beads only)			X								X								X (mats only in cutter sets)	X		
Stencil Planet stencilplanet.com 908-771-8967 877-836-2457																					X					
Sweetfields, Inc. sweetfields.com 760-522-3422 877-98-SWEET			X																							
The Baker's Kitchen thebakerskitchen.net 419-381-9693	X			X		X	X			X	X			X	X	X	X	X (liners only)		X	X	X	X		X (plain only)	X
The Cookie Cutter Shop thecookiecuttershop.com 360-652-3295	X						X						X													
Victoria Larsen victorialarsen.com 425-258-6812																					X					
Wilton wilton.com 630-963-1818 800-794-5866	X			X (sugar beads only)		X	X						X	X	X	X	X	X	X	X	X		X (mats only)	X		X

index

METRIC CONVERSION CHART

Volume Measurements			Weight Measurements			Temperature Conversion	
U.S.	Metric		U.S.	Metric		Fahrenheit	Celsius
1 teaspoon	5 ml		$1/2$ ounce	15 g		250	120
1 tablespoon	15 ml		1 ounce	30 g		300	150
$1/4$ cup	60 ml		3 ounces	90 g		325	160
$1/3$ cup	75 ml		4 ounces	115 g		350	180
$1/2$ cup	125 ml		8 ounces	225 g		375	190
$2/3$ cup	150 ml		12 ounces	350 g		400	200
$3/4$ cup	175 ml		1 pound	450 g		425	220
1 cup	250 ml		$2 1/4$ pounds	1 kg		450	230

Equivalents are not exact; figures have been rounded up or down for easier measuring.

By weight, a cup is not the same for all ingredients. Volume equivalents, above, apply to liquids only. Dry ingredients should be scaled using the following approximate equivalents for 1 cup: all-purpose flour, spooned, tapped, and leveled (about 5 ounces, 142 g), granulated sugar (about 7 ounces, 198 g), firmly packed light brown sugar (about $7 1/3$ ounces, 208 g).